Praise for Jacques Fleury's "Chain Letter to America…"

"A powerful strike on the doors of Justice. The courageous author painted his vision, and suggested understanding and consciousness of our historic and present social reality. Before anybody from any medical society in the Roman Empire, a descendant of a slave performed the first major open heart surgery in America. There is an axiom: 'Know the cause of the illness, and you will be able to apply the proper medicine.' I know this: When we understand that we are the Human Race, there will be no place on Earth for Eris and Ares. Please, keep fueling the wings of Your Quill, and let the world know that it soars safely ~ blown by winds of reality, and aesthetical light. In reverent appreciation…"

-Andre Emmanuel Bendavi ben-YEHU --Poet, Translator

"Quite a tirade of prose and poetry of the state of the United States in the early 21st century. I thought we would be beyond all that, but it has come back to haunt us. I was enthralled with every word. Jacques Fleury's scholarship and writing ability are far above the average. Really worth paying attention to…a metaphor for refugees from all kinds of calamities trying to find a safe place, a calm place in their life where they can rest and think of the life around them… Inspiring words about the harshness and beauty… all around us … Fleury really said a load in this broadly sweeping exposé of modern life awakening. It's good to see his superlative writing again… Kudos!"

--Ronald W. Hull, Ed.D,
Author *of Hanging by a Thread*

"I grew up in a black, white, and yellow world... Differences in color and nationality are what makes life interesting. I go to a very diverse church because I know that's what Heaven is going to be like… as for color, I am not blind but I am so grateful the Lord made us diverse as it's a blessing and not a curse. In His eyes, all of us matter. I Praise Him for giving me such wisdom."

Dr. John M. Domino
Author of *Reflections from the Great Depression* and WWII

"Polarization and violence in our country make increasingly urgent a greater understanding of our history. No one can confidently predict that things will return to 'normal', or that non-racist forces will seamlessly replace President Trump after his one or two terms in office. So what lessons and what inspiration from our past can we draw upon to help us in our present circumstance?"

--Neil Calendar, Adjunct Professor of English,
Roxbury Community College

Books by Jacques Fleury

Sparks in the Dark: A Lighter Shade of Blue, A Poetic Memoir

It's Always Sunrise Somewhere and Other Stories

Chain Letter to America: The One Thing You Can Do To End Racism

Anthologies as Contributing Author

HOME Anthology

Class Lives: Stories from Across Our Economic Divide

CHAIN LETTER TO AMERICA:

THE ONE THING YOU CAN DO TO END RACISM

A Collection of Essays, Fiction and Poetry Celebrating Multiculturalism

---

Diverse Voices of Sociopolitical History, Ethnicity, Race, Class,
the Immigrant Experience, the Arts, the Environment, Philosophy,
Psychopathology, Pedagogy, Empowerment, Spirituality and more...

From Boston Globe featured Author of *Sparks in the Dark*

Jacques Fleury

authorHOUSE®

AuthorHouse™
1663 Liberty Drive
Bloomington, IN 47403
www.authorhouse.com
Phone: 1 (800) 839-8640

Published by AuthorHouse 10/10/2019

ISBN: 978-1-7283-3037-2 (sc)
ISBN: 978-1-7283-3036-5 (e)

Library of Congress Control Number: 2019915723

Print information available on the last page.

Any people depicted in stock imagery provided by Getty Images are models,
and such images are being used for illustrative purposes only.
Certain stock imagery © Getty Images.

Photo of Jacques Fleury by Jon Heinrich, whose photographs of nature and earth dwellers are captivating.
His photos adorn our eyes with earthly elegance; from mountains to flowers, from animals to carnivals and
makes us want to preserve what beauty we have left. His art transcends the bleak and the ordinary to reveal
something we all live for: hope! Visit his photography portfolio online at www.jonheinrich.com

Cover Art by Mary Lou Springstead , who is a visual artist originally from Florida, who currently resides in
Middlesbrough, UK. She is a nasty woman who is inspired by mythology, psychology, social and environmental
justice, Surrealism and Outsider Art. Visit her art portfolio online at: www.marylouspringstead.com.

This book is printed on acid-free paper.

For my mother, Marie Evelyne Toussaint:
The most beautiful woman in the world, who through her love, wisdom and
compassion has helped lead me out of the dark and into the light...

"What we need in the United States is not division; what we need in the United States is not hatred; what we need in the United States is not violence and lawlessness; but is love and wisdom, and compassion toward one another, and a feeling of justice toward those who still suffer within our country, whether they be white or whether they be black…let us dedicate ourselves to what the Greeks wrote so many years ago: to tame the savageness of man and make gentle the life of this world."

Robert F. Kennedy (1968)
Days before his assassination

'The winds of grace are always blowing; it is for us to raise our sails.'

--Rama Krishna
19th century Indian mystic

"Although change is often unwelcomed,
It is what we usually learn the most from…"
--Jacques Fleury
21st century American Romantic

Photo Credit: JimKociuba.com
Maple Breeze, 2019, Acrylic on Canvas, 36 x 48

Table of Contents

"Even in our sleep pain that cannot forget falls drop by drop upon the heart, and in our own despair, against our will, comes wisdom to us by the awful grace of God."

Aeschylus

Preface

In the post new millennium decades since the September 11th, 2001 devastating and alarming mass attack on the United States of America and the shocking election of Donald Trump in the 2016 U.S. election, we have seen increasing islamophobia, mainly because they are seen as a geopolitical source from which the 9/11 terrorist attacks were orchestrated. Also due to Trump's anti-immigrant campaign rhetoric tethered with his one dimensional and mostly unilateral solution and promise to build a wall along the U.S. Mexican border and his crude alleged allusion to the African diaspora (the genetically traced birthplace of humanity) as "sh*t hole" countries, we have also seen growing hostility towards people of color as well as immigrants in America, a sentiment which has been metastasizing incrementally to other parts of the world outside the United States.

Basically, a plethora of U.S. citizens are forgetting that all of us, who are not indigenous American Indians, are descendants of immigrants from Europe, Asia, Latin America and African countries; who came here in search of a less tumultuous and fundamentally more moderated life where they could enjoy economic, social political and religious freedoms.

We are witnessing a monumental resurgence of immigrant migration from Latin American and Asian countries, particularly in Mexico, China and Syria, countries who are experiencing menacing economic and sociopolitical conflicts. And because American born descendants of immigrants have forgotten or have chosen to forget their immigrant roots mainly as a result of assimilation, they have fallen prey to President Donald Trump's anti-immigrant, anti-minority rhetoric; which has created an atmosphere of fear and vulnerability particularly within groups of people of color and undocumented immigrants living and paying taxes in the United States of America. Hence in the face of ensuing hegemony, xenophobia, and the aggregating rise of nationalism; that which have not been seen since the rise of Adolf Hitler in Nazi Germany during the outbreak of World War II, I decided to write this book as a form of meditative exploration of my internal malaise resulting from America's external commotions.

Sic passim, you will find sociopolitical allusions and benefits of using mindful awareness, education, and positive action to inspire and mitigate prominent divisions among a disparate but historically bonded American society and to foster and promote *understanding* and *compassion* for each other, our environment and our all-encompassing humanity.

Jacques Fleury, 2019

Introduction

"First and foremost, I would like to make it clear that this book is not necessarily meant as some type of polemical plebiscite for or against our sitting president. I am quite aware that racism did not begin nor will it end with President Donald J. Trump. This book is also not about partisanship, namely the contentious power play between the democrats and the republicans. This book is also not about white versus black, brown or yellow racial clusters. What this book *is* about is raising conscious awareness to our collective humanity and respective contributions to our country, with added focus on our multiculturalism and fundamentally our shared American constitutional ideology: **that we are all created equal in this country**. In the midst of political and racial divisions in America, I heard a republican congressman speaking to the media, he said: "*With open eyes, open ears, open mind and you walk away with some understanding...*"; which echoes my intent for writing this book: mutual understanding of one another's sociopolitical history and polygonal personal perspectives and values as Americans; while honoring our first amendment right to freedom of expression and to redress our combined grievances with one another through open minded and open hearted conversations. This notion would optimistically bring about mutual understanding of each other beyond racial and cultural barriers. If you take one thing away from reading this book, I hope it's that our numerous races, ethnicities, beliefs and values manifested through comparative historical and contextual exploration serve as a miscible advantage or a harmonious mixture when added together; that could conceivably *strengthen* and not *threaten* this critical juncture in a country birthed in individual freedom and equality."

In the following pages, you will find a series of essays, fiction and poetry written between the election of Obama and the administration of Trump; offered to you as a panoramic canvas of my experiences as a Haitian-American immigrant and an omâge to other immigrants and descendants of immigrants of this country (e.g. African, Haitian, Asian, Irish, Russian etc...) and their inarguable contributions to the cultural and economic bastion that is United States of America. The Africans' indispensable contributions of slave labor and later contributions as soldiers, scientists, inventors, and artists; the Haitians' contributions as the first free black nation that inspired the slave revolution in America and elsewhere when they staged the only successful slave rebellion against the French and winning their independence. They also fought in the American revolutionary war, helping to defeat the British for which they are memorialized in Savanah, Georgia in a colossal monument featuring the then little boy who would be the first emperor of Haiti—Henri Christophe—beating on a drum and marching into battle. **Venerated sociologist, civil rights activist and cofounder of the National Association for the Advancement of Colored People (NAACP) in 1909, W.E.B. Dubois**, whose father was *Haitian*, was the first black man to earn a doctorate from Harvard in 1895 and **Haitian trader Jean Baptiste Point Du Sable** was credited with the founding of the American city of Chicago! The Asians weathered the Chinese Exclusion Act of 1882—which was a federal law prohibiting all immigration of Chinese laborers—mostly due to complains from white American laborers scapegoating them for high unemployment rates among "white men"; this *after* they helped built the transcontinental railroad which would aid American travel and trade economy by way of westward expansion connecting the east to the west. The Irish endured *"No Irish Need Apply"* indignities to contribute as well to the building of the transcontinental railroad and later joined the Russians in making indelible contributions to literature among other seminal achievements.

Since the civil rights movement of the past in the mid-20th century, replicated in the Black Lives Matter movement of the present in early 21st century, and even in the purported greatest democracy in the world, we have seen violence used as a subsidiary method as a desperate attempt to silence "the other" in America's racial schism. However, as the fêted revolutionary writer Gorge Luis Borges stated, "Violence is the last refuge of the weak."

The use of political power to intimidate, subjugate and oppress "the other" is and has always been an unequivocal reality in our beloved American country. We have seen it to a great extinct in the form of capricious and racist systemic policies designed to disempower the so called "minorities" (which I believe as a marginalizing misnomer) and empower the "majority." But what is political power?

According to Dr. Gene Sharp, author of *The Politics of Nonviolent Action*, political power is "…the totality of means, influences and pressures including, authority, rewards, and sanctions available to achieve the objectives of the power holder, especially those of government, the state and those groups in opposition." A textbook manifestation of this scenario is what we are currently experiencing with President Donald Trump's administration and the coercive partisan power play between the democrats in the House of Representatives and the republicans in the senate. A situation that can only be remedied if the people refuse to accept and consequently exercise their freedom of speech rights as Americans and demand bipartisan cooperation for the betterment of *all* Americans, regardless of whether they are aligned with the democrat or republican party; thus affirming the fact that we all live in one *united*, not *divided* country.

In the book; Nonviolent Struggle. 50 Crucial Points by Srdja Popovic et al, a Serbian political activist who abetted the toppling of Serbian president Slobodan Milošević, echoes my latter point regarding the power of the people by proclaiming that, "…ultimately power in society comes from the people's obedience…and those people-each of whom is individually a small source of power- can change their minds, and refuse to follow commands."

In America's history, we have witnessed how the power of nonviolent protest of maligned African Americans effected the United States unconstitutional segregationist Jim Crow laws that kept "blacks" and "whites" segregated but allegedly "equal" We have seen the effects of the civil rights movement—led by Martin Luther King Jr. among others—that desegregated the country and re-affirmed African Americans their constitutional right to vote in 1965—minus all the conjured up and mostly southern barriers like literacy tests designed to keep them from the polls—almost a century after the 15th amendment to the constitution was ratified to that end.

All together, we have seen nonviolent protest change the narrative in America by way of the *abolitionist movement* in the 19th century, the *civil rights movement* in the 20th century and the *black lives matter movement* in the 21st century; which yielded and are still yielding results and proving that nonviolent protest works (consider Gandhi of India or Mandela of South Africa) despite Trump's claim that "protesters" are "useless." Maybe someone should remind him that America was founded on the principals of protest in the form of the Boston Tea Party as the colonies railed against taxation without representation by the British monarchy.

Besides being an affirmative missive of our collective humanity… this book is a reconciliatory nod to our past and a meditative extrapolation, interjection and celebration of our present day United States or **'US'**. Enjoy!"

Essays

"For me, I used to be shy towards journalism because it wasn't poetry. And then I realized that the events that I covered in essays that became journalism were actually great because they inspired me, and they became my muse."

Alice Walker

Race in America: How We Got Here and How We Move Forward

"Our ability to reach unity in diversity will be the beauty and the test of our civilization."

--Mahatma Gandhi

Ah, **racism**, that foggy ugly feeling that everyone feels but hardly anyone wants to admit to or talk about. Hence while I have your attention for at least a little while, let's talk about it. And it all begins with accessing the retrograde memory of history.

"Historical scholarship has become Balkanized into dozens of subfields…many of them virtually inaccessible to lay readers…" I so very much concur with this assertion from James M. McPherson of the New York Times book review that I resolved to use it as the starting point of my attempt at writing about history; which I will attempt to make "accessible" to "lay readers" like myself. So bear with me…we'll navigate this often complex and oversaturated field together.

But before I even begin to address the history of humanity during and post enslavement of Africans, I MUST mention the history of African countries pre-colonial slavery as thriving empires that produced some of the wealthiest Africans in history, particularly the wealthiest of them all, Musa I of Mali or Mansa Musa during the middle ages (circa. 1280 – c. 1337), the tenth emperor of the Mali Empire—who was said to be worth an estimated 400 billion dollars—and of whom prominent Harvard University academician Henry Louis Gates said on the ABC TV show The View, made American computer mogul and philanthropist Bill Gates look like he's on welfare with an estimated net worth of $103.7 billion as of August 2019.

Several other pre-colonial states and societies in Africa include the Ajuran Empire, D'mt, Adal Sultanate, Alodia, Warsangali Sultanate, Kingdom of Nri, Nok culture, Mali Empire, Songhai Empire, Benin Empire, Oyo Empire, Ashanti Empire, Ghana Empire, Mossi Kingdoms, Mutapa Empire, Kingdom of Mapungubwe, Kingdom of Sine, Kingdom of Sennar, Kingdom of Saloum, Kingdom of Baol, Kingdom of Cayor, Kingdom of Zimbabwe, Kingdom of Kongo, Empire of Kaabu, Kingdom of Ile Ife, Ancient Carthage, Numidia, Mauretania, and the Aksumite Empire. At its highest point, and preceding European colonialism, it is projected that Africa safeguarded up to 10,000 diverse states and self-governing clusters with unique languages and customs. But why just take my word for it, for more information, visit:

https://en.wikipedia.org/wiki/History_of_Africa#cite_note-http://newswatch. nationalgeographic.com/2013/10/31/getting-to-know-africa-50-facts/-2

Now that I have established at least a modicum of Africa's history pre-colonial slavery, let us now delve into its peoples' preeminent entombment brought on by the transatlantic slave trade mostly during the 17th and 18th centuries by European powers competing with one another for overseas Empires.

It was 400 years ago on August 23, 1619 that the austere **slave** ship aptly called *White Lion* landed at Point *Comfort* (yes, I'm aware of the irony), Hampton, Virginia. On that ship were the very first registered inception of subdued and enslaved Africans during colonial era America. Presently, this site is now known as Fort Monroe National Monument, and the year 2019 marks its 400th centennial. It is at this very site that this historic event will be venerated as a restorative day of reckoning and understanding. But, before we can address the inexorable consequences of slavery and racism (e.g. discriminatory practice such as Jim Crow segregation, economic inequality, gerrymandering or voting district manipulation to favor one party or class, redlining or denials of loans, insurance or other services to certain racialized groups in targeted areas. —which, like it or not, has become part of America's integrated identity—we must first regress back to re-examine how we got to where we are in twenty-first century, 400 hundred years later. "You can't talk about slavery as a relic of the past" said Price Thomas, Director of Marketing and Communications at the Montpelier Foundation in Charlottesville, Virginia, in a PBS News interview. Which I am in utter concurrence with, for slavery is arguably singlehandedly responsible for today's racialized classifications of "white", "brown", "yellow" and "black"—which I will elaborate on further later—and, as a perpetual force, has systematically affected and permeated all our lives often for the best, if you're labeled white and most likely for the worst, if you're labeled as anything other than white.

Although some historians has traced the inception of slavery in the south as far back as 1526. In a Washington Post article on September 7, 2019 titled "Before 1619, there was 1526: The mystery of the first enslaved Africans in what became the United States", Gillian Brockell wrote of the very first known instance of slavery in North America. She went on to say, "Spanish explorers brought 100 slaves to a doomed settlement in South Carolina or Georgia. Within weeks, the subjugated revolted, then vanished." With the advent of our current political climate of sectionalism in Trump era America, the jarring matter of slavery and its inherent odious connection to racism based on skin color has never been more important in the post new millennium.

Nonetheless, before we begin, we must define what it means to be an American. In his book, *American Character: A History of the Epic Struggle Between Individual Liberty and the Common Good*, Colin Woodard defines what it means to be an American. He states that in America lies a balance of forces of individuality and collectivism, despite our balkanized culture and geography. More specifically, he says that in America, "We are in aggregate one of the most individualistic...cultures on [the planet]...we put great faith in human capacity, innovation and virtue and remain vigilant against...an overreaching government." Colonial America was mostly a self-governing agrarian wilderness society who lived by the credo of "rugged individualism" which has, throughout history, formed the basis of American thought. Back then, having landed on a mostly uncultivated land and sparsely populated areas—partly due to European deceases that reduced the natives—people fended for themselves. However, the onslaught of slavery brought another form of "thought" connecting our human potential to class and racial boundaries; which, essentially, are just lies we are taught in order to justify and preserve our assigned and inherited positions in the hierarchical echelons of society, although precarious as they maybe. From this phenomenon, evolves the top one percent and then the rest of humanity. How is this acceptable in a country birthed in the doctrines of equality? Hence "individualistic" thinking eventually led to "collectivist" ideologies of inferior versus superior groups of races, classes and growing self-aggrandizing sentiments that necessitated instituting boundaries based on skin color.

Howard Zinn, in his seminal and indispensable book: *A People's History of the United States,* starts off chapter two on slavery and racism with the subtitle: "**Drawing the Color Line**." In it, he juxtaposes slavery and racism as coexisting evils in colonial era America, stemming from European colonization and calculated malfeasance all in the name of profit proliferation for a budding capitalist economy and confounding racial hatred of anybody not prima facie "white." He begins his riveting narration by starting of—rightfully—with a quotation from a *black* American writer named J. Saunders Redding, who renders an eerie and ominous description of the advent of the first known "slave ship" to North America in 1619, which must be quoted fully to manifest its foreboding effect:

> Sails furled, flag drooping at her rounded stern, she rode the tide in from the sea. She was a strange ship, indeed, by all accounts, a frightening ship, a ship of mystery. Whether she was trader, privateer, or man-of-war no one knows. Through her bulwarks black-mouthed cannon yawned. The flag she flew was Dutch; her crew a motley. Her port of call, an English settlement, Jamestown, in the colony of Virginia. She came, she traded, and shortly afterwards was gone. Probably no ship in modern history had carried a more portentous freight. Her cargo? Twenty slaves."

In relation to the racist ideations the English settlers utilized to partly justify the enslavement of the African people, Zinn unambiguously spotlights the conception that there is nowhere else in the world where "...racism has been more important, for so long a time, as the United States." And posits the obvious question: "Will blacks and whites ever rid themselves of mutual hostility and ultimately live together in mutual peace and harmony?"

Among the justifications Europeans used to justify their participation in the slave trade was that Africans had been enslaving each other hence the axiom "What's good for the goose, is good for the gander." Which naturally leads to the other question, "If the Africans all decided to jump off the Proverbial Bridge, would the Europeans follow suit? But in any case, Zinn elaborates when he applied a probable explanation from the research of Basil Davidson in his book, *The African Slave Trade* where Davidson contrasted African slaves vs. English slaves when he elucidated that "the 'slaves' of Africa were more like the serfs [or the working class] of Europe. It was a harsh servitude, but they had rights which slaves brought to America did *not* have, and they were 'altogether different from the human cattle of the slave ships and the American plantations.'" Zinn continued with a substantive example from Davidson by describing a scenario in the Ashanti Kingdom of West Africa for example, that "a slave might marry; own property; himself own a slave; swear an oath; be a competent witness and ultimately become heir to his master…" and further more… "An Ashanti slave, nine out of ten, possibly become an adopted member of the family, and in time his descendants so merged and intermarried with the owner's kinsmen that only a few would know their origin." To further substantiate this narrative, Zinn offers the following quotation from slave trader turned antislavery pioneer John Newton who spoke of the stark differences between African and European slavery as a testament to what he witnessed in what is now known as Sierra Leone:

> The state of slavery, among these wild barbarous people, as we esteem them, is much milder than in our colonies. For as, on the one hand, they have no land in high cultivation, like our West India plantations, and therefore no call for that excessive, unintermitted labor, which exhausts our slaves… [and] no man is permitted to draw blood, even from a slave [unlike in the colonies where slave beatings were quite common.]"

In addition to describing the markedly apparent dissimilarities between the "mild" conditions of the African slaves and the demoralizing harsh conditions of the slaves on the English colonies in North America, he acknowledges that he is *not* endorsing African slavery, however he was sure to point out *how* it differed vastly from the involuntary servitude in the American colonies; "which" he said, "was lifelong, morally crippling, and destructive of family ties without hope of any future." He further elaborates on this distinguishable difference stating that, "African slavery lacked two elements that made American slavery the most cruel form of slavery in history: [a] the frenzy for limitless profit that comes from capitalist agriculture; [b] the reduction of the slave to less than human status by the use of racial hatred…where white was master, black was slave… [and] with it developed that special racial feeling—whether hatred, or contempt, or pity or patronization—that accompanied the inferior position of blacks in America for the next [400] years." He concluded.

The New York Times Magazine, on the 400th anniversary of the arrival of the first slave ship in North America, sat around the news room and brainstormed a brilliant idea to devote an *entire* issue—to be written mostly by people of color—of the celebrated (yet at times controversial especially with issues relating to black people), magazine to understanding the sociopolitical and economic impact of slavery in America's past whose influence can still be felt in the present. The article is called "The 1619 Project", which studies both the subtle and observable influences and bequests of slavery in modern day America. Much like Zinn's introduction to slavery in *A People's History…* it begins with a jarring verbatim quotation:

Sometime in 1619, a Portuguese slave ship, the Sao Joao Bautista, traveled across the Atlantic Ocean with a hull filled with human cargo. Captive Africans from Angola, in South Western Africa…."

Hence begins the "1619 Project", an ambitious, revealing, acerbic, and didactic article by New York Times Magazine writer Mary Elliot; in which she recounts the harrowing story of race in the Americas but more specifically in North America. According to Elliot, as the slave ship traversed to Mexico, a demi number of its "cargo" had died before the ship was usurped by the English pirate vessels. The rest was boated off to Point Comfort, a port contiguous to Jamestown, then the capitol of the British settlement of Virginia. A settler by the name of John Rolfe penned a letter to the Virginia Company's Sir Edwin Sandys claiming that in August 1619, a "Dutch-man-of war" (The Man-O-War is a British expression for a powerful naval warship that was intended for battle and not for mercantile purposes) landed on the settlement and "Brought not anything less than 20 negroes,.. Which the governor and cape merchant bought for victuals." The antiquated word "victuals" meaning a stock or food supplies.

"The African were most likely put to work in the tobacco fields that had recently been established in the area…" Elliot surmised. She goes on to describe a nascent system whereby both African and Europeans were accustomed to trading merchandise and persons through the Mediterranean for hundreds of years. But she emphasized the notion that bondage was not then determined by race. She described the trans-Atlantic slave trade, a system that was incepted in the 15th century, inaugurated an entity of involuntary servitude that was made profitable, ethicized and treated like one would treat an heirloom: passed on from one generation to the next.

She echoes Howard Zinn's sentiment of "…the reduction of the slave to less than human status" when she *too* pontificates that the "enslaved were not seen as people but as commodities to be bought, sold and exploited." Human beings as means to an end amidst that demoralizing period of human subjugation through white majority colonial suppression.

The following is a direct statement quoted verbatim from the Times regarding the 1619 Project which helps illuminates the project's most fundamental objective:

By The New York Times
Aug. 13, 2019

The Fourth of July in 1776 is regarded by most Americans as the country's birthday. But what if we were to tell you that the country's true birth date, the moment that its defining contradictions first came into the world, was in late August 1619?

That was when a ship arrived at Point Comfort in the British colony of Virginia, bearing a cargo of 20 to 30 enslaved Africans. Their arrival inaugurated a barbaric system of chattel slavery that would last for the next 250 years and form the basis for almost every aspect of American life. The 1619 Project is a major initiative from The New York Times memorializing that event on its 400th anniversary. The goal of the project is to deepen understanding of American history (and the American present) by proposing a new point of origin for our national story. In the days and weeks to come, we will publish essays demonstrating that nearly everything that has made America exceptional grew out of slavery.

[For access to the "essays" as well as link to live stream presentations published as "The 1619 Project" issue of the New York Times Magazine, please see the bibliography]

Even as the August 18th, 2019 issue of the New York Times's "The 1619 Project" became an international sensation in the media, sold out on newsstands (twice), snatched by curious readers who hitherto had not realized the "impact of slavery in America and more specifically on African Americans", sociopolitical, religious and racial divisions rages on and are currently rancid and rampant in Trump era America and presumably with no end in sight. Although America was founded on the racist principals of the destruction and displacement of indigenous Native Americans and the enslavement and oppression of African Americans, it appears that most have self-servingly forgotten or consciously or subconsciously ignored the gritty teeth of history in this country. Thankfully, academic feats like The 1619 Project and others like it to come, will be there to remind them.

Ray Raphael, in his absorbing book: *Founding Myths: Stories That Hide Our Patriotic Past* which aims to expose the often audaciously extolled falsities and deliberately hidden truths of American History. He presented an in depth analysis of the movie "The Patriot" starring Mel Gibson. But as often happens with Hollywood's attempts at historical cinema, the truth gets lost in special effects.

This notion of constructing American history centered on fallacies is a typical one, and it can materialize in books as well as films, which tend to portray mythical narratives, romanticizing America's perplexing and byzantine past as happy slaves and benevolent masters living together in perfect harmony which, essentially, is a blatant incongruity.

If the past informs the present, then the present has to inform the future, and that's where the need for truth, not falsities comes in. When it comes to our historical past, if everyone share a general knowledge of it, than no one has to repeat it. But if you don't *want* to see it repeated, then *protest* it when you see it happening around you, *to* you, to your loved ones and within your communities.

Even pop icon Beyoncé Knowles chimed into the racial dialogue when she affirmed the perception that "Racism is so American that when we protest racism, some assume we're protesting America." This was relatively evident in what President Donald Trump tweeted about "the squad": the four U.S. democratic state representatives who happen to be women of color and who vehemently protest the Trump administration's often racist policies and rhetoric, of them he said, "They hate America!" and since that is so then, "why don't they go back to the crime infested countries they came from…" All because they are exercising their freedom of speech, which was ironically written by those whom I surmise "*loved* America" and for those "who *loves* America also." Freedom to express dissatisfaction with government is among the ideologies written in the Bill of Rights that make us all unambiguously love America so much…am I right? But Trump, as usual, changes the narrative to create division rather than understanding. And when he is asked plainly, "Are you a racist?" His steadfast answer is usually, "I am the least racist person anywhere in the world" which can be seen on a video posted in The Guardian, see the bibliography for the link to the video.

In Trump becoming so defensive about anything having to do with race and racism is clearly categorized and thoroughly explained in the book: *White Fragility: Why It's So Hard for White People to Talk About Racism* by antiracist educator Robin DiAngelo and with a forward by Michael Eric Dyson.

DiAngelo describes "white fragility" not necessarily as a personal weakness but as a means of deflecting having any type of dialogue on race in order to maintain the status quo of a country where the white majority benefit vastly from the plague of systemic racism. It's the inefficacious rejoinders white people have when their ill-conceived racial ideologies and stereotypes are confronted and the way in which those types of reactions uphold racial inequity. Deny, deny, deny to put it more bluntly. She elaborated that "white fragility" is not limited to "bad people". It alludes to the self-protective actions that some white people take when faced with a racially charged encounter; white fragility is categorized by emotions such as anger, fear, and guilt, and by conducts comprising argumentation and silence. These behaviors, in turn, function to restore white tribal equipoise and inhibit any significant racially nonsectarian dialogue.

"The loveliest trick of the devil is to persuade you that it doesn't exist." As said by the prominent French literary figure Charles Baudelaire in his 1864 tale, "Le Joueur Généreux" ("The Generous Gambler") in which the main character meets and converses with a manifestation of the Devil. In this instance "racism" is the "manifestation of the devil" and its demonstrated existence needs to be addressed and not concealed but if it can "convince" you and I that it does not exist, than it can continue to insidiously dominate and wreak havoc on our reality in the most surprising ways and tethered with the most devastating affects like we're seeing now in Trump era America—with professed racial cleansings by avowed white supremacists—in the form of rampant mass shootings causing people to run pell-mell in every direction—killing races all across the hateful spectrum, white, black, yellow and brown alike.

An edition of the Boston Metro dated August 26, 2019, the article titled "Joe Walsh becomes second Republican to Challenge Trump in 2020 GOP Primary", describes Walsh as a "conservative former U.S. congressman turned talk show host…who criticized Trump… [and] has strong support among Republicans, as a bully…unfit for office." But in his anticipation of "criticism" for "his past affiliation with the Tea Party, a confrontational populist splinter group of the Republican Party…Walsh recalls his past criticisms of President Obama that went beyond policy variances, "There were plenty of times I went beyond the policy…differences… and got personal…and hateful." Seeking to make amends to undoubtedly help his own bid for the presidency and to show unlike Trump he can admit when he's wrong, he brazenly declared, "I helped create Trump. There's no doubt about that: the personal ugly politics. I regret that. And I'm sorry for that. And now we've got a guy in the white house… [and] that's all he does."

"Throughout history, it has been the inaction of those who could have acted; the indifference of those who should have known better; the silence of the voice of justice when it mattered most; that has made it possible for evil to triumph." Declared Haile Selassie, Ethiopian regent from 1916 to 1930 and emperor from 1930 to 1974. He is an essential figure in contemporary Ethiopian history. For evil to triumph, the good must be silenced. If you ignore your history, you become akin to a tree without roots. The lessons of history's past can better inform and prepare us to make a more "just" history in the present and for our posterity.

Those of us who are relatively in parlance with American history are somewhat cognizant of these types of racial tensions that lead to racial violence throughout America's antiquity. First with the usurpation of African slaves from their homeland and brought to the America's bound in chains, then in Nat Turner's slave revolt inducing bloodshed on all sides, then in the civil war that would end slavery in the United States, the retaliatory formations and actions of white nationalist groups like the Ku Klux Klan, who terrorized and murdered innumerous numbers of African Americans, then in the civil rights movement spearheaded most prominently by Rosa Parks and Martin Luther King among others where the world got to see on television black nonviolent protesters fire horsed, beaten with clubs and attacked by vicious dogs and even sometimes killed, now in the 21st century, between the election of President Barack Obama and the administration of Donald Trump, we're seeing the protests reappearing as the Black Lives Matter movement, which is once again being meant with rancor and vehement violence. In the wise words of literary iconoclast Maya Angelou, "History, despite its wrenching pain, cannot be unlived, but if faced with courage, need not be lived again."

Speaking to my own experience specifically in the public school system, what *I* was taught of black history in America did not venture too far beyond "Oh, yeah, we had slaves" and "Oh, yeah, we also had Martin Luther King…any questions?" And of course, we all had one burning question: "Is that going to be on the test?!" As high schoolers, our interest in history then often never went beyond *are we going to be tested on this?* Another notion that always seems to irk me is the idea of the sectionalism of black history—that black history is somehow separate from the rest of the country as opposed to being *part* of the country. However, the truth of the matter is if it happened in America than it is *American* history; whether or not it happened to a black American or a white American. Just as America became sectionalized during the civil war as southerners and northerners, history is seemingly sectionalized as black history and white history.

Back in high school, I remember having a white history teacher—that is a white man who taught history but can also be re-defined as a *white* man who taught "white" history—named Mr. Wynn and all he did was blow a lot of wind as he sleep walked through his lectures and at times even blatantly and audaciously yawning! He did not seem "excited" or "passionate" about his subject and to his credit, he did not convey the message that he wanted *us* to be "excited" or "passionate" about it either. It wasn't until I had a *black* history teacher—that is a black woman who mostly taught black history—that I began to feel any pangs of interest and excitement for the subject matter. Her name was Mrs. Robinson, (and yes I am aware of the Paul Simon song of the same name…which I coincidentally used to listen to quite often on my headphones) and she was a no nonsense teacher who was determined to have us "learn" something. The only magnanimous and indelible memory I have of her was when she gave the class a research paper assignment on two protuberant figures in black history: Booker T. Washington and W.E.B. Dubois. Finally, I thought, someone other than Martin Luther King, who hitherto was my only point of reference when it came to black history. After I wrote the paper, I concluded that these post slavery civil rights iconoclasts has two very distinctive characteristics: on the one hand you have Booker T. who wanted blacks to stay in their place, cooperate with white political rule as long as they could have access to technical training in order to secure employment. Dubois on the other hand, hailed hell with that! He wanted FULL equality for black people **period**! He held America's feet to the fire by flailing in its face its constitutional decree that all man are created equal and therefore all are entitled to the same baseline decree of equality. It was this momentous moment in my entire four years of high school that I became "excited" and "passionate" about history. I became more interested in college, but the experience was lack luster due to the usual surplus of college "distractions" and an overabundance of course choices. However, after, college, I started writing for local newspapers and literary magazines, just as I had done in high school and it was through writing about the history of Haiti, black history month and the history of the American civil war that I inexorably learned far more than I ever did before.

Over the last decade or so leading up to our current inimical political climate, I have found myself wondering about the evolution of race and racism and consequently I did some curious reconnoitering. I discovered that the concept of race and the standardization of racism was preeminently introduced by a French aristocrat by the name of Joseph Arthur De Gobineau in the mid-19th century in his 1400-page (someone had a lot of time on his hands) book entitled An Essay on the Inequality of the Human Races in 1848 in which he utilized the now defunct pseudo-scientific theories of *race biology* otherwise known as "scientific" racist theory: which propagated the belief that experiential proof exists to reify or justify racism, racial inferiority or racial superiority. He also developed the concept of the Aryan Master Race, a farfetched concept that bestowed power and privilege to the Caucasians but predominantly among Germans and those from northern and north western Europe from putative or supposed Nordic or Aryan races which were mostly found in Scandinavia, Northwestern Europe and countries neighboring the Baltic Sea, for instance the Germans and Finnic peoples, who resided in the independent states of Finland and Estonia.

The precept of the sovereignty of the "Nordic race" and the Northwestern European nations that were concomitant with this hypothetical race predisposed the United States' Immigration Act of 1924 (which efficiently barred or harshly restricted the immigration of Italians, Jews, and other Southern and Eastern Europeans) and the later Immigration and Nationality Act of 1952 which included restrictive measures such as increased review of prospective immigrants, increased deportations, and more rigorous naturalization measures and it was also present in other countries outside Northwestern Europe such as Australia, Canada, and South Africa. By the 1930s, the Nazis determined that the Nordic race was the most superior branch of the "Aryan race" and constituted a master race. Gobineau's writings were quickly extoled by white supremacist, pro-slavery Americans like Josiah C. Nott and Henry Hotze, who interpreted his book into English but omitted nearly 1,000 pages of the original book, particularly those parts that negatively described Americans as a racially mixed people. Rousing a social movement in Germany named Gobinism.

But why do we refer to "white" people as Caucasians? Well, according to Wikipedia, the term was popularized by the German scientist, naturalist and anthropologist Johann Friedrich Blumenbach, who was among the premiere pioneers to reconnoiter humans as a facet of natural history. In 1795, he separated the human races into five categories listed verbatim from the site:

- The Caucasian or white race. European, Middle Eastern, and North African origins.
- The Mongolian or yellow race, including all East Asians and some Central Asians.
- The Malayan or brown race, including Southeast Asian and Pacific Islanders.
- The Ethiopian or black race, including sub-Saharan Africans.
- The American or red race, including American Indians.

For more information, visit: https://en.m.wikipedia.org/wiki/Johann_Friedrich_Blumenbach

Caucasians literally refers to people native to "The Caucasus /ˈkɔːkəsəs/ or Caucasia / kɔːˈkeɪʒə/…an area sandwiched between the Black Sea and the Caspian Sea and once primarily recognized domiciles for the people of Armenia, Azerbaijan, Georgia and Russia. It is home to the Caucasus Mountains, comprising the Greater Caucasus mountain range, which has archeologically been measured as a natural barrier between Eastern Europe and Western Asia.

For more information, visit: https://en.wikipedia.org/wiki/Caucasus

In Russian, the word "Caucasian" is a collective term referring to anyone descended from the native ethnic groups of the Caucasus. In Russian slang, people of the Caucasus are (ironically) called "black" despite their fair skin, this name calling comes from their relatively darker features.

Ironically Armenians, who are considered Caucasian because they originate from the Caucasus, were denied the status of being considered "white" when they came to America. They had to petition for "white privilege." During 18th and 19th century America, the status of "whiteness" had to do with more than just your skin color, it also encompassed your social economic status, things like whether or not you were a property (possessing a slave for example) or business owner (trader for example) could make or break your entitlement to "white privilege"; even if you were visibly "white" by appearances alone.

However, the ideology of the white race as a superior race and the black race an inferior one is non sequitur to the genetic scientific evidence that has traced the very first known civilization in the deserts of Sub-Saharan Africa 50,000 years ago. Subsequently, there was a migration to Asia due to a severe drought and then the return of some back to Africa, which partly explains why some modern day Africans bear Asian facial features and characteristics. The 2003 PBS miniseries *"Journey of Man"* extrapolates further on this significant but mostly largely overlooked part of our history. The ideology of white supremacy is bequeathed the mistaken notion that people of African descent are somehow inferior to every other race on the planet. This was largely based on polygenesis and eugenics, among other archaic pseudoscientific racist theories of yesteryear.

According to Lobban C. Fluehr, **polygenesis** is "a theory of human origins which posits the view that the human races are of different origins (polygenesis). This view is opposite to the idea of monogenism, which posits a single origin of humanity. Modern scientific views no longer favor the polygenic model, [which has been replaced] with the monogenic 'Out of Africa' theory and its variants being the most widely accepted models for human origins."

Eugenics, on the other hand, is derived from the Greek word meaning: "well-born". It is "a set of beliefs and practices that aim to improve the genetic quality of a human population by excluding (through a variety of morally criticized means) certain genetic groups judged to be inferior, and promoting other genetic groups judged to be superior." According to Francis Galton, who coined terminology in 1883. This concept of selective breeding is closely linked to white supremacy and has been universally used in the past in Europe and North America.

The African civilization—hailed as the first known genetically traced people 50,000 years ago---had been thriving long before their European annexation and subsequent extraction from Africa, notably known as "The Mother Land." Historian Howard Zinn reaffirms this premise in *A People's History* of the United States when he said, "In fact, it was because they came from a settled culture, of tribal costumes and family ties, of communal life and traditional ritual, that African blacks found themselves especially helpless when removed from this." It was this concept of racial inferiority, along the fact that the Africans too held slaves (although under dissimilar and less draconian conditions as I alluded to earlier) that the Europeans used as among the basis for the enslavement of the African people.

Wanting to give the reader an idea of what the captives endured, Zinn quotes the narratives of a man by the name of John Barbot, who towards the dwindling years of the 17th century wrote of slave conditions along the edges of the Gold Coast:

> As the slaves came down to Fida from the inland country, they are put into a… prison near the beach, and when the Europeans are to receive them, they are brought to a large plain, where the ship's surgeons examines every part of every one of them, to the smallest member, men and women being stark naked… marked on the breast with a red-hot iron, imprinting the marks of the French, English or Dutch companies…[then] bonded slaves are returned to their booths where they await shipment, sometimes 10 to 15 days…

During their harrowing journeys to the Americas, they were parked like sardines into the constricted spaces where they often lived in their own feces in stifling stench where some suffocated and at worst some even chose death over bondage, committing suicide by leaping into the shark infested waters below.

The practice of capture and enslavement was sanctioned by the Catholic Church according to Zinn, who, in wanting to exposes the hypocrisy of so called "Christians"—as any self-respecting truth teller would—reported an instance when a priest wrote to another in a vexing attempt at clearing his conscience. In 1610, Father Sandoval from the Americas wrote to Brother Louis Brandon who was at a religious function in Europe to inquire if "capture, transport, and enslavement of Africans was legal by church doctrine." In return, in a script stamped March 2, 1610, he replied that "This is a matter which has been questioned by the Board of Conscience in Lisbon [largest city in Portugal], and all its members are learned and conscientious men [including] Bishops…and very learned Fathers…never did they consider the trade as [illegal]. Therefor we and the Fathers of Brazil buy these slaves for our service without any [hesitation]...

In consideration of the above scenario of a Catholic priest with a crisis of conscious regarding the sale and acquisition of another human being, it is my experience that usually if you have to ask whether or not something is right or wrong… then it's most likely *wrong*. Having grown up in Catholic school, I unfortunately experienced their hypocrisy first hand and apparently it began many centuries before I was born.

In relation to how the African slaves to some extant (with some exceptions for rebel slaves) came to be tamed in the British colony of Jamestown, Virginia, Zinn offered a most probable explanation. He concluded that there were a plethora of factors at play which made it possible to subjugate Africans in Jamestown. 1) The colonizers were in dire straits for field hands, 2) Capturing and subduing the Indians proved surprisingly difficult being that they were in their own element, 3) It was not easy to make use of white slaves, and 4) Black workers were made possible in large numbers by unscrupulous slave dealers and they being easier to tame due to the psychological and physical trauma they endured crossing the Atlantic, rendering them in a state of shock and stupor. "…is it any wonder that such blacks were ripe for enslavement?" Zinn queries his readers, in—I'm guessing—an earnest quest to cultivate empathy and understanding; perhaps in anticipatory attempt to counter the possible judgment that the enslaved were conceivably just weak and, even more farfetched, willing.

Speaking of history's ancient civilizations and their inevitable bump into racism, the story of Christopher Columbus and the **Indigenous American Indians** is a vital and an inexorable part of this dialogue.

"Arawak men and women, naked, tawny, and full of wonder, emerged from their villages onto the island's beaches and swarm out to get a closer look at the strange big boat. When Columbus and his sailors came ashore, carrying swords, speaking oddly, the Arawaks ran to greet them, brought them food, water, gifts. He later wrote of this in his log:

> They…brought us parrots and balls of cotton and spears and many other things, which they exchanged for the glass beads and hawks' bells. They willingly traded everything they owned…They were well built…They would make fine servants…With fifty men we could subjugate them all…"

Hence begins the indispensable book: *A People's History of the United States* by historian and former Boston University college professor Howard Zinn. This particularly book was required reading on the college syllabus of my U.S. History class. Unlike other historic texts, it recounts America's history from the point of view of the people, the governed rather than the governors. When you read it, you get a more intimate and incisive feel for the marrow of America's birthing tales; which are, in more traditional texts, are aggrandized sometimes beyond comprehension or recognition by history experts like Zinn and later Ray Raphael (author of Founding Myths: Stories That Hide Our American Past) who are cognizant of what "really" happened. Both Zinn and Raphael extrapolates that American history is rampant with inaccuracies, exaggerations and downright lies! Reading these books will sure to open your eyes and force you to question everything you "thought" you knew about the complex history of our beloved country. Yet another story would also intercept these "false" narratives of history and would essentially serve to further demythologize the story of Christopher Columbus as "the founding father" of the Americas and shed light on how "America" acquired its namesake.

According to research on Wikipedia, "**Amerigo Vespucci**: [ameˈriːgo veˈsputti (Italian); Americus Vespucius (Latin)—who was born in the Republic of Florence on March 9, 1454 and died in February 22, 1512)—was an Italian voyager, investor, navigator, and cartographer (mapmaker). While Sailing for Portugal circa 1501–1502, Vespucci proved that Brazil and the West Indies were not Asia's eastern borders (as originally thought by Christopher Columbus) but a detached, uncharted land corpus colloquially known as the New World. In 1507, **the new continent was called America eponymously subsequent to the Latin version of Vespucci's first name Americus.** But how America was named is not as important as the principals on which it was founded.

As I've mentioned before in the introduction to this book, America was founded on the principals and practice of racism, which existed long before the concept of "race" (which was not clearly defined until mid-19th century by Joseph Arthur de Gobineau among others long after the onset of slavery); which I will elaborate on later. When Christopher Columbus landed in the Americas, namely Hispaniola (present day Haiti and the Dominican Republic) he and his troops terrorized the natives through rapes, kidnappings, enslavement and nonchalant brutalities, like chopping off a child's head for flimsy excuses among other acts and flinching practices of violence.

Personal affronts, land thefts and decimations of indigenous American Indians did not only happen in 1492, when Columbus first arrived in the Americas. As a New Englander, it was interesting to learn of the history of the desperate and despondent Pilgrims—who fled England for the Americas due to religious persecution—and their eventual mostly "grim" encounter with them at Cape Cod and Plymouth plantation when they disembarked from the prickly and shabby shipping vessel known as the *Mayflower* back in the fall of 1620. But before we can get into the "what", we essentially have to begin with the "who, when and where" of the Pilgrims' journey.

According the History Channel DVD *The Mayflower*, in England, the official state religion in 1534 was the Church of England. This happened after England's break with the Catholic church when Pope Clement 7th declined to terminate the marriage between King Henry the 8th and Spanish born Catherine of Aragon, daughter of Isabella I of Castile and Ferdinand II of Aragon —who was Queen of England from June 1509 until May 1533 as the first wife of Henry 8th—so that he could marry Anne Boleyn, who would be Queen Elizabeth I's mother. Hence Henry the 8th established himself as the head of the church replacing the catholic Pope in Rome. He defied him by assuming supremacy over religious matters.

In 1533 their marriage was consequently declared invalid and Henry married Anne on the judgement of clergy in England, without reference to the Pope. Now without the Pope in power, what was to become of the divisive issue of religion in England?

For more information, visit: https://en.wikipedia.org/wiki/Catherine_of_Aragon

King Henry the 8th's unprecedented break from the Catholic Church delighted the English Protestants who took this as a sign that England would be joining the Great Protestant Reformation of Martin Luther and overthrow the old Catholic Church dogma altogether. They exclaimed that "God has all the power and we have none!" This would result in the great split of the Western World in the 16th century between the Church of England, the puritans and the separatists.

The puritans—although leery that certain elements of the Catholic Church was still present in the new Church of England, like Bishops and copious use of Catholic ornamentations and functions—still believed in the new church but wanted to change some of these pesky Catholic remnants. The separatists—on the other hand—believed that the Church of England should not exist on the moral and religious doctrine that the church shouldn't be connected to civil power period. Both puritans and separatists did not believe in holding saint days, such as traditional holidays like Christmas and Easter.

In 1607, King James I declared that you can't have political stability unless you have religious unity. The separatists or English Protestants disagreed and facing persecution, fled to Holland, Netherlands from Scrooby, England where separatists rejoiced in religious tolerance. There they formed a non-conformist community printing seditious pamphlets in Leiden, Netherlands, expressing their objection to the religious intolerance and authoritarian practices of the Church of England and anonymously sending them to King James I in England in 1617. Once King James discovered where the printing of the pamphlets were coming from, in a thinly veiled threat, strongly suggested to the authorities in Holland not to house religious subversives in their whelm; that is if they wanted their hitherto amicable relationship to remain as is for their own sake. They complied and began to galvanize raids and arrests of the separatists which then resulted in them fleeing Holland for the Americas.

Meanwhile, before the pilgrims even arrived, the only successful English settlement in the Americas was in James Town, Virginia in the year 1617, with a population of about 2000 Europeans. However, in stark contrast to the European population, there were about fifty million natives. Virginia was an immense area over which England claimed and developed. The pilgrims' journey to the Americas began between August and December of 1620. They had to return once due to another ship called the Speedwell—which they brought in addition to the Mayflower, faltered; thus delaying their journey by a month or so. They then decided that the Mayflower—with ceilings about five feet high was really a merchant cargo ship not designed to transport passengers—would have to be suffice. The ship carried about 102 passengers with 35 to 45 crew members. They constructed the Mayflower Compact as a governing body until proper legislation could be establish as the settle in their new home.

The pilgrims first landed at Cape Cop, Provincetown on November 9th, 1620. But after only a little over a month, due to unremittent scuffles with the Indigenous Natives—compounded by their inability to find sources of freshwater—decided to traverse to other terrains and on

December 11th, 1620 ended up in Plymouth, Massachusetts where they established their first colony with the natives in a sometimes tense and precarious relationship. After an English speaking native American named Squanto—who learned English after he was kidnapped by the English and brought back to England in the town of Cornhill for three years until his escape back to the Americas only to find his entire family decimated by European diseases—who translated and mediated between the English pilgrims and the Wampanoag Native Americans. The Wampanoags' taught the English a method of growing corn by burying herring fish with the corn seed to help fertilize the crops. They called their creator "Kiehtan" and held the deer among their high status foods. The famous story of Thanksgiving was originally called a "Harvest Festival" in 1621. And since the area only had wild turkey (with no access to domestically grown turkey from Europe) and being that the deer was held in high regards, they most likely feasted on venison or dear meat and NOT turkey as we've been led to believe. The Harvest Festival—or "Thanksgiving" as it came to be known, was to celebrate the apprehensive alliance between the pilgrims and King Massasoit. Born circa 1590, near present day Bristol, Rhode Island, U.S.—and died 1661, near Bristol), He was a revered Wampanoag Indian chief who all through his life sustained peaceful relations with English immigrants in the area of the Plymouth Colony, of Massachusetts.

Hence as I have demonstrated in the previous narratives regarding the treatment of the Indigenous Natives first by Christopher Columbus, then by the British colonists, who killed them amass both with their diseases and with weaponry, European entitlement and racism both played a huge role in the subjugation and annihilation of the natives of the Americas. The question is, with the persistence of racism even today, in the year 2019, how do we utilize the lessons of the past to move forward toward a more racially just tomorrow? For that, I turn to modern day intellectuals with fecund ideologies and guidance on the racial justice issue like African American author Van Jones.

Looking back throughout America's history of racism, Yale University graduate, CNN politico and New York Times best-selling author of *Beyond the Messy Truth: How We Came Apart and How We Come Together*, Van Jones surmises that, "America's problems are bigger than Donald Trump. And they long predate his rise." He extrapolates that politics across all party lines set the stage for "Trump's ascendance." He expounded that since the 1990s inaugurated policies that virtually destroyed tons of American lives—among them were dire trade deals, unrestricted maneuvers on Wall Street, and the augmentation of jails, and infinite warfare which inevitably bore ominous circumstances of home and job lost and hopeless chances for pay increases.

"As unnerving as it is to have an erratic narcissist in power, any analysis of his rise must start with an acknowledgement that both parties have been letting the American people for a very long time." Jones resolved. Although he decidedly put the blame of Trump's rise at the door steps of both Republican and Democratic political parties, he wanted to make it clear his position and determinants on not only the Trump administration's dystopic oligarchical style of government—or ruling characterized by life conditions rendered particularly ruthless, as from dispossession, domination, and fear—but on President Trump himself when he stated, "The Trump presidency has polarized the discourse, jeopardized our standing on the world stage, and inflamed hostility along racial, gender and religious lines." He alluded to a particular Trump behavior that most if not all are familiar with when he said, "…individuals at both ends of the political system are growing uneasy with his tweeting, tantrums, and temperament."

However, his most pressing point is not just the enigmatic fact that we've elected someone like Trump as our president, but how we go about dealing and conversing with one another in response of that fact? "What are we to learn from this?" He beseeched. The first thing we have to do according to Jones, is blow up conventions that dictate, "Always attack your opponent's views even if he or she made a good point" or "Expose your opponent's weaknesses, conceal your own." He acknowledged that "conservatives, moderates and progressives are equally guilty of this." Including himself, he earnestly admitted. "What we need now," he said, "is not politics of accusation" but "politic of confession", a new convention in which all sides can begin to take responsibility in conjuring up this calamity we've all find ourselves embroiled in and move in the direction "towards a more positive populism."

The Trump administration is conceivably a pejorative response or "confession" to the Obama administration, as was the Obama administration a pejorative response or "confession" to the George W. Bush administration and so forth… As with any transitional shift of a governing body, the allegiance or lack thereof and the satisfaction or lack thereof with the preceding administration will often determine the political pulse of the American populous for successive elections. However the one pesky constant subtext of often thinly veiled "confession" in anything having to do with America is unequivocally *racism*.

Ta- Nehisi Coates, best-selling author and National Book Award winner in his book, *We Were Eight Years in Power*, offers Bill Cosby's take on the issue of racism from one of his ubiquitous talks to black audiences across the U.S., in which he tries to motivate and mobilize black people from feeling like disempowered victims to becoming empowered victors while navigating America's race partiality crisis, "As Cosby sees it," Coats wrote, "the antidote to racism is not rallies, protests, or pleas but strong families and communities. Instead of focusing on some abstract notion of equality, he argues, blacks need to cleanse their culture, embrace personal responsibility and reclaim the traditions that fortified them in the past." To thrive rather than dwindle by binding together despite slavery's demoralizing legacy; whose "… long legal existence created the American caste [or social rankings based on the privileged few] system that endures today" according to Detroit Free Press Columnist Rochelle Riley in an article titled "Why America can't get over slavery, its greatest shame", published Feb. 8, 2018.

However, Coats seemingly has a bleak premonition of the fate of black activism in American society when he reflected that, "The civil rights generation is exiting the American stage.." he said, "Not in haze of nostalgia but in a cloud of gloom, troubled by the persistence of racism, the apparent weaknesses of the generation following in its wake, and the seeming indifference of much of the country to black America's fate." In light of those realizations, Cosby's admonitions of structured self-restraint, ethical cleansings, and self-sufficiency proffers a way of escaping the scourge of limitations imposed on them by racism. "…a promise that one need not cure America of its original sin in order to succeed." That it does not necessitate racism to be eradicated but reinforces the notion that it can be *overcomed*, as Martin Luther King Jr. espoused. An ideology that reinforces the powerful impetus of togetherness within the black community, particularly in as a defensive action against the detrimental forces of racism.

"We survived slavery because we held on to another. The moment we found freedom, we began to commit suicide." A sentiment expressed by Dr. Teseh Loane Keto as quoted in Iyanla Vanzant's best-selling book: *Acts of Faith: Daily Meditations for People of Color*. She expounded on this notion of togetherness as a people (although this notion **must** be applied across the spectrum of skin color) when she said, "We are connected to one creative source. This source creates a responsibility for, accountability to and dependence on one another. The moment we allow the self to believe that it can do without other people we create [a] kind of loneliness and depression… [that makes life seemingly] not worth living." Understandably it can be hard to stick together when ghettoized and Balkanized members of the relentlessly underserved black communities—having nowhere else to turn—turn on one another; as they navigate the realities of withstanding centuries of systemic oppression and mass incarcerations under the American weather of majority power.

Frederick Douglas, a self-educated former slave, abolitionist, orator and advisor to President Abraham Lincoln once said, "Power concedes nothing without a demand." And America, as with most large dominant forces, is a magnanimous stage for the proliferation of power plays. For ALL Americans to participate in the highly extoled great American Dream—and benefit from its associated wealth—there must be a structure in place to shift the balance of power and redistribute the wealth from the top to the bottom. This notion is becoming quite important to young college grads—who in some instances—will not work for a company that has not taken an oath of "social responsibility" according to a segment I saw on PBS News Hour. These millennial iconoclasts are determined to hold big business' feet to the fire and ascertain that they don't value profit over people as most often do and that they are also willing to redistribute the wealth by "sharing" the profits with mid and low level employees who— diligently on a daily basis—contribute to the company's success. Still change is not readily acceptable and is quick to be dismissed as undoable, this notion assuaged and reflected by spiritual blogger and author Mary Deturris Poust when she said, "We cling to the comfortable, rather than step out into the possible." Yes! Racial and economic equity *can* be POSSIBLE!

The matter of economic equity is resonated by editor-in-chief Joshua Cohen in an issue of the Boston Review: Forum 2 entitled "Work, Inequality and Basic Income" when he spoke of the need for pervasive economic security when he said, "We are in a fight about the future and it is important to be clear about the larger purpose of that fight. Suppose, then, we think we are aiming at a freer society, in which greater economic security reduces vulnerability and subordination…that is not a bad start in describing a world worth fighting for." And I couldn't agree more…

There needs to be a way to manage the daunting ideology of the participation of the nation's wealth for the common good, especially since it was the commoners who helped build that wealth to begin with. In an another article of the same issue of the previously mentioned Boston Review entitled "Redistributing Wealth and Power", Connie Razza, director of Strategic Research at the Center for Popular Democracy, make a logical argument regarding the dissemination of capital and clout among the American populous. "Algernon Austin has shown that, for more than half –century, African American unemployment rates have been roughly twice as high as white unemployment rates. Structural racism—both within the labor market and in education, housing, and other related areas—largely account for this disparity." Among her stated reasons attributed to this "structural racism" that has affected certain "racial and ethnic groups" thus contributing to them being omitted from the labor force are the unequivocal facts that the pernicious corpus of confinements and bias against those with criminal records "which disproportionately impacts African Americans."

Her most pressing declarations, however was her bold assessment of the Trump administration's threat to "our social net" as they attack employee privileges, reasonable recompenses, and unrestricted partnerships with unions; the mobilization of municipal goods to private regulators and lastly to prioritize the "interest of wealthy corporations and individuals." Which threaten the civil rights of the bottom 99 percent, particularly minorities.

"It just feels like we're still waiting" said Boe Montgomery in the Washington Post article "In Trump Country, a Group of Coal Miners Rebel over Lost Jobs", published Sept. 2, 2019 by Tim Craig. What Montgomery, who is a mine worker, is "waiting" for according to Craig is "Trump's vow to revive the economies of depressed communities" as he touted during his 2016 presidential bid. In Cumberland, Kentucky, there's a nationwide battle over workers' rights. The Trump administration "failed to spark a revival in communities like Cumberland that formed his political base in the 2016 election." Craig wrote.

Basically, we are now in the twenty-first century and when it's all said and done, these are the days you'll remember: swelling and seemingly inexorable racial, sociopolitical and religious divisions running rampant in Trump era America. Atavistic xenophobia is back--did it ever leave?—an old racial reality with younger angrier faces has been re-hatched with temerity and we hope it will compel us to unity rather than tear us apart; as we continue to learn to celebrate our contrasting multiculturalism instead of being castigated for our differences. Although America was founded on racist principles of the destruction and displacement of indigenous Native Americans, and the enslavement and oppression of African Americans, it appears that most have self-servingly forgotten, consciously or subconsciously ignored the gritty teeth of history in this country. I saw a sign held by a young white female protester during the freedom of speech rally on the Boston Commons that said: **"Racism is not over, but I'm over racism."** This is a testament to the resistance against intolerance.

The "Black Lives Matter" (BLM) movement is not in competition with the "white Lives Matter" movement simply because of course All Lives Matter but racism dictates that Black Lives Matter Less and White Lives Matter More and so that's why the movement exists. The BLM movement is having its moment in the sun by speaking and standing up for equity for the designated bottom feeders of society who refuse to run, but instead, get angry. They hail and wail and with them I also question: "what is going on?" We need a shift in direction!

"Many sides! Many sides!" say Black people are lazy but moon town sun down we're working like crazy; fighting for our inalienable rights as "equal" members of society. Our clock never seems to stop turning; we're confused about the American promise: work hard and you'll get some relief but does "relief" comes for those who do not look like the majority? But who am I? Just a maligned Haitian-American citizen whose voting voice barely makes a seething sound.

Way back when, chiefly Africans worked 400 years around the clock building the American capitalist economy. It is documented that slave labor made an 80% contribution to the building of the grand American wealth. And when Abraham Lincoln tried to remedy slavery with the onslaught of the Civil War and won, he was assassinated and the White Lives Matter More movement was born. Never mind the fact that when America decided to free itself from the tight grip of British oppression, the first person who died for the American cause was a Black Bostonian by the name of Crispus Attucks on March 5th, 1770.

Never mind that Black people have fought in every American war, even when they were told that their "inferior" genetics made them a liability and unfit to serve, hence they essentially had to fight to fight. Never mind that after the American World War II triumph, when returning soldiers were handed hefty G.I Bills-which is designed to help service members, eligible veterans and their families cover the costs associated with getting an education or training--that allowed them to partake in the American dream that resulted in being able to buy houses in the suburbs with two car garages during the booming 1950s and subsequently the Black soldiers were denied their G.I. Bills and instead faced further indignities by having to endure separated but "equal" Jim Crow laws and a discriminatory practice that was generated by the civil war called The Black Code which meant that Blacks seeking jobs were to be turned away. A practice similar to the "No Irish Need Apply" signs during the influx of Irish immigrants in the early 1820s. Which makes one wonder, how does a race that endured 400 years of slave labor, toiling seventeen hour days under the sun, while light skinned Blacks waited on Whites inside the plantation houses, and in the post slavery years were turned away when they sought legitimate employment be stereotyped as "lazy"? Besides, scientific evidence has traced the genesis of the human race and eventual diaspora all the way back to Africa 50,000 years ago, (aka The Mother Land). Hence this mere fact would argue that indirectly we are all connected.

Never mind that my Haitian ancestors fought in the American Revolution and were finally memorialized in Savannah, Georgia for their heroic service. Never mind that the ruthless emperor Napoleon Bonaparte used the monetary funds he attained from the slave labor on the Island of Haiti to fortify the American cause against the British. Never mind that Haiti's victory over the French inspired American slave revolts in the form of Nat Turners rebellion and more successfully the Civil War; which resulted in the passing of the 13th, 14th, and 15th amendments meant to ensure Black equality in America. Yet, here we are, in the 21st century, over 150 years post slavery, we are back in the streets fighting to matter. I once heard an unmasked white nationalist (as most of them are these days) asserting with a deceptively docile smile on his face, that he acknowledges the inherent worth and dignity of all people BUT… particularly people of European descent. Go figure.

The world is restless as wars for justice and equality go on and on the domestic front; regular folks have formed movements to unify a diversified and increasingly divided America juxtaposed with President Donald Trump's stance to "Make America Great Again" but for whom? For Blacks? For Hispanics? For Asians? For Muslims? For All immigrants? For the poor and disenfranchised? For whom? Perhaps we can "all" make America great by making our own unique voices heard by making moral and ethical contributions to one another; by aiding and not abetting the American cause, the American promise of life, liberty and the pursuit of happiness which belongs to all Americans. Period. Let's not forget all of us, who are not American Indians, are descendants of immigrants. All of our ancestors came here from somewhere else, whether it was on the Mayflower or on Ellis Island in New York harbor overlooking the Statue of Liberty, we owe our lives here in America to the intrepid liberty seeking trajectory of the immigrant; whether they be white, black or otherwise.

Because of racial inequality and bias, affirmative action became one of the contentious "wins" blacks achieved in America as a result of the **civil rights movement** (which coincidentally benefitted numerous white women in their own melee for equal pay and employment opportunities) and of which African American Supreme Court justice Clarence Thomas said, "Openness and comfort in multi-cultural places is part of the self-understanding of the American ruling class. So the combination of elitist exclusivity and a racial esthetic leads to affirmative action." In other words affirmative action is not as much pro-equality as it is pro-impression management or cultivating a facading schematic environs to control how things "look" in terms of the white and black visual ratio; this then gave rise to the crude "token black" ideology in which one or two blacks are strategically placed in a mostly white setting so that the organization won't prima facie appear "racist." We see this manifested in live TV news anchors, sitcoms and dramas where a plethora of black, yellow and brown personalities are scattered among the usual sea of whiteness on television.

I am quite aware that a plethora of Americans, White or otherwise, have been indoctrinated— or taught to uncritically accept biased ideas, opinions, and beliefs of a particular group—rather than educated about our social-cultural and economic structures. For example some have been indoctrinated to think that Black people are lazy and some choose to believe that without question. One of the remedies I can think of is to be honest with yourself about how you have been consciously or subconsciously indoctrinated or taught about others who are different from you, and then, the most difficult part of all, have a DIALOGUE with that person, then reevaluate your preconceived notions or fallacies and start fresh. I truly believe that it will be at

that point you can move from being indoctrinated to being "educated" about other human beings who are truly not that much different from you; being that we are all members of the same race: the human race.

Yet, still I concur with the French playwright Moliere's inspirational words "It is not only what we do but also what we do not do for which we are accountable." Hence you are responsible for looking away when wrong is being committed just as you are responsible for getting involved when wrong is being committed. So don't just sit there, do something! Start by having a conversation with someone perceived as different from you from a prima facie stand point and see what happens. There can be social progressivity in practicing political civility. What I mean by that is diligently adhering to our American constitutional pledge of freedom of speech inherent in our first amendment rights and our democracy. We may not always agree, but as free Americans, we have pledged to at least listen to what each other have to say.

My heart is brimming with pride to be a Bostonian after the inexorable display of unity on that hot summer day, the August 19th Freedom of Speech Rally where hate groups were expected to make a strong showing, but less 50 showed up to Boston's 40,000 strong; which proves Bostonians treat each other as family, and like most families, there maybe some in fighting, but when it comes to hostile intruders, we stand together in defiant unity.

"Today Boston stood for peace and love, not bigotry and hate. We should work to bring people together, not apart." said Mayor Martin J. Walsh, boldly denouncing the intolerance of the alternative right wing (alt-right) extremist movement. I would like to personally thank the Mayor, the Boston police department and Boston police commissioner William Evans for the preemptive protection of our beloved city.

"99.9% of the people were here for the right reason, and that was to fight bigotry and hate,"

Commissioner Evans said. It is because of this intrepid display of unity that l am a proud Haitian- American citizen and Bostonian. It is because of this fervent display of unity that I am hopeful and optimistic that one day the poor, marginalized and disenfranchised members of society will finally rise from the ashes of assigned adversity to eventually bask in the glory of human dignity through monetary self-sufficiency and finally find liberty, equality and fraternity for all of humanity.

The father of that young White woman who died fighting racism and hatred in Charlottesville, Virginia at the hands of neo-Nazis and white supremacist implored us all to STOP THE HATE!

Stop holding onto the past like a child holds onto a security blanket and forgive each other.

Bishop Desmond Tutu famously said, "When the law of an eye for an eye operates, all the people will end up blind." It is imperative that we learn to surrender our thirst for that transient "feel good fix" known as vengeance! Because realistically, an eye for an eye *will* leave everybody blind, as Bishop Tutu alluded to. In any situation, positive or negative (for this purpose mostly negative), there is a lesson to be learned. If you've been burned than maybe next time you'll consider wearing oven mitts. You must learn to forgo the notion that once you've been wronged by someone, than you hold *anyone* who looks like that person accountable; whether he or she be white, brown, yellow or black. For your own peace of mind and moral integrity, you must treat each situation individually, learn the lesson to be learned from *that* particular interaction and move on. Both you and the rest of society will be the "better" for it.

To understand the evolution of entrenched systemic racism in America—that is the implementation of racist policies that benefit the racially privileged "whites" over everyone else—we must be willing to understand and accept the country's founding based on historical *facts*, and not historical *myths*. America was founded on its "original sins" of the decimation and displacement of Indigenous Native Americans and the abduction and enslavement of African Americans; "facts"—not "myths"—that would establish the rise of racism in the United States, resulting to how we got to be where we are today: utterly stupefied as white supremacist march orgulous in our streets. Automobile and assembly line pioneer Henry Ford—himself the son of Irish and Belgian immigrants—had the vision and wisdom to know that we as a people are stronger together when he said, "Coming together is a beginning; keeping together is a process; [but] working together is success."

At the end of the day, we all matter and when it comes to the "States" we are all stronger when we are "United". Russian doctor, playwright and short story writer Anton Chekhov once said, "Man will become better, when you show him what he is like." I fervently hope that certain aspects of this narrative vividly "showed" you what "our collective humanity" looked like over our hitherto social history of racism up to our present day reality. Whether we like it or not, we are all broken pearls along the roundabout road of life, and by "seeing" one another from roundabout perspectives dissimilar to our own, we can conceivably have a sudden "revival" of compassion and understanding for our collectively "broken" natures and THAT—my fellow humans---is how we move forward *together*! It might serve you well to remember what the German-born Jewish-American theoretical physicist Albert Einstein —who himself while visiting America in 1933 amidst the rise of the German dictator Adolf Hitler decided to stay and became a U.S. citizen—once said, "Learn from yesterday, live for today, hope for tomorrow."

Why We Still Need Black History Month

"We are caught in an inescapable network of mutuality, tied in a single garment of destiny. Whatever affects one directly, affects all indirectly." —Dr. Martin Luther King Jr.

In an article by Mema Ayi and Demetrius Patterson from the Chicago Defender, they wrote that "actor Morgan Freeman created a small firestorm...when he told Mike Wallace of 60 Minutes that he finds Black History Month (BHM) ridiculous." Freeman goes on to say that "Americans perpetrate racism by relegating Black history to just one month when Black history is American history." I agree with Dr. Martin Luther King Jr. that as Americans we are tied together "...in an inescapable network of mutuality...Whatever affects one [of us]... affects [all of us] as Americans in this country.

As you can clearly see, a month dedicated to Black history continues to stir controversy. The point of the matter is we can't continue to ignore the fact that—although we have made progress towards racial unity—we still have ways to go towards racial, harmony, understanding and tolerance if not acceptance.

Scholars and historians such as Conrad Worrill, chairman of the National Black United Front repulses the commercialization of the celebration, stated Ayi and Patterson. However, they go on to say that "but [Worrill] agree that Black Americans still need February and every day to reflect on the accomplishments of Black Americans who contributed countless inventions and innovations into society."

But why do we still need—even in the twenty-first century—a month set aside to recognize Black history in this country? Perhaps you can look within your respective hearts for that answer.

In an article titled "We Need Black History Month Now More Than Ever" by Peniel Joseph and published on CNN.com on Feb. 2, 2017, he reifies the necessity of a month designated to remind all Americans of why the month is important, not just for African Americans, but for all Americans participating in a democratic society and especially in consideration of sitting President Donald Trump who—while trying to "honor" the month described its yearly gathering as "our little breakfast"—had so little knowledge of, the self-educated former slave, abolitionist and advisor to President Lincoln, Frederick Douglas, that he spoke of him as if he was still alive (Douglas died in 1895); which drew the ire of many according to Joseph.

"Black History Month, created by the Harvard trained black historian Carter G. Woodson as Negro History Week in 1926, is more vital in our own times than ever for at least three reasons." He said. He continued by stating, "Its descriptive intervention allows us to embrace the fullness of American and world history on a previously unimagined scale. By allowing the voices of black women and men, icons and ordinary people, to join in our larger democratic story, we come to see how African-Americans expansively transformed the United States. The struggle for black dignity, both its triumphs and travails, offers a universal story through the particular experiences of African-Americans, one that immigrants, women, people of color and LGBTQ communities can all relate to. Black history is also prescriptive; it offers a window into how civil rights struggles can fundamentally change democratic institutions for all people."

Radio personality Cliff Kelley offers an explanation as to why we need Black History Month. Loosely translated, he said that we need it because capricious historians conveniently leave out certain parts of history that does not corroborate their version of history, which I think consist mostly of dead White men. Blacks are virtually removed from it to substantiate the White historical agenda. Plenty of Black youths do not know their history. Most of them think that their history begins and ends with slavery, wrote Patterson and Ayi.

State Representative David Miller (D- Calumet City) asserted that Freeman was right in saying that Black history should be a year round thing. "We've shaped America," he said. And that Black History Month should serve as a reminder of our legacy. The recently deceased Howard Zinn wrote in his book A People's History of the United States, "There is not a country in world history in which racism has been more important than the United States." He poses the question "Is it possible for Blacks and Whites to live together without hatred?" And when it comes to the evolution of racism he had this to say, "...slavery developed into a regular institution of the normal labor relations of Blacks and Whites in the New World. With it developed that special racial feeling—whether hatred or contempt or pity or patronization— that accompanied the inferior position of Blacks in America… that combination of inferior status and derogatory thought we call racism." He goes on to say that "The point is the elements of this web are historical, not 'natural.' This does not mean that they are easily disentangled or dismantled. It only means that there is a possibility for something else, under historical conditions not yet realized."

In an article in The Phoenix titled "Is There Hope in Hollywood? Three controversial films tackle race in The Age of Obama," Peter Keough extrapolates the medium of films are making an effort to bridge the race gap by portraying Blacks as heads of state—in movies like Transformers 2, 2012 and Invictus—although the contexts in which a Black man becomes President is often marred by catastrophe in which case the White leader is killed. Or Blacks are still being portrayed in glaring stereotypical roles as in Precious, with racist clichés like when Precious steals and eats an entire box of fried chicken. The undercurrent of racism is evident even from well-meaning Whites like Joe Biden, when he opposed Obama for President. Biden declared that "[Obama] is the first mainstream African-American who is articulate, and bright and clean and a nice looking guy" Similarly, another fellow democrat and senate majority leader Harry Reid in his book Game Change, said of Obama that America is ready for a Black President, particularly because he is "light skinned and speak with no Negro dialect." This leads me to extrapolate that despite all that Blacks have contributed to the making of America, our contributions seemingly become extraneous compared to our prima facie colorful appearance. And I am compelled to recall what Dr. King Jr. so eloquently stated that Black people should be judged "by the contents of their character" and not their skin color.

Many modern conveniences are directly related to or derivative of the inventions of Black inventors and pioneers: **Daniel Hale Williams** became the first individual in the history of humanity to successfully operate on a human heart, **Charles Drew** discovered how to separate blood plasma, leading to the development of blood banks facilitating life-saving transfusions, I.R. Johnson who invented the **bicycle** frame in 1899, the **electric trolley**, the **dustpan**, **comb**, **brush**, **clothes dryer**, Sarah Boone who invented the **ironing board** in 1892, **Jan Ernst** Matzeliger who revolutionized the shoe industry in the U.S. in 1883 when he invented a machine that attached the upper leather portion to the bottom portion of the shoe, John Lee Love who invented the **pencil sharpener** in 1897, **walkers**, J. A. Burr who invented the **lawn mower, IBM computers, gas masks**, Garrett A. Morgan who invented the automatic three-way **traffic lights**, the fountain **pen, peanut butter, George E. Carruthers** who designed the ultraviolet camera used in space to photograph the moon's surface, **Frederick McKinley** who developed refrigeration of railroad cars and trucks and the portable x-ray machine, **George Washington Carver** who modernized southern agriculture by developing a plethora of products from peanuts and sweet potatoes, **Dr. Patricia Bath**, in 1985, invented specialized tools and systematic procedures for the treatment and removal of cataracts. And, on a less serious note, George Crum who invented the potato ship and Kenneth Dunkley who invented 3-D viewing glasses and holographs, Lisa Gelobter who invented web **animation-online videos**, And thanks to the Academy Award nominated film, Hidden Figures, we're now all conversant with the amazing contributions of the black mathematical geniuses Katherine Johnson, Dorothy Vaughan, and Mary Jackson whose work helped make Neil Armstrong the first man on the moon! And Guion Stewart Bluford, Jr. who became the first African American astronaut in 1983.

All of these achievements have become part of our daily lives here in America and elsewhere as a result of African-American contributions to the economic and scientific stronghold known as America and sadly, we still need Black History Month to remind us!

I sought out some thoughts and comments from local community leaders and young activists on the issue of why we still need Black History Month. I was inundated with a wealth of responses!

Dr. Carolyn L. Turk, an African-American woman and Deputy Superintendent of Cambridge

Public Schools stated that "We have moved from celebrating Negro History Week to celebrating

Black History Month…these celebrations are…needed and should continue, but I am also a strong advocate for the contributions of African Americans to be recognized…throughout the year, across content areas and to be inclusive of local community history. Knowledge of our past helps connect us to our present and provides hope …for the future…if we are to continue to build on the [legacies of those who came before us].

Bob Doolittle, a white youth pastor living in Cambridge said: "Black History Month can and should take Martin Luther King day and make it thirty days of celebrating how the right kind of force leaves a legacy of increasing enjoyment of one another by those who are different."

Shani Fletcher, a bi-racial woman (African- American and Caucasian) of Teen Voices Magazine offered her thoughts… "Black History Month is an opportunity for everyone to celebrate the

African-American experience and the role of Black people in the history of the United States… Quite literally, Black people built this country, and our communities' contributions are a major part of its culture."

Marla Marcum, a white doctoral candidate at the Boston University School of Theology had this to say: "I can give you a concrete example of why Black History Month is vitally important: … This extremely bright young woman—a freshman at MIT—who graduated from one of the best high schools in Massachusetts upon finding out about Coretta Scott King's death asked 'Was she Martin Luther King's sister?' Are we content that this young woman (and so many others) has been taught something about Dr. King, yet she understands so little of his context that she learned nothing at all of his life? Of course our education system should be integrating Black history into the broader curricula, but when it had not happened even in the best public school systems, I think we need to recognize the critical importance of continued attention to Black History Month."

The fundamental nature of Black History Month based on these spectrum perspectives is to celebrate variety and inclusiveness of all people, build on the prophetic and heroic legacies of our ancestors who fought for our freedoms today, recognize that Black History Month is essentially American history despite racial diversity, acknowledge an honor the contributions of African-Americans to this country, advocate for change in our public school systems to include more Black history in their curricula. Dr. Martin Luther King Jr. once said: "Our lives begin to end the day we become silent about things that matter" and that "Injustice anywhere is a threat to justice everywhere." Black history is not separate from American history. As Americans, we are all one blended entity. We need to bridge the interpersonal and inter-racial gap in a highly mechanized society so… "TAKE OFF YOUR HEAD PHONES AND CARE!!!"

The memory of history is often picky. BHM serves as a reminder of its often-colorless state of existence.

So, do we still need Black History Month? The answer is a resounding "Yes!" As long as Blacks are portrayed as stereotypes in the movies, as long as Black contributions to the bastion that is America are marginalized or altogether ignored, as long as Black leaders like former President Barrack Obama are seen as "acceptable" by Whites simply because he is light-skinned and speak without Negro dialect, Black History Month will continue to be necessary and indispensable.

How Haiti Won Its Place in Black History:

The first independent nation in Latin America and the first Black-led republic in the world shaped the African-American identity

"Injustice anywhere, is a threat to justice everywhere. Darkness cannot drive out darkness; only light can do that. Hate cannot drive out hate; only love can do that."—Martin Luther King Jr.

In the two years since the earthquake that devastated Haiti, a country already marred by political depravity and economic hardship, scholars have shed light on the profound connection between Haitian and African-American history. The Haitian people's triumph over slavery and their achievement as the first Black republic have inspired African Americans in their own melee against centuries of slavery and modern-day inequality rooted in racist ideology.

First and foremost, I would like to chart some of Haiti's history from my point of view, as well as from the point of view of Haitian scholars. I lived in Haiti for the first 13 years of my life until my parents brought me to America to escape the Jean Claude "Baby Doc" Duvalier's brutal dictatorship. I grew up in a middle-class family and both my parents had their own houses and were landlords. My father was also a well-known fashion designer with about twenty or so employees who made all my clothes and an avid businessman with his own retail store and dry cleaning business in the Haitian capital of Port-au-Prince, which was then adjacent to Versace's Department Store. I went to a private catholic school and both my parents' separate households and respective families had attending servants. My father also had U.S. residency status and frequently traveled and lived in both Haiti and the United States for both business and to satisfy U.S. residency requirement standards. Although my father was well connected politically, I remember the fear in my parent's eyes when it came to expressing ideas about politics. No one was allowed to speak unfavorably of the government; we all lived under a conspiracy of silence.

In America, I found that most of the Haitian kids I came into contact with were greatly ashamed of their Haitian identity because they had been misinformed by the American media or knew very little of Haiti's iconoclastic place in history. These negative ideas were reinforced by the lack of attention paid to African-American history in American schools. I don't remember being taught much of Black history in either high school or college. Partly due to the recent spotlight on Haiti, I've began to study Black history independently. What I have discovered has helped me to understand the correlation between the Haitian Revolution and the African-American experience of railing against a system of racial inequality.

In his book "Avengers of the New World: The Story of the Haitian Revolution," historian

Laurent Dubois argues that Haiti's revolution posed a challenge not only to the French but also

to "the existence of slavery itself." The Haitian revolution inspired people of color in other countries who were waging their own wars against oppression and discrimination and set a precedent for the antislavery insurgencies to come, particularly in the American south.

Toussaint Louverture, a former slave, became a military leader in the Haitian revolution against the French occupiers who had long enslaved the Haitian people. The 2009 film "Egalite (equality) For All: Toussaint Louverture and the Haitian Revolution" chronicles Louverture and the Haitian army's fight for freedom. After Louverture's capture by the French and his subsequent imprisonment and death, his fame reached new heights and he has frequently been compared to George Washington for his bravery and military acumen.

After Louverture's death, Jean Jacques Dessalines, who had served as Louverture's principal lieutenant, became the new leader of the revolution. The Battle of Vertieres on November 18, 1803 marked the last major battle of the revolution, and the first time in the history of humanity that a slave army had won their freedom. Dessalines, who became known the Father of Haiti, was the first ruler of the newly free country. However freedom often comes with a price, and for Haiti it was a hefty one. America joined France in forcing Haiti to pay "reparations" for France's economic "lost"—since production and trade from the island constituted about 70 percent of France's economy—and required Haiti to pay $150 million dollars in 1825 which they did not finish paying off until around 1947. This financial demand entombed the country in chronic state of debt an ensuing poverty compiled with the economic and political isolation of the international community that would contribute the devastating state of the Haitian republic until this day. Also the American occupation from 1915 to 1934 made a profound impact on Haiti's sociopolitical and economic detriment.

For a more detailed recount, visit: https://en.wikipedia.org/wiki/History_of_Haiti

A recent book, also by Laurent Dubois, "Haiti: The Aftershock of History," argues that even centuries after the revolution, Haiti continues to be punished by the international community for its successful slave insurrection, hurling the country into a cycle of debt, isolation and political instability. Dubois' book also highlights the Haitian people's triumphs and resiliency in their ongoing fight for autonomy and equality despite the devastation caused by the earthquake.

According to the Interim Haiti Recovery Commission (I.H.R.C) website, Haitians have observed some positive progress since the earthquake. Clean water has become more readily available since the recent outbreak of cholera. Although unemployment remains a pressing concern, an investment from a Korean garment maker is expected to create about 20,000 jobs in the country's northeast region.

One of the commission's most crucial goals is to gain the confidence of international donors by promoting government accountability and transparency, no easy task considering the country's history of corrupt leadership. So far, only half of the $4.6 billion in redevelopment money promised for 2010 and 2011 has been acquired and disbursed. The commission also reports that most of the donated money has been attributed to "non-governmental organizations and private contractors," a fact that the commission considers to be problematic.

Former President Michel Martelly, who was once a popular musician, was reported to have fared better than his predecessor, Rene Preval, who was criticized as an impediment to Haiti's redevelopment goals. In the fall of 2011, Martelly promulgated a plan to provide rental subsidies to 30,000 residents of the six tent cities and to begin construction of new housing developments.

Significant progress is also being made in the areas of health and education. The NGO Partners in Health has unveiled a plan to build a new teaching hospital in rural Haiti. To improve educational opportunities for Haitian children the inter-American Development Bank will direct $150 million in aid money towards training teachers and building and repairing schools.

As rebuilding efforts continue, Haiti will need a profusion of international support to continue on its path towards political and economic stability. In the past, outside help has often proven to be self-serving and to the detriment of Haiti's people. Now that Haiti is in the international spotlight, government transparency and accountability has never been more important.

Although the country has seen great adversity, Haiti's monumental achievement as the first Black republic has earned the country a permanent place in African history. Haiti's unsurpassed legacy of successful rebellion against slavery will leave a revolutionary dent in the hearts and minds of oppressed, maligned and aggrieved people everywhere.

Life in Haiti Just 8 Months after the January 2010 Earthquake

"Life doesn't have to be a strain or struggle."
--Marion Anderson

In the aftermath of one the biggest tragedies in Haiti—a country already known for persistent political unrest and economic depravity—the country still lacks the ability to meet basic human needs. Long after the media coverage of the January 12th earthquake has ceased and Haiti's fifteen minutes of fame appears to have faded, one thing remains the same: the resilient and perpetually thriving spirit of the Haitian people.

I interviewed my cousin "Betty" (for the purpose of anonymity), who recently came to America for a month of respite and reflection after the catastrophe in Haiti. She seemed surprisingly well-adjusted, and at times was even jovial and comical. Her spirit reflects that of the people in Haiti as they strive to return back to a normal life. I am painfully aware that the term "normal" in this context may take different meanings given the dire conditions the people have to endure in the poorest country in the western hemisphere. A large number of people in this country live beyond their means just to keep up appearances and convey a façade of financial security when often the true reality denotes a much more humble economic situation.

"The people's spirits remains high," Cousin Betty said, "women are still getting their hair and nails done and going on with life as usual." She also mentioned that people are still having "Rarras." A Rarra is when a group of people take to the streets dancing with drums, and other Haitian musical instruments, and as they go through the neighborhoods other people join them. This is something I experienced myself having grown up in Haiti for the first thirteen years of my life before I came to America. Although the Haitian people have always maintained an attitude of "Joix De Vivre" which is French for "Joy of Life", the world and particularly the American people and the news media has just begun to recognize the undying fire that is the Haitian spirit. In the darkness of times, it's a guarantee that you will see a Haitian dancing on a cloud. I recently saw journalists and celebrities, who after coming back from visiting Haiti; speak emphatically of the Haitian people's positive and mirthful dispositions.

"While it looked like life resumed on the streets, the trip was sobering for me," said Bill Lin, Director of Corporate Contributions for Johnson & Johnson who recently went to Leogane, Haiti, which is a city west of Port-au-Prince and at the epicenter of the Jan. 12th earthquake. Lin was interviewed by Melissa Waggenspack in an article on the internet where she emphasizes the pressing needs of the Haitian people. Lin goes on to say that "So many people are displaced and are still living in tent cities. The need for housing is so tremendous." When asked about the health concerns of the Haitian people, Lin responded "Hurricane season began on June 1st, presenting a new threat to those who are still living in tent cities…there is a great concern over the spread of waterborne disease…that is why, in Haiti, Johnson & Johnson is providing more assistance for housing than we have during previous disaster relief efforts."

When I asked Cousin Betty about how she experienced the earthquake and the ensuing aftermath. She had this to say, "I was at home when the quake hit. Our house shook but did not fall. However because of the anticipation of aftermaths, we were forced to sleep on a football field for 4 to 5 days. Then we returned back to our own yard to sleep in tents. Today, we still sleep in tents just to be on the cautious side. However, during the day, we stay in the house.

Although now, we keep the doors open in case we need to exit the house in case of aftershocks."

Regarding American aid to post-quake Haiti cousin Betty said, "American aid helped provide first-aid to those under debris, there were a lot of amputees, there were 2,000 amputees in a two month period." And regarding donations, she said that the people are very frustrated because even though they are getting all this money in earthquake relief aid, as usual there is no account of where the money is going. She also said that "most of the money goes to non-profits like Habitat for Humanity, but actual help is slow in progression."

In an article by Maria Sacchetti of the Boston Globe, she writes about how in Petionville, Haiti, a once prosperous suburb of Port-au-Prince, people are sleeping in rat infested tents with "reeking latrines" and also how basic human needs like food and water is still scarce. She describes a situation when the water ran out: "In scorching heat, a group of angry parents… marched to the winding road above the camp armed with empty containers, a sawed-off garden hose and pans. They busted open an exposed pipe and collected the water that gushed from it."

"There is not much help," Sacchetti writes quoting Benice George, a 50-year-old construction worker, cradling his 1-year-old son. He ended up using the water he collected earlier to cook spaghetti on a campfire, his family's only meal for the day, "We're not living like human beings," Benice said. In terms of the donated monies and what has been done so far in Haiti, she wrote: "Across the Caribbean nation, less than 4 percent of the debris has been cleared since the powerful… earthquake and some 1.6 million people are living in tent camps in the middle of hurricane season, despite 1.8 billion in earthquake aid according to U.S. government and United Nations figures."

The current crisis in Haiti is finally catapulting its glaring political maladies into view for the whole world to see. For years not much has been done to intercept the corruption that has plagued the Haitian government and its people. At times, America has either looked the other way, except when intervening has been mostly in their best interest.

"Paul Farmer, founder of Boston-based Partners in Health (PIH) and a deputy special envoy for the United Nations, recently told a congressional panel that less than 3 percent of aid has gone directly to the Haitian government, and urged lawmakers to increase such disbursement," writes

Sacchetti. And when it comes to America's complex and often problematic relationship with Haiti, Sacchetti writes, "In the past [Paul Farmer] said, US and other policies have sometimes bypassed Haiti's leadership, weakening it and contributing in part to the crisis today."

Another problem that plagues Haiti's recovery efforts is that most countries have failed to deliver on Haiti aid pledges as reported by CNN.com. International donors promised $5.billion after the earthquake; only four countries have distributed any money, less than 2 percent of the money that's been promised has been delivered, the U.S. pledged more than $1 billion and distributed nothing with the money tied up in the congressional appropriations process. Although much hasn't been done in terms of helping earthquake victims meet basic human needs like permanent housing, food and water, there is a glimmer of hope for the children of Haiti is the form of the Life is Good Kids Foundation (LIGKF).

"The Life is Good Kids Foundation is working with Haitian childcare providers to make sure that nothing destroys the joy, playfulness and optimism of the children," says head playmaker and chief executive officer Steven Gross. "Sadly, the children of Haiti will need to overcome many opticals and when you face those opticals with optimism, you're more likely going to be able to figure out creative solutions." He also spoke of a group of people called "Guerye Jwa" which is Creole for "Joy Worriers."

"The Guerye Jwa are going to tent cities in Port-au-Prince and they are playing with the children in a very intentional way and the children come to life when the Guerye Jwa come to town."

When I asked him how LIGKF is funded, he said, "All of the work in Haiti is funded by the Life is Good Kids Foundation through the sales of a special Haiti T-Shirt with the Haitian flag and Life is Good character holding the flag." You can help by purchasing a T-Shirt on their website at www.lifeisgood.com.

Haiti is a country that has been victimized for years, however its people refuse to become victims. Haitians have contributed greatly to America and at one time even provided the U.S. monetary assistance during America's revolutionary war. The Haitian people that live here in America are mostly hard-working, law abiding people. Most of the men and women work as health care paraprofessionals and even doctors, nurses and nurse's aides taking care of America's elderly population and a plethora work as cab drivers getting the people of America from point A to point B. Now, Haiti and its people need help more than ever before. One way you can help is by joining the Annual Urban Walk for Haiti which happens in late March or early April. I happen to be the Official Poet and Publicity Agent for the walk which was intended to raise money and awareness for PIH, a ubiquitous organization spearheaded by

Harvard University Professor Dr. Paul Farmer, as mentioned earlier, designed to help third world countries like Haiti meet basic human needs but particularly it helps build schools and hospitals in poverty stricken nations like Lima, Peru and Haiti.

So help keep the spirit of the Haitian people strong. One way to do this is by participating in the upcoming Urban Walk for Haiti or contribute financially. For more information or to make donations visit www.Partnersinhealth.org and www.walkforhaiti.org.

The Legacy of the Black Soldiers of the Civil War

"Cowards die many times before their deaths, the valiant never taste of death but once."

— Shakespeare, Julius Caesar (II, ii, 32-37)

The contributions and achievements of black people throughout American History have often been overlooked in traditional history textbooks. Although I was educated in American schools from the eighth grade through college, an empirical and systematic knowledge of black history eluded me. I began to educate myself about African American history by pouring over history texts in public libraries.

It was during this time that I discovered the crucial role of black soldiers in securing victory for the Union during the Civil War, and in doing so, preserving the United States as we know it today. Black men, who had been considered disempowered chattel, partook in a winning army, aiding in the emancipation of four million slaves.

Scholars still debate the causes of the Civil War. Confederates contended that they fought for the right of secession and the capacity to build an autonomous nation. Unionists argued that they went to war to prevent Southerners from disassembling the United States. For black soldiers however, the war was about slavery, and the aim of war was its abolition.

Black men had to overcome many obstacles to join the Union Army, one such barrier being a law dating back to the late 1700s that precluded blacks from fighting in the U.S. Army. The first black volunteers were refused by white military leadership, who considered black men to be incorrigible, irresponsible and child-like barbarians, unfit to be soldiers. Eventually, the Union Army permitted black men to serve, but under draconian conditions. The first black soldiers were made to serve in segregated battalions under white commanding officers. The federal government attempted to pay black soldiers lower wages than whites, and they were subjected to blatant forms of prejudice and abuse on campgrounds.

Despite hardship and discrimination, the loyalty and tenacity of black soldiers upheld their merit on the battlefield; their performance was grudgingly extolled even by their Confederate adversaries.

One such group of black soldiers was the 54th Massachusetts Volunteer Infantry Regiment, the first all-black battalion recruited in the North.

"Six hundred Union soldiers raced towards Fort Wagner in South Carolina. The men were wet, tired and hungry. It was July 1863 and the 54th regiment was one of the first units of African

American soldiers fighting in the Civil War." So begins historian Carin T. Ford's book,

"African-American Soldiers in the Civil War: Fighting for Freedom." The 54th regiment was led by Colonel Robert Gould Shaw, a white man from a privileged Boston abolitionist family. Today, the 54th Massachusetts Volunteer Regiment Company A is a Boston-Based non-profit organization. Members of the 54th take part in re-enactments and civic education efforts.

Last August, I attended the 54th's celebration of the 150th anniversary of the Civil War at Fort Warren on George's Island. I had a chance to meet and speak with members of the 54th, some of whom are descendants of black Civil War soldiers. These soldiers' pivotal roles in the outcome of the Civil War left a lasting legacy of intrepid defiance against racism and injustice. Historian Christian Samito argues that prior to the Civil War national citizenship existed only as a vague concept. Basic civil rights were far from universal, factors such as race, gender, slave-status, and immigration status determined the "rights and privileges" that an individual could enjoy.

The Union victory paved the way for the passing of the 13th amendment in 1865 which ended slavery in the United States, the 14th amendment, which awarded blacks equal protection under the law and the right to hold political office, and the 15th amendment, which granted black men the right to vote. These Civil War amendments created a new order by recognizing nearly 4.5 million blacks as national citizens and freed men as voters.

Although white and black soldiers — at least on the prima facie level — came together in battle, in the post-war years black men continued to be plagued by racism and inequality. Civil War historian Joseph T. Glatthaar claims that black soldiers saw their fight in the Civil War as a beacon of hope for equality in the coming years. Glatthaar believes that the continuation of racist policies and the failure of the reconstruction era to bring about meaningful changes "provoked a pattern of selective memory that continues to trouble America today." He proclaims that blacks' desire for equality after the war severed the hard-fought bonds forged between black and white soldiers during the war.

Some historians, such as Kenneth C. Davis, believe that "The Civil War never really ended." In his book, "Don't Know Much About the Civil War," Davis writes that our country's "racial chasm is the most pernicious legacy of America's slave past and the Civil War." Davis believes that the first step towards healing the wounds inflicted by slavery and racism is for Americans to understand them.

Today, we need Black History Month as a reminder of African American contributions to this country. But why should we think of black history only one month out of the year? African

Americans' contributions to the fabric of America are ongoing. America has shown much progress in overcoming racism by electing the first black president of the United States, Barack Obama. But as black Americans, we must not become complacent in our continuing quest for equality beyond the boundaries of status, class and race; Black History Month is a perfect reminder.

Soliloquy to America

"There are two ways of spreading the light, to be the candle or the mirror that reflects it."

—Edith Wharton

I'd like to shed some "light" on a few things I've had on my mind for quite a long time. I am first and foremost a poet. A poet speaks through the mouth of truth with a poetic tongue through keen observations and scrutiny of society and that's exactly what I will do.

These are the days you'll remember, a new year has dawned and we hope it will bring us together and with a sense of wonder. I am sorry that Dr. Martin Luther King Jr. did not live to see President Barrack Obama reach the mountain top. I am sorry he did not live to see interracial harmony through marriage and integrated communities once made illegal by injustice, malevolence and intolerance. The children of Africa have risen to the highest heights of America when United States citizens elected Barrack Obama. But as often is the case, the more things change on the superficial level, the more they stay the same on a much deeper, darker level. Unfortunately, racism is here to stay and is still played out most often, but not always, in a more subtle way.

The "occupy" movement is having its moment in the sun by speaking and standing up for equity for the bottom feeders of society who refuse to run, but instead, get angry. They hail and wail and with them I also question: "what is going on?" I don't understand why the earth is on fire! Injustice wakes up, injustice stands up, injustice refuses to fall; children playing on lands ravaged by war; mothers sleeping next to coffins; come sun down, the pain doesn't go away; we can see it trembling in the dark, thirsty for medication, but the government claims that there isn't enough money to keep the pharmacies open. We need a shift in direction!

Flip flop flip flop! Some say Black people are lazy but moon town sun down we're working like crazy. Our clock never seems to stop turning; we're confused about the American promise: work hard and you'll get some relief but we are being led by official thieves and opposition, so it's time to cry out in protest for a change in direction. But who am I? Just an inner city Black immigrant who has no vote, shivering in the winter without a coat. I look around me and I see misery snarling in the faces of the homeless and the hopeless; I see children being born fatherless into a world of deprivation; begging for a blessing, waiting for God to dawn an opening.

Way back when, chiefly Africans worked around the clock building America while wishing they could all go back to Africa. I look around and I see politicians listen to the people who elect them with the patience of short order cooks. I see mounting government expenditures and U.S. national debt killing our American Dream and radicals importuning, "How did the president's speech go over, with an audience stock full of political imbeciles?" All clapping while he sprayed salt on his lies, talking like a poem: saying nothing saying everything while holding haughty fundraisers to generate generosity from those of us already in a state of economic paucity.

So I am coughing these words, for the homeless Jo Black or White he's still my Bro; selling Spare Change News the only way they know; an honest way of life to eat away the strife. I am coughing these words and it's nothing Sudafed can feed; for all the young Black men wrongfully accused and jailed; gather your tears in protest and use it as bail. The world is restless as wars for justice and equality go on and on the domestic front, regular folks have formed the "occupy" movement to take back America from the powerful and malevolent; to take back the American promise of life, liberty and the pursuit of happiness.

I see mothers, fathers and children weeping hungry for equity, hungry for a piece of the American Dream. I watch in stupor as young Black brotherhoods gather from the statue residue of Dr. Martin Luther King Jr., an archetype of freedom, liberty and equality, to continue their own struggle against racism and inequity! The futures of our country are playing on the playgrounds as equals, for now unaware of the inherent hatred and inequality stemming from their disparate skin colors. I am sad seeing wealthy white fat businessmen forever feasting on caviar while the rest of us look on like gaunt pitiable dogs; forcing me to ponder "When will the rest of us finally get a taste of opulence and luxury?"

Let's not make the U.S. election a "black and white thing" by simply doing "the right thing" as you see fit. For people of color everywhere, maybe in the next century, King's dream of justice and equality will finally become a reality. But, that doesn't keep me from having hope and optimism; that one day the poor and marginalized of society will finally rise from the ashes of abject poverty and essentially bask in the glory of human dignity through monetary self-sufficiency and finally find liberty, fraternity and equity for all of humanity!

Dialogue on Race Relations in America: An Interview with "Jane Doe"

"There is power in naming racism for what it is, in shining a bright light on it.… naming it allows us to root it out of the darkness and hushed conversation where it likes to breed like roaches. It makes us acknowledge it. Confront it."

Jesmyn Ward

I recently joined a writer's group from the website meetup.com. The first day I attended the group, I was considerably late. Upon entering, a la true Jacques fashion with my cyborg glasses, looking like the black guy from Star Trek, the members (who happened to be all white) looked up at me in a frozen state, tight grin in place. I felt uneasy. But I sat down, started to be my jovial, gregarious self, and eventually I had them in tears with laughter. In the midst of the chilly reception, however, one woman radiated warmth and openness right from the beginning. Her name was "Jane Doe" (for the purpose of anonymity). During the group's second meeting, she waited until everyone else left, sat me down and proceeded to tell me that she too saw how the members tensed up when I first walked in. She said she felt "bad" for me because all her white cohorts saw was a big black guy in their presence. Being a big black man in Boston, I am used to being subjected to that subtle yet unmitigated racism, often inherent in the white community. I then asked Jane if she would be willing to give an interview regarding race relations in America from a white perspective. She agreed, and here is what followed:

Jacques Fleury: Can you tell me a little about your personal and professional background?

Jane Doe: My father was a minister, so we moved around a lot growing up. My mom was heavily engaged in our church and was a stay-at-home mom. The church we belonged to was the United Church of Christ, one of the most liberal church denominations. I've spent most of my life performing. I majored in music in undergrad and theater in grad school. I went to New York and pursued performing professionally, but it was tough. So for most of my adult life, I had to have survival jobs to keep myself afloat.

JF: Where did you grow up and how was the issue of race dealt with at home?

JD: I grew up all around northern Ohio until I was 14. Then we moved to Florida where I went to high school and college. My mom and dad always told me that we – everyone is the same. No one of us is any more or any less than any other person. My parents walked the walk and talked the talk!

JF: Growing up, were you exposed to people of color?

JD: I remember having wonderful classmates who were African-American and Asian. In the early 1970s, we lived in a suburb of Cleveland called Painesville, where I came into greater contact with people of color.

JF: Did the media ever affect your perceptions of black people?

JD: I remember some of the sitcoms from the mid-to-late '70s that seemed pretty stereotypical of African-Americans in particular. It was pretty obvious they weren't being written or directed by the people they were representing. It was embarrassing. Because my dad was a fairly socially concerned kind of guy, I was very aware of things like Dr. King being shot. I was pretty young, but pretty aware because I think it was discussed within our family and in his pulpit — the why's and how's of it all. Also, at the time, television was just beginning to bring the entire civil rights struggle into our living rooms and I remember watching people getting fire hosed and not understanding why.

JF: What were you taught at home regarding black people and how did that affect your attitude towards blacks as an adult?

JD: How I saw kids treating other kids at school was very hard for me to take. My parents were lucky enough to meet Dr. King and they felt truly inspired by the experience. So all of the messages I got from them were of compassion and love, while what I saw in school was very different. But I think, because they really treated every person they met with respect, that was the message that got through.

JF: Have some of your perceptions changed about race over the years and if so, how?

JD: I'd say the biggest thing that changed in my mind is the understanding that I was born into a group [Caucasian] that is inherently racist. Because of the way things were done in this country four hundred years ago, the group I belong to just assume a place of superiority to this day — and most of us don't even know it. We take for granted walking into a restaurant or a store and not being made to feel uncomfortable simply because we walked in. I cannot ever really know the African-American or the Asian or the Hispanic experience, but the one thing I can do is have compassion, because fear gets you nowhere.

JF: Why do you think some individuals in the white community are so afraid to talk about race?

JD: It's about personal discomfort and accountability. If we actually admit that there is a problem, then we might be part of that problem. By believing that the situation is so much better than, say 40 years ago, we're kidding ourselves. Just because the racism isn't obvious doesn't mean it's not there. But changing perceptions, talking about it, realizing that we make assumptions about people due to the color of their skin is embarrassing and painful to talk about, I think. And I think that scares people. I think that people are motivated by either compassion or fear. Most people would rather just assume that everything's okay as long as they aren't impacted by it.

JF: Do you observe subtle racist behavior from your white cohorts towards blacks?

JD: I see it all the time. White people don't even know they're doing it; it's just part of who they are. Obviously, I'm making a vast and sweeping generalization, but I've seen and heard a lot of condescension toward people of color. Jacques, I watched it happen when you walked into the café and an entire table of white people visibly changed their body language when you sat down. By the power of your wonderful personality, those people eventually relaxed again. But it was palpable.

JF: I've come to accept the reality that none of us living in America are completely immune to racist ideologies; do you think that's true?

JD: I have to admit that what makes me personally most uncomfortable doesn't have to do with race per se, but more about class. It's the extremes of class that rankle me: from "white trash" to the rich. Some part of me feels that I am part of the "underclass" as I so often feel... treated like a second-class citizen in various situations. But it's fluid, never constant. So often these situations involve personalities, who deal with their insecurities by treating others as subordinates. I try to see them as doing the best they can, though when one is being treated badly, it's difficult to remember.

JF: America shows progress in race relations by electing Barrack Obama. What more do you think needs to be accomplished in mitigating nascent racial disunity towards more racial tolerance, understanding, and harmony in this country?

JD: Well, besides the fact that white people need to be slapped awake after a 40-year nap... I think that racism, unfortunately, has been rearing its rather large and ugly head over the past three years. Electing Obama was amazing and wonderful, but the dormant racism in our country has come out via the Tea Partiers and the hard shift of the Republican Party to the right. At last year's State of the Union address, when Rep. Joe Wilson shouted, "You lie!" at President Obama, I thought, "Wow, now that's a racist." Do you think that would have ever happened if President Obama were white? I don't think so. It's like that representative felt he needed to put that black man in his place. It was an incredibly disgusting display, I thought. I feel pretty down about race relations in general. It doesn't get talked about, and I don't know what the solution is to get the dialogue going. It's like, "Let's all just pretend it's okay."

As the Sun Sets Over Port-au-Prince

"If you look just at the decades after 1934 [referring to the American occupation between 1915 and 1934], you know it's hard to point to really inspired and positive support from outside of Haiti, to Haiti, and much easier to point to either small-minded or downright mean-spirited policies."

Dr. Paul Farmer,
Harvard University
Founder of Partners in Health
Author of: *The Uses of Haiti*

In Haiti I grew up taking blood baths, basking in the epoch of oppression. My nation was occupied by the French, and despite my French influence, I consider myself a Creole poet and not a French Creole poet. My Caribbean spice rack is stocked full of flavored stories, which I will gladly tell you just enough of to satisfy your hunger for the knowledge of the courage of my people; since my blood was once the color of slavery. But now, since I left Haiti for America, I dream the dream that every American dreams: to sleep on the pillows of justice, freedom and opportunity. After all, aren't we all entitled to happiness? So now, watch me run from the lasso of the unjust, just to make it under the wire of justice.

The great Cuban poet, Joseito Fernandez, who penned the lyrics to the popular song "Guantanamera" wrote, "...with the poor people of this earth, I want to share my faith." Like him, my heart has been oppressed and wired, my vocal cords tapped. But like the great Rhythm and Blues singer Marvin Gaye so eloquently said, "True artists suffer for the people", and so I am going to continue to say what I need to say, even if it means some suffering along the way.

In 1492, Christopher Columbus landed on the island of Hispaniola and gave it its name. Taino

Arawak Indians, who referred to their homeland as "Hayti" or "Mountainous Land", originally inhabited the island. In 1697 slaves were sent to Haiti. The island was cherished by European powers for its natural resources, including cocoa, cotton and sugar cane. The French shipped in thousands of slaves mainly from West Africa to harvest the crops. In 1804, after a slave rebellion led by a man named Bookman in 1791, Haiti became the first free Black nation in the world under General Jean-Jacques Dessalines, who declared himself Emperor. America feared that the slave rebellion in Haiti would ignite anti-slavery insurgencies in the U.S. southern states, and as we all now know, eventually it did. Perhaps this is one the many of multifarious reasons why America's relationship with Haiti is strained to this day.

The Uses of Haiti, a book by Harvard University professor Dr. Paul Farmer, chronicles

America's long and perplexing history with Haiti. Tourism flourished in Haiti from the 1950s to 1986, practically ending with the Jean-Claude "Baby Doc" Duvalier mutiny. Haiti's main tourist attraction is La Citadelle Laferierre built on mountains overlooking Port-au-Prince. It has walls 130 feet high and is the largest fortress in the Americas, and was designated by the United

Nations Educational, Scientific and Cultural Organization (UNESCO) as a world history site in 1982. It was built to keep the newly independent nation from French incursions, which never materialized.

Yet still, sometimes I wonder, "Why can't I easily co-exist with my inner tropical child?" Maybe it's because in your eyes I am nothing but a stereotype, a risk that most in power would rather not take. I am nothing if not the product of Neo-Freudian philosophy, so don't criticize my personality. An honorable part of me knows that I'm more than just an island "bro" without the afro. What I am is a Caribbean soup stock full of vegetables with circumscribed roots; so come take a spoonful of my flavor, I am more than just a Caribbean brother. My forefathers were more than fugitive slaves, they were purple tropical birds adorned in the mythical, waiting to go on sabbatical, while our Haitian land remained fallow, praying, and begging for something sacramental. They treated us like debris, even after we facilitated their safari. Sometimes I feel like I want to be magical, so that I can live life invisible to the hatred, hypocrisy, racism, sexism and classism that permeates my existence. To insolent interchanges of ignorance, to an overflow of content and arrogance, I surrender. I linger like a disturbed dissenter. I want to be a paradigm;

I want to be a prolific producer. I don't want to live my life like a silent singer and I hope you don't either.

Growing up partly in Haiti with mostly marred memories of mango trees and my macabre childhood swaying in the lazy wind, was no walk in the park, more like a walk in the woods. As we know, the woods are much less manicured than the park. In the woods, it is not always clear what lies ahead. One minute you may be leaping with gaiety downhill, and the next minute you may find yourself straining and striving to reach a summit. Don't get me wrong, on Haitian terrains, there were certainly moments of triumph (fabulous cuisine and a colorful culture), but unfortunately they were equally matched, and often surpassed, by moments of failure (living under the constant weather of fear and intimidation).

The government was an archetype for this ideology. As the tyrannical government oppressed the people, the people then reciprocated by oppressing each other. To my chagrin, I realized that the mentality of the Haitian people was "Every man and woman for himself or herself," and trust was actually non-existent. In Haiti, we were all subjected to living within a conspiracy of silence.

"See no evil, speak no evil," because "evil" had the people under panoptic surveillance. This could have been a family member hired as a spy to turn their own in, should they speak unfavorably of the government.

You see, in Haiti, dialect was in handcuffs. Fear tore souls to pieces and left them scattered along the scorching pavement and dark dirt roads for hungry dogs to feed on. Imagine a place where a teacher is without students, and his only freedom is to be ignorant. His voice is but a squeak in the fading forests, while the tongue of dissension lies entombed at the bottom of an empty well, waiting for a subversive echo to give its voice a chance at change. Even though dialect of dissension in Haiti is gagged, its voice is an intricacy of words, loaded to snap its constraint and recoup its power!

The guts of the Haitian nation have exploded since the devastating earthquake back on January

12th, 2010. Its long, dirty yet valiant and pioneering history sprawled, snarling and unsympathetic, in discordant bliss all over the ubiquitous dirt roads. All the humanitarians who rushed over to help the aggrieved people could almost hear the debris hiss, as the apathetic summer air suffocated Creole fireflies. Sounds of volatile youths banging their heads against scarcities echoed like gun shots in the empty fear-filled streets, while the savage beat cops known as "ton ton macoutes" strutted around town. Baby Doc, rueful that he couldn't fly, fell prey to domestic maladies and was exiled to France.

"Garcon!" mama used to call me.

"Yes, ma ma!"

With fear fighting to hold back her valiant voice she said, "Never walk bare foot on cold concrete and never EVER talk too quick!" Then I was forcing sleep, was stifled by what was supple. One day mama woke me up and said, "Time to go America!" Then I tried smiling, but my big parched patois lips felt raw.

Voices of Liberation: The Changing Role of Haitian-American Women

"If you're going to write, then write a novel with a Haitian woman in it and try and describe her accurately. When you can do that, you can write about people"

--Jeff Buckley

Haitian Women, in Haiti, are terribly oppressed, both economically and psychologically. I know this first hand having grown up with five women in Haiti and by often observing their delicate task of navigating in a sea of sharks: the male oppressors who limit them to being subservient and objectified. But, as Bob Dylan sings, "The times they are a changing…" Now Haitian American women are exploring their own disparate identities, abilities and attainting psychological, spiritual and economic autonomy from Haitian male chauvinism, classism and oppression.

I want to start out by qualifying my statement, by declaring that I am aware that not all Haitian-American males are oppressive to the women in their lives. I, for one, am an example, since I consider myself a male-feminist in direct contradiction to the often-Haitian male chauvinist. Having evolved from the roots of oppression, Haitian women are basking in their newfound freedom in the United States and they are growing out of the limitations once set on them in Haiti, branching out to achieve success and independence in the United States. Yet, they still have to deal with their former oppressors, the Haitian males who still refuse to see and accept them in their new roles as heads of their own families, and who at times ask to drive the cars that the working Haitian women pay for, even though the women are making the car payments.

The oppressive Haitian male in the United States is experiencing a cultural shock to his outdated mentality that places women at the bottom and man at the top when it comes to the power structure that used to put women at a disadvantage in Haiti. My own mother has been approached many times by Haitian males who often proposition her to be their "woman", and by this I mean they want her not only to continue to work to take care of herself, but they also want her to make time to cook for them, wash their clothes, drive the car that she pays for while the males stay home, watch television, and sneak other women to her bed while she's working to financially support them. Haitian men are often surprised when my mother decides to decline their generous offer. One even told her "I know why you don't want to be with me, you enjoy being free don't you? Because if you were to be with me, I would have to know your whereabouts every hour on the hour!" which is the typical behavior of most Haitian males back in Haiti and even in the United States today. Some Haitian women tolerate this domineering behavior from the Haitian males in order to keep them in their lives. For some, their identities are empty without the often-suppressive presence of a man, any man. Perhaps it's because they have grown accustomed to that type of subservient relationship, and perhaps it's because very early on, as my mother has told me, they are taught to acquiesce and "behave" out of fear of financial and/or physical punishment. Even when enduring physical and psychological abuse, some woman prefer to stick by their man because they really believe, as they did in Haiti, that having a man is more acceptable to society then being single. They are somehow perceived to be more "respectable" even if it costs them their freedom.

The uneven balance of power between the oppressive male and the suppressed female leads to the desperate and dangerous act of emasculating the male so that females can empower themselves. In Haiti, there are narrow choices for Haitian women if at all, but in the United States the choices are widened to accommodate their yearnings of living independently from men and to free themselves from the anchoring chains of subservience, and to reach ultimate levels of competency when making their aspirations a reality. To be endued with power, in the United States, women have gained the temerity to challenge the limitations imposed on them by Haitian males who thus infringe on their civil liberties and yearnings to pursue boundless happiness through their own personal achievements.

Essentially in the dawn of the new Millennium, Haitian women are reaping the rewards of acclimating to living in the United States, fundamentally finding spiritual freedom and coming as close to social and economic equity as possible since leaving oppression in the form of economic and psychological misery in Haiti. They are proving that they can be both iconoclastic and diplomatic in their torrid pursuit for justice, economic and social equity in the face of the officious male mentality. They have proven to be good communicators by being neither too passive nor overtly aggressive, but rightfully assertive. Some women are still so angry about having been oppressed by Haitian males in Haiti; that they have stopped dating them or limit their interactions with them all together. They have sought other ethnicities like Caucasian, Portuguese and so forth as partners. The Haitian males in the United States still try to flex their dominating muscles on the Haitian women who have reached a higher level of being by creating a life for themselves independent of the males. They have two or three jobs, are often homeowners and entrepreneurs who also happen to be mothers. In Haiti, being some man's wife and somebody's mother is usually a woman's main identity, but in the United States, they have shed those restraints to explore other parts of themselves, like innate desires to take on leadership roles like pastors, artists, doctors, lawyers, engineers and last but not least, single mothers. They no longer feel the need to be trapped in bad marriages in order to have some sense of identity.

Today in the United States, Haitian women are finding their truest identities outside of the unequivocal scorch of oppression from the Haitian males to live exhilarating lives that include, but are not limited to, being mothers, breadwinners and essentially survivors!

American Fiction: The Evolution of Women in Colonial Literature

"When you look down into silence, you see no friend;
When you lift your gaze to space, you hear no echo.
It is like striking a single chord it rings out but there's no music."

--"Literature: A Rhapsody" Lu Ji

I started writing poetry in high school and was encouraged to continue to do so by my mostly female peers and mostly women teachers. I learned that I could be an "emotional" man without consequences like being ostracized or called "girly." And so because I identify with women on an emotional level, I studied American literature in college that focused on the relationships between women and men in the 19th century American south.

We know that the past essentially and inevitably informs the present. My hope in writing this article is to establish a juxtaposition of the oppressive and subservient relationships between men and women in the past with the oppressive and subservient relationships between the men and women in Haiti even in the present day. I would like to illuminate the growing trend towards social, spiritual and economic equality between men and women in contemporary society.

I consider myself to be somewhat of a male feminist and with good reasons. I grew up partly in Haiti and I was mostly raised by women. My mother and her four sisters had a great deal to do with the man I have become. I feel a certain level of kinship to women. Perhaps it's partly because I am a sensitive poet and have a propensity to be rightfully and infallibly "emotional." In Haiti, being an emotional male is neither encouraged nor tolerated. If you are indeed an emotional male, you best hide it or risk being ostracized from your family and community as well as being labeled a "massissi" or "faggot." As a result, I kept my emotions to myself and took everything that was thrown at me with the stoical silence characteristic of the typical Haitian male. I was even praised by my aunt for this detrimental albeit desirable behavior.

"Jacques is a good little boy", she said. "He never shows any emotion." And so during my formative years, I learned that emotions were "bad" and stoicism was "good." However, all that changed when I came to America.

During the mid- to late-19th century, almost a hundred years since the U.S. won its independence from England, the white women of the American south were fighting their own private war. In particular they waged a war to be free from male sovereignty and oppression and societal constrictions. Indeed, society played a great role in restraining those women; nevertheless, the battles and wars inside their own homes played a greater role in their restricted and limited lives than the society at large. It was the sum of the incidents that contributed to the women's rebellion. The conditions in which these women were forced to live, the women's diverse rebellious acts themselves, and female unknowing collusion helping mitigate the emotional and spiritual oppression of women in today's society.

In order to understand the preceding critical elements, an understanding is needed of the meaning of marriage in the southern states during the nineteenth century. One needs to understand how divorce was perceived and dealt with, the domestic laws of that time, and what a good marriage is and what isn't. Three stories involving three remarkable nineteenth century women will be discussed to examine these social dynamics: The Yellow Wall Paper, by charlotte Perkins Gilman (1899), The Revolt of Mother, by Mary E. Wilkins (1890) and The Story of An Hour, by Kate Chopin (1894).

"One's defined role in marriage and gender were key factors in determining a woman's constitutional rights…in parts of America." wrote history connoisseur Timothy Crumrin, in his Internet article "Women and the Law in Early Nineteenth Century Indiana." He also states that, legally speaking, women were detained the role of being "dependent, subservient and unequal." These women were strong, intelligent and deeply spiritual, however, they were condescended to and bestowed such titles as "lunatics and idiots" according to Crumrin.

Moreover, Crumrin further elaborates on the marriage issue by affirming that rights normally enjoyed by a woman were often withdrawn when she married. He further expounded on that idea by stating that once a woman became married, she was said to be coming into "a state of civil death". He maintains that divorce was downplayed during the first half of the nineteenth century.

In order to legally separate, one must have been able to prove signs of "extreme cruelty." The reader must ask several pertinent questions: who and what defined "extreme cruelty" then? What the laws defined as "extreme cruelty" then that only warrants separation, may in fact be considered a criminal act today that justifies criminal confinement. A good wife was defined as someone who did what her husband told her to do. If a wife disobeyed her husband during that time, he had a legal right to kill her. What constitutes that kind of rationale? There's a fine line between "extreme cruelty" and murder —which brings Crumrin to defining the laws and regulations of that time.

During the nineteenth century, the U.S. government had domestic laws referred to as "Cult of Domesticity." In Mary K. Cayton's article "Gender Roles and Relations" published in the Encyclopedia of American Social History, she discusses how in the early colonial era, the father ruled with his wife as his assistant. Towards mid nineteenth century, this ideology was substituted for a revised version that the wife was to dominate the home environment and the husband was solely the bread winner. To this end, relieved from any other domestic affair, the mother was to create a "home sweet home" atmosphere for the father to come home to, but not to be a part of. Cayton goes on to say how the mother was responsible for the care and morale of her sons and daughters "who would become virtuous citizens of the new nation."

As the father continuously removed himself from daily domestic affairs, consequently, "The doctrine of separate spheres" or cult of domesticity writes Cayton, "promised women greater respect in family matters, though it restricted the scope of their activity to the home." In scrutinizing this statement, one can infer that it foreshadows women's' erosion of power over their lives for the years to come.

Further more, Barbara Kantrowitz and Pat Wingert in their article "The Science of a Good

Marriage," explores the idea of what a good marriage is and what it isn't. Although the article offers insightful discourse about what a good marriage is by current standards, the basic concepts of it can still apply to marriages from the 1800's. They speak of "the myth" of marriages in which couples hope to meet and fall in love with an extension of themselves; in that the scenario would assimilate the "perfect" key to go into the "perfect" lock. They go on to say, "And then there is the reality of marriage, which, as any spouse knows is not unlike what Thomas Edison once said about genius: one percent inspiration and ninety-nine percent perspiration." They elaborate on the subject by extrapolating that anger is not the real poison in a marriage and that the "real demons are criticism, contempt, defensiveness and stonewalling."

Consequently, the preceding statement relates to the stifling conditions of those southern white women. They were often criticized and their ideas were either not taken seriously, treated with contempt, or be altogether dismissed. Their husbands' defense systems were 'what I say goes,' "Stone walling" was a stoical stance to their wives grievances, which was a commonality among husbands of that time period.

A lot has changed since those bad old days of male domination, socioeconomic oppression and disparity, contempt and downright psychological abuse towards women in the 19th and 20th centuries. Women of the 21st century have evolved post women's liberation movement of the 1960s and 70s. The publishing of books like the New York Times bestseller: *Founding Mothers: The Women Who Raised Our Nation* (2005) Cokie Roberts, prove that the women who helped forged the path to post-revolutionary American prosperity were a force to be reckoned with in all their iconoclastic and pioneering glory. Today, they are heads of households, doctors, lawyers, scientists, engineers, professional athletes and yes, some still choose to be stay-at-home moms to raise the future leaders of our world. In spite of all their advancements however, their fight for full equality as fruitful contributors to a still mostly male dominated society remains imminent.

African-American Fiction: Zora Neal Hurston Explores Identity, Love, Race and Religion in Her Seminal book *Their Eyes Were Watching God*

"I lost many literary battles the day I read 'Their Eyes Were Watching God.' I had to concede that occasionally aphorisms have their power. I had to give up the idea that Keats had a monopoly on the lyrical."

--Zadie Smith

"Ships at a distance have every man's wish on board. For some they come in with the tide. For others they sail forever on the horizon, never landing until the Watcher turns his eyes away in resignation, his dreams mocked to death by Time. That is the life of men. Now, women forget all the things they don't want to remember and remember everything they don't want to forget. The dream is the truth. Then they act and do things accordingly."

So begins Zora Neal Hurston's epic story about an emotional and spiritual journey of self-discovery. Through my incessant study of literature and the craft of writing, I have learned that what grabs a reader right from the onset of a story is by having a fully formed voice and vision that prepares us to go along for the ride; that we will be transported elsewhere to another reality. The book is a dichotomous exploration of variant thematic ideologies of love and hate, wrong and right in black literary historical genre as manifested in the American cultural and sociopolitical past and in its effects on posterity.

"A graduate of Barnard…, Zora Neal Hurston published seven books—four novels, two books of folklore, and an autobiography—more than fifty shorter works between the middle of the Harlem Renaissance and the end of the Korean War, when she was the dominant Black woman writer in the United States. The dark obscurity in which her career than lapsed reflects her staunchly independent political stances rather than any deficiency of craft and vision," writes Henry Louis Gates, Jr. in the afterward to Their Eyes.

Hurston, whose life spanned between the year 1891 and 1960, was a novelist, folklorist and anthropologist. Her fictional and factual writings of Black Heritage remain unparalleled. "Their Eyes Were Watching God" is Hurston's most highly praised novel and is considered a classic among the best of Black literature.

Their Eyes re-counts the story of Janie Crawford's burgeoning selfhood through three marriages with loving empathy and stinging urgency. Janie, who is described as "fair- skinned, long haired and dreamy as a child" advances in years to anticipate better treatment than she actually receives; that is until she has an unexpected encounter with an amusing, smooth and fast talking younger roustabout named Tea Cake, who entices her into an emotional and spiritual journey that will change her life forever. He proffers to her an opportunity to see herself and life through his eyes without being regrettably adorned with the formerly disparaging labels of being "one man's mule" or another man's wall flower through her previous two marriages.

Over the course of the story, the character of Janie unfolds, as she will learn that she does not have to succumb to living a life ripe with rife, acrimony or maladroit romantic dreams. Towards the end of the story, the reader will learn in Janie's words: "two things everybody's got tuh do fuh themselves. They got tuh go tuh God and they got tuh find out about livin' fuh themselves," since her character struggles with the incessant panoptic surveillance and potentially spirit crushing criticism of her neighbors.

Every good writer or story-teller has to have motif and Hurston's Their Eyes is swimming in a crystal clear blue- eyed sea of symbolism. In Their Eyes she uses an overworked, underfed and tormented mule to illustrate the dire living conditions of her main character Janie, what she endures on her way to spiritual, emotional, and physical freedom and awakening. Her depiction of Janie's life of strife serves not only to demonstrate essentially the mistreatment of Janie as "one man's mule and another man's adornment", it also attests to the meager living conditions of women, that is to say in terms of oppression and maltreatment, during her time period. Since she died right at the cusp of both the Civil Rights and the Women's Equal Rights Movements, Hurton's Their Eyes would go on to achieve greater respect and acknowledgement as an indispensible part of Black literature.

Also in Hurston's novel, I was particularly enthralled by her use of Black vernacular speech (i.e. go tuh God…livin' fuh theyselves…) to chronicle her Black female characters' coming to the best of their being or emerging consciousness. In his afterward, Henry Louis Gates offers a keen observation of some of the most indispensable key elements regarding the deceptively simple trajectory of Hurston's story. He writes that "The Charting of Janie Crawford's fulfillment as an autonomous imagination, Their Eyes is a lyrical novel that correlates the needs of her first two husbands for ownership of progressively larger physical space (and the gaudy accoutrements of upward mobility) with the suppression of self -awareness in their wife. Only with her third and last lover, a roustabout called Tea Cake whose unstructured frolics center around and about the Florida swamps, does Janie at last blooms…"

In other words, towards the end of the story, Janie did not find love and happiness as presumably defined by her first two husbands by the often superficial veneers of status and ownership of fancy property, ironically she found the bond of love, God and community living by a swamp with a mere unrefined and uneducated vagrant whose only means of sustaining Janie was through a daily dosage of love, laughter and whatever he could muster with his bare hands to put food on the table.

Therefore in honor of Black History Month, you will find that in "Their Eyes Were Watching God" concurrent themes of Hope, love, and an affirmation of Black Heritage are enough to make you want to put Their Eyes on your reading list this February.

Irish-American Fiction: The Loss of Innocence in James Joyce's "Araby" and Ernest Hemingway's "Indian Camp"

"Better pass boldly into that other world, in the full glory of some passion, than fade and wither dismally with age."

--James Joyce

Ah, Childhood, a time when our slates were clean and fresh like the morning dawn; a time when we saw life very much as we saw a new toy, something to be observed and explored. This innocence lasts up until that moment when, one day, everything changes; the tooth fairy's mask falls off and we see "mom" and Santa Claus becomes just "dad." The stories "Araby" by James Joyce and "Indian Camp" by Ernest Hemingway depict the stories of two boys who are on this passage from innocent childhood to early adulthood. The stories capture that period of time when each of us was innocent and optimistic about everything. But once the truth comes to light and exposes the harsh realities of life, one of the boys surrenders his "innocence" to "insight," while the other remains a child.

Nick, in "Indian Camp," is a young boy who is about to embark on a boat trip with his father, a doctor, who is on his way to see a woman who has been in labor for an extended period of time. Because he is the nearest physician, Nick's father agreed to go and help the woman even though he is without his tools. He takes Nick with him, believing that the experience will be good for his son.

The boy in "Araby," who is nameless (perhaps implying that he represents every adolescent boy), is lovesick for a young woman. Once he realizes that going to a bazaar in Araby could mean possibly buying the young woman a gift, and thus enhancing his imagined relationship with her, he is absolutely inspired. Though he does not know what lies ahead, he welcomes the opportunity. Hence it seems to me that the boy is making an unconscious decision to grow up.

The train in "Araby" and the boat in "Indian Camp" facilitate the boys' journeys, symbolizing the crossing over to the adult world. The train, which is faster, symbolizes the "Araby" boy's expedited rate of mental growth. While the boat, which is slower, symbolizes Nick's delayed mental growth rate. The water Nick travels over has a diffused, vast surface, leading to all possible destinations; this represents Nick's uncertainty, vulnerability, and his tendency to "follow the wind."

The bridge the "Araby" boy travels on represents a symbol of determination and self-governing attitude; bridges lead to a specific destination. The boy made a conscious decision to go to

Araby; thus the bridge portrays the lovesick boy's sense of direction and possibly further development ahead.

The "Araby" boy's journey from innocence to insight is again hinted at when he reaches the bazaar. He says, "I could not find any six-penny entrance, and fearing that the bazaar would be closed, I passed in quickly through a turnstile, handing a shilling to a weary looking man." The phrase "passed in quickly" here hints that the boy is ready to leave childhood. This is shown and expressed when he decides to use the "adult" turnstile when he could not find the entrance reserved for children.

On the other hand, Nick demonstrates unwillingness to leave childhood. After his father delivers the baby, he asks his son, "How [does he] like being an intern?" to which Nick responds, "All right." Nick's words are belied by the fact the he is "…looking away so as not to see what his dad was doing." This gesture has much impact because it shows that Nick is not ready to step into his dad's shoes or the adult world just yet.

The "Araby" boy has no father to shelter him from the experience of growing up; thus hastening the passage from child to adult. Nick, on the other hand, has a father to protect him. I find that children often grow up faster when they lack adult supervision and protection. The drawback for these children is that they are robbed of their childhood that much sooner.

As I read "Indian Camp," I anticipated that Nick was going to be exposed to something so profound that there was no way that he was going to walk away from it not having grown up a little. However, on his way back with his dad, he asked him, "Is dying hard, daddy?" and to that his dad answered "No," and that it "depends." These questions represent a mirror of his true innocence. In the end, he felt sure that death was not going to knock on his door; which hints to the reader that Nick did not grow up at all, he remains still a child.

In contrast, the "Araby" boy did seem to get something from his experience. At the end of the story, he thinks to himself, "Gazing up into the darkness, I saw myself as a creature driven and derided by vanity, and my eyes burned with anguish and anger." It's at this point that I feel he undergoes the transition from "innocence" to "insight." Despite the "darkness" that he was in, which implies the confusion and deception imposed on him by the adult world, he finally manage to see "light." He was able to see himself, like adults often do, as a victim of life's many disappointments — but finds that with each disappointment, one tends to get more insightful about life. It's like driving a car and being lost. Life happens when you try to find your way out.

So, unlike Nick in "Indian Camp" who kept his innocence, lover boy in "Araby" inadvertently traded in his innocence for insight. This reminds me of the axiom: "life without risks, is no life at all."

Russian-American Fiction: Life, Liberty and the Pursuit of More Stuff in Leo Tolstoy's "How Much Land Does a Man Need?"

"The richest man is not who has the most, but who needs the least." Anonymous

There once was a man from Haiti, we'll call him Francois to protect his identity, who came to the United States; to pursue economic liberty.

Now most of us are aware of what coming to a new country means. It means, in case you're not aware, having to start all over again. For example, if you used to live in a house of great magnitude in your country, in this country one might have to start out by being a border in somebody else's apartment. This particular man started out with nothing. He had no car, money or a place of his own. He lived with his sister at the time and was in the process of looking for some type of employment. Now this man, at the beginning, was content with just being in the States. Material possessions like cars, fashionable clothing, expensive furniture and home entertainment systems were not his priority.

Then a few years later, things started to change. By that time he had gotten a job, and was paying his sister some rent. His ambition, however, was to use most of his money to buy home entertainment systems, new clothes and ultimately a car. Now keep in mind that this man has only been in this country for three years and could barely speak English. He figured that if he had all of these things, he could write to his family in Haiti to tell them how he had attained instant success. He wanted all things that he never had back in his country and was willing to do anything to get them and get them fast. He figured that if he was empowered by material things, then nothing else could touch him. The devil, with all his temptations, then makes his grand entrance into his life and wreaked havoc.

This brings me to Leo Tolstoy's revealing story, "How Much Land Does a Man Need?" This particular story was written more than a century ago. The situation described in the previous paragraph took place in today's world however the similarities are uncanny.

In Tolstoy's story, he describes a land owner who can never get enough land. A few acres more always appear to be more attractive and at the time the one thing that he 'thought' would make him happy. The paradox in that though is the more land he has, the more he is unhappy because he is too busy thinking about getting more land to really enjoy the land he already has. Pakhom, the landowner, asserts that, "If I had all the land I wanted; I wouldn't fear the Devil himself!" It was at that point that he inadvertently, like Francois, beckons the devil himself with all his temptations.

Francois ended up purchasing a new car, signed a contract for a membership at a popular health club and had by that time accumulated all kinds of bills and was feeling like a "big man." His friends in this case played the devil's advocate in encouraging him to do all of these things. They told him that having all these things meant that he would look like he has money, which meant that he could then have all the women he wanted. Then all of a sudden, he lost his job. Since he didn't have any skills or speak any English, he could not find one soon enough. Apparently, the money he was spending on material things, he should have invested in an education. He was forced to sell his car, his entertainment system and was reduced to buying second hand clothes, all contrary to his previous illusionary status. He could not be extricated from his contract at the gym, so they submitted his name to a collection agency which would stain his future credit report. Hence in the end, how many material possessions did Francois really need? He probably needed just enough to be comfortable and content. What he shouldn't have wanted was to be overly comfortable yet highly stressed; which would only bring inevitable misery.

In Pakhom's case, we see him succumbing to the same situation at the end of the story. So like Pakhom, Francois lost his priorities along the way. He confused what he needed for what he wanted and in the end it was what he wanted that finally destroyed him.

Pakhom, in "How Much Land Does a Man Need?" towards the end surrenders to the devil's temptations, this time in the shape of an older land owner. The land owner tells him that he can own as much land as he can walk in a day, but the catch is that he has to return to the place where he started from before sundown. Pakhom sees this as a great opportunity to acquire more land and thought that he was going to walk on as much land as possible, but carefully so he wouldn't bite more than he could chew. He then, however, succumbed to the devil's wishes by walking on more land than he's able to walk back. He barely made it to the spot where he started, and when he did he fell right onto that spot and had a heart attack!

How much land would one say Pakhom needed? Just enough to bury him in, which is about six feet. Pakhom, like Francois, lost sight of his priorities. He confused what he needed for what he wanted and what he wanted ended up destroying him.

The biggest mistake that people make in contemporary consumerist society, among all the surrounding temptations, is failing to differentiate between necessity and luxury. There is an axiom that "God never gives you more than you can handle." So whatever you have now is probably what you "need" to survive. The epiphany I had after reading Toltoy's story was don't chase somebody else's waterfall, when you have a nice fountain in your own backyard.

Diverse Voices of Literacy: A Talk with Jewish Writer and Harvard University Alumni Douglas Holder of the Somerville Writers Festival

The autumn chill has dawned. Soon we will all be in search of something warm and toasty to heat up our bodies. But I want to tell you about something that will heat up not only your bodies, but your minds and souls. Something warm and "literary." I'm talking about the annual Somerville News Writer's Festival that took place on Nov. 11, 2007 at the Dilboy VFW Hall in Somerville and hosted by Jimmy Tingle who once appeared regularly on "60 Minutes", "The Tonight Show with Jay Leno", in addition to his own comedy special on HBO and whom I once appeared on the same stage with while giving a reading from my book: *Sparks in the Dark* at a Roxbury Community College literary, visual, and performing arts festival.

In the past, the Festival has attracted writers from Hollywood and Pulitzer Prize Winners and was co-founded by local author-publisher and Harvard University graduate Douglas Holder, who is also a member of the Bagel with the Bards: a group of poets and writers who meet every Saturday at the Au Bon Pain in Cambridge/Somerville to share their works, resources, and create good vibes with each other. Some of the other writers participating this year are Haitian American writer Danielle Legros Georges, festival co-founder Timothy Gager, Lo Galluccio, Gloria Mindock and Douglas Holder just to name a few. Holder had also been among my most influential mentors and featured me on his show on SCAT (Somerville Community Access Televison) TV show "Poet to Poet, Writer to Writer", as well as publishing my poetry and personal interview in the Somerville Times *and* the Boston Globe in a generous effort to promote my poetic memoir *Sparks in the Dark* which was released back in 2008.

Jacques Fleury: Can you tell me when and why was the Somerville News Writers Festival established and what role did you play in this FABULOUS literary project?

Douglas Holder: The festival started in 2003. I was writing for The Somerville News, and the new owners came aboard and I was made Arts/Editor. The owners, the Norton and Tauro families wanted a higher profile for the paper. I had the idea of a Writer's festival, and I contacted Tim Gager. Gager and I proposed it to the board, and they were on board from the start.

JF: How do you keep the festival running? Who are your sponsors and most ardent supporters?

DH: Porter Square Books and Grub Street have been consistent supporters. The Somerville News does the lion share of funding.

JF: What method do you use to attain and select your writers?

DH: We want people who are respected for their writing, and can bring people in. Both Tim and I are connected in the Poetry and Fiction communities, so getting people hasn't been that hard.

JF: Can you tell me a brief synopsis or interesting anecdote of a few of your writers, particularly the ones that you know personally like Tim Gager, Lo Galluccio etc...?

DH: Well Lo is going to read the poetry of the late poet Sarah Hannah.

Hannah committed suicide last spring and was scheduled to read at the festival. Lo will read from Hannah's work and from her own.

JF: What are your aspirations for the festival? What do you hope to achieve in the next five years?

DH: I hope to achieve another five years. Tim has plans to have a workshop sponsored by a local college.

JF: Do you think that the writer's festival is necessary and why?

DH: I think it is a good thing for Somerville- a showcase for national and local talent. It is a focal point for the writing community.

JF: What do you get from co-hosting the festival?

DH: Well of course I get publicity from it. Also I enjoy hosting, and introducing many of my friends and fellow writers.

JF: What have you seen the writer's festival done for the writing careers of past participants?

DH: Well many of the writers are very established, so the festival really doesn't affect them. I am sure the less established have gotten more recognition--and hopefully sold a few books. I hope the festival gives recognition to some of the emerging writers we have. The big names like Perrotta, Almond, Wright, Pinsky etc... do it out [of] a sense of service to the community.

JF: I know in the past the festival have sparked the interest and participation of popular a Hollywood actor and Pulitzer Prize winners. Do you have any high profile writers this year?

DH: Robert Pinsky will be receiving the Ibbetson Street Press Lifetime Achievement Award; Former US Poet Laureate Tom Perrotta, his screenplay "Little Children" was nominated for an Oscar, and of course Steve Almond, etc...

JF: You do so much for the artistic family, how do you balance work, a personal life and your active participation in the writing community?

DH: I don't have kids so that helps. I have a flexible job AND AN UNDERSTANDING WIFE DIANNE ROBITAILLE. IT IS ALL A LABOR OF LOVE.

JF: I read that Henry Roth have greatly influenced your writing. Can you tell me why?

DH: Well he wrote about being Jewish, and he wrote beautifully about food. I did my thesis at Harvard on him. I am very interested in Jewish-American literature...I am Jewish. Both food and being Jewish often shows up in my work.

JF: In your opinion, what do you think makes a good writer?

DH: A good writer is someone who makes you cut yourself while shaving, as you read their work. A good writer is evocative, leaves you with something, [and] captures a person, place or thing…

JF: What advice if any do you have for up and coming writers?

DH: Read, Read, Read. Write, Write, Write. Study. Study. Study. Get an internship in a lit mag, join writers groups, attend readings, and immerse yourself in the writing life.

JF: Is there anything that I did not ask that you wish to address? And merci for this interview!

DH: That's about it.

For more information please visit: www.somervillenewswritersfestival.com.

The Healing Power of Music: Shea Rose Blends the Revolutionary Sounds of Rap, Rock and Jazz and Gives Us Something Eclectic and Unique

"Where did all the female hip hop artists go? We need to find the next generation and make sure their voices are heard." –Queen Latifah

Although the charts are inundated with a plethora of ubiquitous pop artists like Beyonce, Rhianna and Lady Gaga, one tend to wonder…whatever happened to female hip hop acts like Queen Latifah, Da Brat and Salt and Peppa? Perhaps this is a sign of the perpetually transformative trajectory of the musical landscape or perhaps our musical posterity has yet to look back at the derivative sounds that encompass today's music. Nevertheless, new generations of female artists are doing just that, bringing back the hip hop sounds of yesteryear and infusing it with other musical genres to create a fresh eclectic sound and one such artist is Shea Rose.

It was just only a few years ago that Shea Rose began singing. She started out as a poet and progressed to song writing. After leaving her dream job as a writer for MTV in New York City, she began to sing as well upon returning back to her native Boston where she experimented by performing with neo soul and classic rock acts, according to Noelle Janka in an article in Performer Magazine at Berklee College of Music. After listening to her current LP, "Little Warrior", it is clear to me that her oeuvre are drenched in heartache, righteous anger, and communal frustration mitigated by a subtext of humanitarianism, hope and inspiration.

"Music is a Godsend, a life saver thrown out to me at a time in my life when the light at the end of the tunnel was flooded by unrelenting darkness," declares Shea. She goes on to say, "Music has helped me to reconnect with the human condition, my community, humanity and the world at large."

A retroactive assessment of an artist's early years is often the best indication of their musical influences. Her recordings showcase an array of musical influences including Janis Joplin, Marvin Gaye, Amel Larriuex and Queen Latifah, whose hit song "U.N.I.T.Y" she recently rerecorded. Latifah—who coincidentally was determined to find female poets, emcees and musicians—initiated a nationwide search which resulted in her handpicking five fresh talented female voices among six hundred and Shea Rose was one of them. In an interview in Ebony

Magazine, Shea talks about what it was like meeting the Queen, "…it was all about sisterhood and just being you. It was magical." Yet still Shea struggles to define her sound, one of which is Rock 'N' Roll, a genre not accustomed to her prima facie physical portraiture as a Black female urbanite.

"I struggle to describe my voice and my songs when asked because…I'm still discovering me…I can say that I am a soulful…performer with traces of Blues, Folk, Jazz and Rock influences…Or as I often say, 'The Female Lenny Kravitz meets Lauryn Hill." And from listening to her "Little Warrior" LP, I can eagerly concur with her utterance. Songs from "Warrior" like "Go So Hard" and "Jungle Fever" capture an intransigent call for awareness surrounding issues of transcending life hardships and antiquated racist ideologies. And in a world where assertive and confident women are easily called the "b" word, songs like "I'm the Sh*t" is an affirmation of female self-esteem and empowerment. The lyrics and tone of the LP can at times be perceived as austere and astringent to the senses but it is balanced with a fair amount of facetious levity.

As Shea Rose prepares to embark on the echelons of the music industry, she has a clear message for her musical peers. In her interview in Ebony Magazine, when asked about what's missing from music today, she said plainly, "Content. We need more stuff, not fluff… something…kids can take home and really think about." And I couldn't agree more.

The Healing Power of Music: Sweet Sounds from "Sweet Wednesday" to Make Our Modern Day Pains Go Away

"When people refer to 'Back in the Day,' it was a Wednesday. Just a little fun fact for you."

--Dane Cook

I met the neo-folk group Sweet Wednesday back in 2007. I invited them to perform live on my then television show, "Dream Weavers with Jacques," at Cambridge Community Television (CCTV). They are a rare breed of individuals reminiscent of the best of the 1960s and '70s peace and love era and their music is a true reflection of that. They bought my poetic memoir, "Sparks in the Dark," and were inspired to turn three of my poems into songs. These songs are now available on iTunes under the title "A Lighter Shade of Blue," by Sweet Wednesday and Jacques Fleury. The profits from the CD will benefit Haiti charity, St. Boniface. When *Sweet Wednesday* released their CD "Escaping the Pale Moon," in 2012 at Club Passim, an illustrious locale in Cambridge, Massachusetts where legends like Neil Young jammed, I caught up with them for this fabulous interview:

Jacques Fleury: How did Sweet Wednesday come to be?

Sweet Wednesday: We met 12 years ago at the Natick Center for the Arts. The first time we played together there was definitely chemistry there, like electrons being pulled together in orbit around the waters of the muses.

JF: Tell me a bit about your musical background.

SW: I first decided to learn violin after hearing Buskin and Batteau's "The Boy and the Violin." My dad took me to the concert and they were the first group I saw. I was enthralled. My parents had an old classical guitar with two strings and I used to lie on my back in the den and play along with old records and the radio. I eventually got my first guitar for my bar mitzvah from my grandfather. It was an Alvarez that I later wrote a lot of songs on and it even ended up in the Pacific Ocean after a wild night of playing and drinking whiskey. I played in some bands in high school and college and after that. Fronted briefly the band that later became The Ethnics and

That Band in Harvard Square. Jon Natchez, my childhood friend, who played on my first record, is in a really awesome indie band called Yellow Ostrich.

JF: Are you living your American Dream?

SW: I do my best to try to live my dream. It is hard to be an artist; I feel it can have a stigma, like being a bank robber or something. It is so hard to be true to yourself and your vision.

There's a pendulum that you go through where you can be like, what the....am I doing? I should have stayed in school. But then there's the exciting explorer aspect of it, like traveling unknown seas to the new continent. I do feel like, where I came from, people don't totally understand what I'm doing and some people might think me a bit crazy. But I'd rather one day be under the ground knowing that I pursued my vision than worry about what I perceive other people to think.

JF: When did you know that you wanted to become a musician?

SW: It's pretty funny that I became a musician because I suffer from awful stage fright. I remember first playing open mics and wanting to play shows and I was sitting in 1369 in Central Square with my mentor, Janet Connerney, and she told me to write down on a piece of paper all the venues I wanted to play and post it on the wall and picture myself playing there, and it happened. My only regret is that I didn't put U2's 360 Tour on the list. Once you start playing the shows, this whole thing is hugely addictive, but in a good way. There is no rush quite like it.

JF: How would you define the musical genre of Sweet Wednesday? And how do you think it fares in popular musical culture today?

SW: Our influences include Gram Parsons, Natalie Merchant, Neil Young, Pink Floyd. We are an indie band which is a cool place to be right now. With the Internet boom came empowerment to artists. You can sell CDs and book shows online. Indie bands are now winning Grammys and getting thousands of fans bypassing traditional conglomerate media. This is good because a lot of radio stations are still playing the same songs they were playing 30 years ago.

JF: What inspires your songs?

SW: Scotty Melton, a Nashville musician I recently met, compared me to Fox Mulder on "The X Files," having the look of pondering the deep questions of the universe. I found that flattering and I feel that some people are drawn to music to deal with the big questions. Why are we here? What is the point of the cycles of life and death? Why is there war? And also, there's this constant trying to make sense of the past. Inspiration comes anywhere. You could be driving in a car at 2AM outside of Dublin after you just missed running over a giant hare. You could be locked in the bathroom before your wedding day. You could be in Acadia National Park after a night of too many beers or writing on a napkin in a restaurant in Belgium.

JF: Can you talk about your recent tour?

SW: Had a great southern tour this past fall. We fell in love with the south. You can find inspiration on the streets. I saw one of my favorite bands, Mountain Sprout, for the first time, basking on a park bench in Eureka Springs, Arkansas. We've had wild experiences on tour. We've been chased by vigilante bikers who tried to run us off the road at the Mexican border. We once played at a place that I think was a cult. A gig we got on Craigslist once turned out to be a sex club. Wild things happen in this business.

JF: Do current events affect your music?

SW: You have to be careful with current events because it can make your music sound dated. Compare Bob Dylan's writing to Phil Ochs. Both brilliant, but Dylan's imagery and vagueness and mystery stands the test of time and has new meaning in the present. It is almost as if songs have to have holes in them. What is not said allows the listener to fill in their own meanings. I was influenced by the Iraq war when I first started writing the song Ophelia. In the song, about an army deserter during the revolutionary war who falls in love with the daughter of a Madame who is a loyalist, I was trying to work something out. I was against the Iraq war, I was against Vietnam. Would I have been against the Revolutionary War? Is all war stupid and pointless? Would I have fought in World War II? I was trying to work these things out of how far I go as a pacifist.

JF: Can you talk about your pending CD release party?

SW: We are so excited for our CD release show for our new album, "Escaping from the Pale

Moonlight." The show will be at Club Passim. We're having our friends Red Velvet Slide, Reverend Busker, Susan Levine and more as special guests. Tickets are available at passim.org.

Thank you Jacques! Our website is www.sweetwednesday.com where you can listen to our

songs and get the latest on shows and new releases and our email is info@sweetwednesday. com. Drop us a line we'd love to hear from you!

"The Niceties" Challenges Racial Power Structure & Encourages Dialogue on Race Relations in American Politics & Education

"The most common way people give up their power is by thinking they don't have any."

–Alice Walker

"You have too much power!!!" exclaims Zoe, a black student at Yale University, to her white professor Janine from the theatrical production "The Niceties" which played at the Calderwood Pavilion at the Boston Center for the Arts in the fall of 2018 and is written by Brookline native and Yale University graduate Eleanor Burgess and was directed by Kimberly Senior.

"Niceties" tells the story of Zoe and Janine who meant to discuss the virtue of Zoe's term paper on the effects of slavery on the American Revolution. However, neither woman expected what transpired next: a war of words on race relations in America (yikes!) which garnered national attention and consequently proved capable of ruining both their lives.

"For months I was stuck in an endless succession of unsuccessful conversations about race, over and over and over again," Burgess explains about an incident that actually happened back in the fall of 2015 while she was a student at Yale. It started when a campus email warning student not to wear potentially offensive or "insensitive" Halloween attire caused a ripple effect when a professor safeguarded the idea that the holiday should be a time of intentional "transgression"; that students should be able to express themselves without the pressure to be politically correct.

Burgess began to ponder about how the conversations went so wrong so fast, even within her own assorted range of classmates and friends. She went on to say, "I was obsessed with why my interactions were going so badly between smart and well intentioned people. It made me evaluate, as an undergraduate history major and former high school history teacher, what I was taught, what I believed, and what I taught to others."

The production itself set the stage for the power dynamic narrative and discussion between Zoe and her white professor Janice. They meet in Janice's office with a colossal sprawling desk seemingly perched upon a structure that makes it appear high and imposing, while Zoe sits across from Janice in a chair positioned far below the mammoth sized desk. And the fact that for the most part Janice was standing and hovering over Zoe speaks further to the power structure dynamic between the two.

George Washington hangs on Janice's office wall like a haunting commanding figure from the past and its mere presence communicates power and influence; which Zoe takes offense to when she describes Washington in a manner that brought a visceral jolt to the senses and psyches of the viewing audience as they are pelted with opinions and facts which they are forced to experience and confront.

Jordan Boatman delivered a searing, jaunty, impassioned, and astute performance as Zoe, an idealistic black college student with a resplendent intellect and puissant advocate for diversity in our educational system, exigent in her quest for social justice. She constantly adverted to the practice of racial inequality due to the lack of minorities in the American educational stratosphere. When Janice tells her to "play nice" in order to get ahead in a predominantly white society, she elucidated that it's "unfair" that minorities have to ingratiate themselves to those who oppress them.

Lisa Banes rendered an erudite, emotionally charged, at tines passive aggressive and circuitous characterization of Professor Janice; that is until at the very end when she became more brazen in her opinions on race by blurting out a word that stunned Zoe and the audience. At times, I felt like I wanted to know more of her point of view without her hiding behind her education and status as a tenured professor. I wanted more of what she revealed about her true and unambiguous feelings on race towards the end of the play.

The rapid fire and, not surprisingly, acerbic dialogue kept audiences perched on the edge of their seats, who often responded with gasps of guttural utterances during particularly tense moments. There were numerous allusions to the context of history as it pertains to racial inequality and gaping chasm in our country that prompted my interests in further explorations of racist ideology and practice in American pedagogical society. History is written by the victors and not the victimized. I want to read a different version of history, one that was written on behalf of the oppressed or by the oppressed. The play inspired me to want continue to read books like "A People's History of the United States" by Howard Zen and "Lies My Teacher Told Me" by James W. Loewen, both books criticizing American text books as presenting a transparently Eurocentric and mythologized view of American history and emphasizing the muffled voices of those left out of the history books by presenting a more balanced and historically accurate version of the past. After all, it was a white southern writer by the name of Mark Twain who corroborated this notion when he said, "The very ink with which history is written is merely fluid prejudice."

"America is an engine of racial oppression!" bellowed Zoe to Janice. This prompted both characters to dialogue about racial power dynamics especially in academia but perpetrated by our politicians designing policies to benefit the majority at the expense of the subjugated racial minority.

"A good grade from me would open doors for you..." declares Janice to Zoe and Zoe challenging that notion of why that has to be, why does she and others like her have to continually be subjected to partitioned, biased and monolithic pedagogy being dispensed by privileged white educators?

In order to decrease what Zoe perceives as "micro aggression" in academia—a term devised in

1970 by Psychiatrist and Harvard University professor Chester M. Pierce to describe spontaneous degradations of marginalized groups whether intentional or unintentional — she calls for more diverse primary sources and educators of color in academia, more diverse services on college campuses; a student body that matches the U.S. population, investments in minority businesses and that people who make the law are not necessarily more important than those who live under them. After all, the U.S. constitution dictates that government for the people by the people and that all man are created equal.

"The Niceties" is an indispensable missive to the power of the white majority in this country, it is of transcendent importance and is akin to an uncompromising muckraker, an unapologetic harangue, a stream of opinionized form encouraging us to reconsider our familiar tropes and listen to another point of view. Having seen this timely and important play makes me wonder about why we continue to need plays like this, and why do we continue to need film makers like Spike Lee ("Blackkklansman" 2018) and Michael Moore ("Farenheight 11/9" 2018) all addressing the issues of race and inequality in American society. All these artistic offerings have one thing in common: they all encourage us to talk as well as to listen to each other. Whether we agree with one another or not, it is imperative we come to understand that all feelings are valid and all points views are worth considering, that is if you value the essential premise of our American liberty.

The political right ought not to silence the political left and vice versa, otherwise we all become despotic bullies, the single biggest threat to any democracy. Under the Trump administration, America is experiencing a racially motivated Risorgimento as white supremacists march orgulous in our streets and as the Black Lives Matter movement persists.

We must not give up on one another as impassioned Americans vying for the best possible America, where every voice matters regardless of your skin color or perceived socio-economic power. "The Niceties" implores us all to come together and share, not shout, our different points of views with each other, recognize that we all need to feel equal if we are to sustain our American democracy.

The Purists Ponders Questions of Race & Sexual Identity

Racial stereotypes, racial tensions, complex and conflicted issues of sexuality in the black community all manifested at the Boston Center for the Arts Calderwood Pavilion stage

"I'd never seen anything like it in my life. Someone so blatantly challenging the ideas of race and gender and sexuality. In a way, it was comparable to David Bowie, except that Prince brought that to the black community."

--Edward Enninful

"I need to exfoliate!" Exclaims Analisa Velez as Val Kano in Dan Mc Cabe's innovative and germane new drama The Purists. Directed by Grammy and Tony Award winner Billy Porter and starring Morocco Omari of Fox TV's Empire, the play is a mordant and searing piece of art that begs the question: how well do we really know ourselves and each other minus the proverbial smoke screen of assumptions and stereotypes? It played at the Boston Center for the Art's Calderwood Pavilion in Back Bay's South End neighborhood from Aug. 30th to Oct. 6th, 2019.

The basic premise of the play entails a motley and unlikely group of multiracial-multicultural friends who gather on the front steps of their Queens apartment building to jive about their respective musical passions. In the midst of it all is a former rap star, a hip-hop DJ, a show tunes lover and a couple of rapping girls. However the play nears a Shakespearean crescendo when a rap battle between the two females spark underlying tensions that will have the characters question everything they thought they knew about themselves, each other and the notion of friendship. The play essentially posits the question: is it possible for us to love and accept one another in spite of our differences; whether those differences are musical, sexual, sociopolitical, or racial?

Juilliard School fellow and playwright Dan McCabe wrote a scandalous, acerbic and visceral script speaking directly to the black experience with whites and conversely the black experience with other blacks within the sociopolitical context. Being himself a white man writing black characters perhaps demonstrates his adscititious knowledge and awareness of the black experience pertaining to how they relate to whites as well as to one another. He explores the tacit homophobia and issues of sexuality in the black community while simultaneously juxtaposing the complexities of a race conscious society and the inexorable tensions between blacks and whites who have to live in close proximity to one another.

When asked about his inspiration for the play by Huntington Theater director of New Work Charles Haugland, he spoke particularly of the two main characters, the white musical theater loving "Gerry" played by John Scurti, and the black hip-hop loving "Lamont" played by Morocco Omari:

"I started writing this around the summer of 2015. It started with two characters: Gerry and Lamont. I saw them as interesting people to be together on stage.—very different, but also similar in their ideals and what they believed in… I've always been a hip-hop person, but I also like…musical theater. So I thought it was interesting to have these people on stage that are super passionate about [one thing] and hate the other thing."

And when it came to his knowledge and awareness of the black experience pertaining to how they relate to whites as well as to one another, he said, "[The] theme is two very different people coming together-which had a lot to do with how I was raised." He went on to say, "…I went to a private high school in Jersey where my dad was a teacher. That was a very affluent school, whereas I grew up in the middle class buildings in Manhattan. And down the block from me were the lower income [residents]…I had a lot of different types of people around me…in terms of class and race…"

The Purists is a convulsion of emotional, satirical, and comical, although at times inimical, but ultimately convivial and delightful narrative of the human experience. Towards the end, much like the character "Val", we all needed to "exfoliate" not only to remove "dead skin cells" from the surface of our skins, but the metaphoric removal of our preconceived notions of one another and to embrace new visions of a more accepting and empathetic society regardless of our racial or sexual identities and ultimately to reconsider our notions of "purity"-whether you're a "purely" hyper masculine hip-hop fanatic or a "purely" ultra-androgynous show tunes frenetic --that we can never escape ourselves, no matter how much we try to shed the layers of our true natures by "exfoliating" or chipping away at our often ambiguous and complex humanity. I gave this penetrating production a five out of five stars!

Grammy Winner Bebe Winans Was "Born for This": Celebrating Life, Love & Resiliency at the Majestic Theatre

"Dreams come true, but then things happen that are beyond anything you could dream…."

--BeBe Winans

In the midst of imminent sociopolitical divisiveness, hegemony, jingoism and xenophobia in

America, comes "Born For This", a play about renowned gospel singer and six time Grammy Award winner Bebe Winans's journey celebrating life, love, family unity, and the enduring power of resiliency, which played at the Emerson Cutler Majestic Theatre in Boston,

Massachusetts in the summer of 2018 and was written by Charles Randolph-Wright, BeBe Winans, Lisa D'Amour and directed by Charles Randolph-Wright.

This play can be perceived as a vivid bildungsroman recounting the Detroit childhood upbringing of sensational brother-sister gospel singers BeBe and Cece Winans and their eventual departure from their ubiquitous singing family to Pineville, North Carolina to join Jim and Tammy Faye Bakker's Praise The Lord Network (PTL). There, they would experience inexorable "culture shock" as they learn about love, racism and the traps and costs of fame. The televangelist couple assimilates the role of improbable surrogate family as the siblings hastily escalate to television prominence. After the brother-sister act attain astonishing success with a

PTL rendering of a cover version of the secular hit song, "Love Lift Us Up (Where We Belong)," from the movie "An Officer and a Gentleman", they come against the allure of celebrity and they form a life-long bond with then burgeoning pop star Whitney Houston. Ultimately, BeBe is compelled to learn to mediate the lures of celebrity and prosperity with the things he essentially treasures most in accordance with his religious upbringing.

"We are beyond thrilled to be continuing Arts Emerson's relationship with this remarkably inspirational work," said David Howse, Executive Director of ArtsEmerson. "Our commitment to this piece began in 2013, when we provided BeBe Winans and Charles Randolph-Wright with space for two workshops of what was then a brand new idea for a Broadway musical." The production aimed at constructing this "idea" around an illustrious set, luminescent lighting and thundering musical performances that had the audience quite literally on the edge of their seats from beginning to end. The chemistry between the actors as the Winans family was palpable; thus propelling the entertaining but at times caustic plot that manifested Bebe and

Cece Winans dually painful and joyous journey of self-discovery and eventual salvation and liberation from the trappings of celebrity.

The portrayal of the incomparable Whitney Houston, who befriended the Winans as they strived to climb the precarious rungs of musical success, was mesmerizing, magical, nostalgic and powerful. Her wistful rendition of "Don't live for the applause because you'll get lost" was touching and haunting. Jim and Tammy Faye Bakker's characterizations were gut-busting and uproarious. From Jim's sanctimonious bravado to Tammy's squeaky high pitched voice and super happy disposition or "buffoonery" as described by the Mrs. Winans character. Yes, the Bakerrs helped catapult the Winans to singing stardom, however, this play also sheds light on the Bakker's stealthy, perhaps even nefarious motives for inviting the Winans on their hit television show to begin with: to generate more donations and to attract a broader audience because the show was "looking too white" as Tammy Faye puts it. To do that, they portrayed Cece as a prostitute and Bebe as a drug addict to their largely Caucasian audience without their prior knowledge or consent. The white male singers on the show were not immediately receptive to the Winans, one barking works like "you're standing in my spot BOY!", the other stating that they will tolerate the Winans as long as the "stay in their place" reminding us of present day recurrence of emboldened racism, intolerance and ignorance that has divided the United (?) States of America.

However, later on in the show, one racist redeemed himself by absconding from the grips of ignorance and racism and into the enlightened arms of justice and accountability when he expresses regret for usurping the dignity of the teenage Bebe when he said, "I was taught to think that n...err...I mean black people were evil...I cringed when I had to shake your hands..." And goes on to explain how because he got to know Bebe, he had a change of heart. "I tried to break you" he said, as Bebe was getting ready to leave the television show to pursue singing as a duo with his sister Cece, "But you didn't break". This exemplifies the impetus, faith and resilience as demonstrated by Bebe and Cece along their spiritual and musical journey away from their family.

The issue of race is an emphatic theme throughout this compelling story as it explores interracial relationships. Bebe and a white female singer starts to develop romantic feelings for one another and when the audience starts to take notice of their nascent romance and threats of violence began to pour in, Tammy Faye tells Bebe to end the relationship or she will fire the young woman. When he asks her why, she abruptly exclaims "Because we're in the south!"

This play not only tackles difficult and timely subject matters, but it does so with great staging, spectacular lighting, imaginative props and a live band! The song and dance numbers are exciting, contemporary and well-choreographed; they propelled the trajectory of the plot seamlessly into an emotionally satisfying denouement. Mayor Martin J. Walsh proclaimed opening night of June 22, 2018 as officially "Born For This" day in Boston, Massachusetts. At the end, the ensemble cast along with Bebe Winans interacted with the audience and Bebe gave a moving soliloquy about the true message of the play: unity and love in the face of divisiveness and hate as the racially diverse cast collectively held hands and took a final bow and Bebe addressing the crowd "I know you're going to help us take this play to Broadway!" And I agree whole heartedly, Broadway bound is where "Born for This" should be heading.

Sexuality and Redemption Are Center Stage for Boxing Champ Emile Griffith in the Theatrical Production of "Man in the Ring"

"I keep thinking how strange it is . . . I kill a man and most people understand and forgive me. However, I love a man, and to so many people this is an unforgivable sin; this makes me an evil person. So, even though I never went to jail, I have been in prison almost all my life."

--Emile Griffith

"Sometimes you got the sun in your pocket and you still go out looking for the dark." This among the plethora of earnest and didactic one liners in the Huntington Theatre production of "Man in the Ring" written by Pulitzer Prize winner Michael Cristopher and directed by Michael Greif; which showed at the Calderwood Pavilion at the Boston Center of the Arts in the winter of 2018.

"Man in the Ring" attempts, and to a large extent succeeds, at gifting the audience with a heart shaped emotional odyssey, a little more than a dram from the life of six-time world champion pugilist (fancy name for boxer) Emile Griffith, marred with abysmal tragedies and towering triumphs in his ever ending search for forgiveness and redemption from the darkest parts of his salacious life. The play offers an eagle-eyed glimpse into the boxing great's life stemming from meager origins in the U.S. Virgin Islands of St. Thomas and through his indiscretions, scandals and turmoil—whether having to do with his love life, familial woes or professional setbacks— that came to define his moments of reckoning with his sexual orientation (which could possibly explain why most have not heard of him until now) and his fragmentary search for identity, acceptance and deliverance.

"Emile Griffith is a black Caribbean American…who came to New York as an immigrant hoping to be a baseball player or singer," said playwright Michael Cristofer—whose screenplay credits include "Falling in Love" with Meryl Streep and Robert DeNiro and "The Witches of Eastwick" with Cher and Jack Nicholson—when asked by Director of New Works Charles Haugland about what ignited his interest in Griffith's story. "He was drawn into becoming a boxer—which he didn't have a passion for to begin with—but then found the passion and had a very long career." But more importantly, Cristofer emphasized that his ability to connect to Griffith's story on a personal level was what really singed his desire to write the play, "I've been offered jobs to write about a certain subject or a certain character, and I've felt no connection. Then [I] can't do it. But when that mysterious thing happens and you feel that their voice and your voice have a similar connection, then it can be done."

Cristofer expounds on this "connection" when he went on to say, "I grew up in an Italian ghetto where the definitions of masculinity were strict and I [too] had struggled with my sexuality…

[Like Griffith] there was a sense of wanting to make peace with my past. I saw in his story, a man slipping into dementia and trying to make peace...He was a young immigrant... struggling with his identity while in a brutal sport... [Trying] to find peace amid the love, pain and joy that was his life."

The issues of Griffith sexuality was omnipresent throughout the play, yet it did not obliterate other aspects of his life, for example his complex and at times accusatorial relationship with his mother, his questionable "marriage" and his palpable, sympathetic and searing relationship with his lifelong partner all assembled to make for an extravagantly inventive and studied production.

Described by some pundits as impressionistic, this visually vivid and lavish conception of "Man in the Ring" offers the audience a cornucopia of philosophical, spiritual and mostly convivial and jovial spectacle involving authentic Caribbean song and dance, sunny period costumes and lush set designs and props by David Zinn—Tony Award Winner for SpongeBob SquarePants—that weaved in and out seamlessly on stage right before our very eyes; rendering the impression of a close-up magic act.

Tony Award nominee John Douglas Thompson, whom I jawed with after the show, gave a heartfelt emotional rendering as the older Griffith in tandem with his St. Thomas accent, which he effectively delivered with lapidary clarity. The accent, according to Thompson, took about a month of training to master since Thompson himself was born in England to Jamaican parents and lives in Brooklyn, New York. Some of his film credits include "The Bourne Supremacy", "Michael Clayton" and "Wolves". His portrayal of the reflective and mentally deteriorating Griffith was at times farcical but nonetheless touching, realistic and haunting, evoking compassion in lieu of pity, understanding and benevolence in lieu of judgement and indifference.

Kyle Vincent Terry gave an ebullient, boisterous, nuanced and thoughtful performance of the younger Griffith. A Brown University graduate with a Masters of Fine Arts and whose television credits include—"Elementary", "Bull", "Madam Secretary" among others— commanded the attention of the audience in hypervigilant fashion, replete with youthful adrenaline, esthetical ease, gregarious grace and perhaps inadvertently or even deliberately radiating palpable sexual energy with his pelvic thrusts and well-defined muscular body. The chemistry between the cast was most definitely and unequivocally electric and readily apparent.

This production was able to pluck the heart strings of compassion from some of the most seemingly stoic audience members. One man began to shift uncomfortably in his seat and was soon wiping streams of tears during a particularly poignant moment towards the end of the play.

Hip-Hop artist and music mogul Sean "Diddy" Combs once said "great art" should make you feel "uncomfortable" especially when you are sharing the experience with other people around and I can definitely attest to feeling "uncomfortable" many times over at the shear emotional rawness that was depicted before me.

The erotic scenes, as uncomfortable as they were at times for me personally, were tastefully and artfully done, as young Griffith explored the physical components of his sexuality, which was purported to be indubitably ambiguous. He pranced around the stage in a devoted regimen of partial nudity. His heavily muscled body glistened, thundered, stomped and commanded our attention like a swashbuckling giant. His physicality simultaneously menacing and alluring in his resilient and youthful attempts to find himself as a black sexually ambiguous professional boxer during the 1950s and 60s, when masculinity was very narrowly defined; on his way to reaching the zenith of boxing stardom.

"Sometimes you have to reach for what you can't reach, sometimes you have to reach for what you can't even see," the older wiser Griffith character earnestly utters which denotes the plays message of faith, hope and optimism, which I found particularly relatable to our current turbulent epoch here in America and elsewhere as the need for macrocosmic hopes for peace becomes more and more pressing. Even 18th century German philosopher Johann Wolfgang Von Goethe centuries before demonstrates concurrence when he affirmed that, "In all things, it is better to hope than to despair."

The theatre was invented as a beacon of hope for the human race; it was designed to help connect us to each other, to mitigate our collective sorrows, celebrate our collective joys and harmonize our human hearts. 18th century English poet Alexander Pope agrees with this ideology when he wrote that the theatre's purpose is to "wake the soul by tender strokes of art, to wake the genius and to mend the heart."

"Man in the Ring" is an affecting primrose heart mending production, imbued with perennial true to life tufts of motley characters, rousing and sensual dance numbers, exceptional and fantastical acting and directing. See it if it ever comes to your town; it may just help you find your own form of redemption.

Playwright Arthur Miller Wrestles with Morality and Hypocrisy in the Theatrical Production of "Fall"

"Let you look sometimes for the goodness in me, and judge me not." —Arthur Miller

Juxtaposed with our current tumult of cultural absurdity, intellectual madness and social chaos, dissident writer and Pulitzer Prize winning playwright Arthur Miller has his own moral conundrum and it's brought to the spotlight in the theatrical production "Fall" which showed at the Calderwood Pavilion at the Boston Center for the Arts in the spring of 2018. The auspicious play was written by playwright Bernard Weinraub and directed by Peter Dubois.

Miller, who penned such ubiquitous tales as "Death of a Salesman", "The Crucible" and "The Misfits", which he wrote for his then ex-wife Marilyn Monroe, was considered the most fêted playwright of the 20th century and was purported to be the "moral conscience" of a nation but he had a secret: a son born with Down Syndrome whose existence he refused to acknowledge.

"Arthur Miller wrote many plays about the sins of a father visited on a son, and as a writer he provided a moral compass for a generation" writes artistic director Peter Dubois. It's just ironic that although Miller penned the narrative of the oppressed, subjugated and marginalized "others" of society, he failed to be the voice of reason and compassion for his own oppressed, subjugated and marginalized disabled son, who himself was considered to be in the category of "other" or outsider if you will.

"Fall" is an emotional tour de force, effectively casted, meticulously directed and with minimalist set designs that are smart, simple and elegant; that which propelled the plot to an inexorable emotionally charged crescendo. Josh Stamberg gives a subdued, pensive, stoical, lovable yet powerful performance as Miller and Joanne Kelly delivered a nuanced, gregarious, quirky, comical yet guttural performance as Miller's wife Inge and Nolan James Tierce was touching and endearing as Daniel Miller. This play puts forth the ideological paradox of the duality of man, that we are creatures of contradictions. On the one hand Miller, a literary hommes de lettres (a man of letters), portrays himself as morally upright in his public life; whereas he perpetrated a morally unjust act in his private life when he jettisoned his own son as he embarked on the echelons of the literary intelligentsia: which is the product of culture and ideology consisting of artists, teachers and writers whose political roles fluctuates between being a progressive or regressive influence upon the development of their societies. Miller succeeded at characterizing himself as progressive in his public life but was regressive in his private life and in doing so exposes a human frailty I can safely declare we can all relate to at one point or another in our lives. Our public façade of morality does not always align with our private practices, we don't always practice what we preach.

In a glimpse of guilt or anguish over his morally regressive behavior, there is a point in the play where Miller builds a chair for his son. His wife besieges him to bring the chair to Daniel himself at the institution where he is receiving care, "YOU give him the chair…" she exclaimed and the implications of "the chair" was not loss on me as it is reminiscent of the "electric chair" given to death row inmates, hence the use of the chair is particularly affective.

The play itself can be perceived as a biographical palimpsest of Miller's original autobiography in which he omitted or "deleted" Daniel Miller. It highlights Miller's decision of omission and its ensuing ramifications. Daniel was an anathema to Miller, his greatest source of guilt and shame and he says to his wife, "Guilt is temporary, shame is permanent"; which gives the viewer an indication of the burden he must have carried over the years.

In "Fall", playwright Bernard Weinraub offers Miller up to our scrutiny and perhaps judgement. Do we see ourselves in him or do we distance ourselves from him out of fear of confronting our own human failings? And when we judge him, we must give adequate awareness to what was considered "acceptable" at the time dealing with disabled persons, they had limited choices, staggering stigma and mistreatment. To judge Miller by today's standards would render our judgement an anachronism in the time period in which Daniel was born, which was 1966. The play reminds us that we have come a long way in overcoming stigmatization and mistreatment of those afflicted with a disability. It proffers the opportunity for dialogue, compassion and understanding. Former president Theodore Roosevelt once said: "Do what you can, with what you have, where you are." Perhaps Arthur Miller did just that but "Fall" posits the question, can we forgive him for it?

The Play "A Doll's House Part 2" Poses a Modern Day Challenge to the Institution of Marriage at the Huntington Theatre

"Your home is regarded as a model home, your life as a model life. But all this splendor, and you along with it... it's just as though it were built upon a shifting quagmire. A moment may come, a word can be spoken, and both you and all this splendor will collapse."

--Henrik Ibsen

"Men leave their families all the time, but when a woman leaves she's a monster!" Exclaims

Nora, the structural character from the play A Doll's House Part 2, written by playwright and Tony Award Nominee Lucas Hnath and directed by Obie Award winner Les Waters; which debuted at the Huntington Avenue Theatre in the winter of 2019.

A Doll's House Part 2 is a re-imaging by Hnath of the original play A Doll's House– which was considered to be subversive when it was originally written back in 1879 by celebrated Norwegian modernist poet, playwright and Pulitzer Prize Nominee Henrik Johan Ibsen. It takes off where the Ibsen play left off, with Nora returning home after a fifteen year absence to face the fractured family she left behind.

"The set-up is there's a woman who left her family 15 years ago. That's kind of the only information you need. The play doesn't get into the specifics of the plot that motivated her to leave," said Hnath in interview with Berkeley Repertory Theatre Literary Manager Sarah Rose Leonard. The play offers a platform putting forth the double standard of what's expected of women versus what's expected of men within the confines and binding "contact", as Nora put it, of matrimony; that men are afforded far more freedom to come and go as they please, in stark contrast to women, who are expected to stay regardless of any rancid circumstances that may be woe them.

"It was shocking to Nora to leave her family at the end of [the original play, not this Part 2 play]

"A Doll's House…" Hnath said, and when he inquired of today's feminist scholars of what would be considered a "shocking ending today?" They unequivocally replied that it would still be a "shocking" thing to do even in the new millennium, "that's still something that is unthinkable"; which brings to mind the axiom "The more things change, the more they stay the same."

"All of the things that were debated and negotiated in A Doll's House are still topics that are debated and negotiated [today]," said Hnath. He goes on to say, "A Doll's House, Part 2 is…a play about how much we've changed, and how much we haven't, in terms of thinking about equality between men and women."

Among the many interesting aspects of the play, one I thought was particularly effective was

Hnath's use of all four characters in the play to present alternating and contradicting arguments on the issue of marriage. The point of views of Nora's husband Torvold, daughter Emmy as well as longtime family nanny Anne Marie all served the plot in balancing out multiple opinions in search for some truth about the institution of marriage and its inter-correlated effects on all the parties directly or indirectly involved. The counter arguments served to create interest and dramatic tension to the viewing audience and between the characters which abetted in propelling the plot forward to an almost Shakespearian crescendo leading to an unpredictable ending.

The staging, by Chicago-based designer Andrew Boyce, was deliberately sparse; thus allowing the audience to be fully engrossed in the world of Nora and those whom she had apparently wounded and from whom she now seeks clemency. The ultra-bright lighting illuminated every nuanced facial expression leaving little room for the characters to conceal their often agonizing emotions. Nora's understanding of the mess she left behind prima facie manifested as farouche rather than fastidious; that is until her ill sense of perception is remedied by her preemptive "victims" determined to set her straight. Nora's nomothetic beliefs vis-à-vis marriage and the opposing perspectives of the family she left bereft of her presence, forms the foundation for the play's entire premise. The audience gets to hear the many sides for and against marriage tethered with their respective arguments which are equally valid in their own rights. The comedic elements of the play made the often tense subject matter and resulting emotions more palatable. Nora is back bearing what was considered a startling (and is considered so even today) syllogism—or a method of proof based on stated premises—about marriage in late 19th century Norway and the audience is left to decide which member of Nora's family best synthesizes with their own attitudes about the subject matter.

Mary Beth Fisher, from the Chicago stage and who appeared in How Shakespeare Won the

West, gave a compelling and nuanced performance as Nora, invoking empathy for the plight of her tormented character. We can be mad at her but we can also laugh with her. While Nora never really offers a verbal mea culpa to the people she had conceivably hurt, she does unequivocally and seemingly seeks to be exculpated when she requests more favors from them.

John Judd, a Chicago actor for many years, rendered a typically stoic yet emotionally responsive manifestation as Nora's husband Torvald. He manages to be both the anchor and the catalyst for Nora's farouche behavior as he considers the hitherto unheard of requests from a wife of her husband. He has acted in many regional theatres including Berkeley Repertory Theater and

Town Hall in Galway, Ireland. Some of his television credits include "Chicago Fire" (NBC), "Empire" (Fox) and "SouthSide" (Comedy Central).

NiKKi Massoud, who has appeared on the New York stage alongside Daniel Craig in Orthello, delivered a deliberately candid and coincidentally witty performance as Nora's daughter Emmy. She is a semi-seminal character who puts Nora in her place, so to speak. She received her MFA from Brown University and trained at the British American Drama Academy.

Nancy E. Carroll, who has appeared on Broadway in Present Laughter for which she won an Elliot Norton Award, gave a grating, at times expletive filled, comedic and dramatic performance as Nora's family nanny Anne Marie; having stayed behind to help the shattered household Nora abandoned. Her film and television credits include Spotlight, Irrational Man and Olive Kitteridge.

Tony Award Nominated playwright Lucas Hnath utilized a surfeit of available resources when constructing this groundbreaking and still timely play. He consulted with eminent feminist scholars in an attempt to attain contrasting points of views regarding the institution of marriage for his character's rapid-fire dialogue and resolute arguments. Hnath also read feminist 19th century writers the likes of Charlotte Perkins Gilman who penned the related story "The Yellow Wallpaper" about a woman oppressed by her domineering husband. A story which I analyzed myself as part of my classic American Literature class in college. All of Hnath's efforts came to fruition in producing a well thought out, evocative and galvanizing play.

The #MeToo movement has blasted the door right open on the plight of women in a male dominated world. Women are coming forward with their stories of feeling the weight of oppression, whether it be in the form of workplace inequality or marital woes, they are ensuring that their voices are heard LOUD and clear! Because according to Nora–who considers marriage to be a great big lie– "When you lie to yourself long enough, you lose your voice." A Doll's

House, Part 2 reminds us that all of us are responsible to ourselves to speak out against subordination and social injustice and given the current political climate, there's no better time like the present. I give this production 5 out of 5 stars.

"Can You Forgive Her?" Well, It Doesn't Matter Really Because She Doesn't Care...in this Dark Comedy at the Boston Center for the Arts

"For things to have value in man's world, they are given the role of commodities. Among man's oldest and most constant commodity is woman."

--Ana Castillo

"Don't let the Indian in!" The aforementioned phrase is one among many caustic one liners that suffuses the Huntington Theatre Company's new play Can You Forgive Her? It is written by prolific writer and playwright Gina Gionfriddo, Brown University graduate, two-time Pulitzer

Prize finalist, and writer for Television shows such as "Law & Order" and "Cold Case." The play is directed by Huntington's own Peter Dubois and is expected to run from Mar. 5th through Apr.24th at the Boston Center for the Arts' Calderwood Pavilion in the South End.

The play is mostly about Miranda, a prima facie heartless and nefarious young white woman who is entombed in arrears, namely college loans, credit cards and a lavish lifestyle she can't afford; which attests to the spirit of the times today since most of us can identify with her quandary when it comes to living beyond our means. During her perpetual quest to keep up appearances by straining to sustain the often precarious echelons of social class and status, she uses her feminine wiles to build several quid pro quo relationships with affluent "Sugar Daddies" with "enough sugar" to help her sustain her debt-ridden existence; that which will implicate her in potentially catastrophic consequences as the narrative dictates.

"This play has a perspective on reality in a sense that these types of relationships actually exist," explained female spectator Zoe Arguello answering to my request for her take on the production. She went on to say, "sugar daddy or rich guy with intellectually and emotionally intelligent female, who use one another assuming that they are balancing out their troubled lives but are living in a fantasy not reality."

Miranda's "reality" is that she's HUNGRY for cash and her appetite is insatiable. In the French Creole culture, she is what we would call a "Piyagé", anyone who will stop at nothing until they clean out your bank account before moving on to their next victim. What the play does, however, is raise the question: "why" Miranda has to be a "Piyagé?" Is she simply a victim of her circumstances, a casualty to her choices or is she tragically aggrieved by a consumerist and socio-economic status obsessed society? Can we forgive her?

In the play, Miranda slighted a man from India whom she kept referring to as "The Indian;" thus alluding to the subtext of her racism. The "Indian" remains nameless throughout the play inferring of how often minorities are seen solely for their ethnicity and not for their humanity. She came to think that this man wanted to kill her because he found out that she has several other "boyfriends" and in her flight she interwove herself into the lives of another couple navigating their own convoluted relationship woes. The characters possess undeniable chemistry and the dialogue is meticulously clever and fast paced. The story is believable and arguably true to our present day realities as depicted on Television shows, within our own families and in the newspapers.

The theatre often imitates life and this is the third play I've seen at the Huntington Theatre that tackles subjects ostensibly ripped right from the newspaper headlines. A Confederacy of Dunces, Disgraced and now "Can You Forgive Her" all have these three subtexts in common: fear of the unknown, dissatisfaction and unrest with present day realities and ultimately confronting our inherent racism. Nevertheless Gionfriddo's brilliance is readily apparent when she manages to render uncomfortable topics whole heartedly laughable. In an interview with Huntington dramaturge Charles Haugland, Gionfriddo spoke about some of the themes that ignited this play.

"I had become fixated on a crime that was a murder-suicide," said Gionfriddo. She went on to say, "A couple went on a date in which the woman had publicly treated the man badly...and it ended with him killing her and then himself." She added that, "I kept thinking 'Oh, I want to know more about this case,' and I really couldn't find out any more, so I created a fictional story to explore why I was so obsessed with it. That is where [the character of] Miranda came from: a woman who finds herself on a very self-destructive path...I wanted to know how she got to that moment."

Some of the concurrent themes range from the self-help book and spiritual search phenomenon; that which Miranda refers to as a "... type of self-improvement cult pyramid...", alcoholism, grief, anger, menopause, living beyond your means, mother/son relationships, differences between the sexes and differences between gay and straight men. In a hilarious scene when

Miranda is "spilling her guts" to the character Graham whom she originally thought was gay and when her assumption was refuted, she screeched: "How could you NOT be gay! You're obsessed with your mother!!!" She went on to say, "I only tell my sh*t to gays! They GET the blackness! I'm humiliated!" She is characterized as being among "active and energetic form[s] of female wretchedness." Miranda, as she describes herself, is "an outsider aspiring to the ruling class." The issue of "class" permeates throughout the play. Some of the other topics range from taking refuge in the joyful innocence of children, to taking jabs at fat families with dressed-up pets; all amalgamated together to make for a hilarious experience.

I believe that the theatre exists to help us navigate the often complex nuances of our lives, reaffirm that we are all connected and as America's founding father George Washington once said, "We are one." Basically we can all relate to these topics of love, anger, hate, the quest for peace and the pursuit of happiness. At the risk of making broad generalizations, I think that we all have a little "Miranda" in us, we can all be cunning, selfish, and hateful and we also all want to fit in and be accepted, even if it means living beyond our means in a flagrant effort to impress others to make being accepted easier.

I was thinking about all of this while walking by the Boston Harbor the other day and I came upon these colorful words written artfully and probably by a local artist. It said: "Nothing's for keeps except that we must keep going. You'll spend your entire life searching, ok? We all want to belong. So let's all get along…" I think forgiveness is an imperative component in our quest to get along. Miranda offers no apologies for her shrewd, duplicitous and selfish ways and yet still, can't we identify with her? And more importantly, can we forgive her? Loved "her" loved the play, 5 out of 5 stars.

Released Just Before the Election of Donald Trump, the Political Play "Disgraced" about Muslim Americans Packs a Personal Punch

"Sooner or later we've all got to confront the reality that we have got to come to understand who we are and what we're doing, and the extent to which we are guided or manipulated by forces that are beyond our control."

--Ayad Akhtar

"For 300 years they've disgraced us! Why can't they understand the rage we've got?!" Declares

Amir, the principal character of Ayad Akhtar's play Disgraced presently which debuted at the Avenue of the Arts' Huntington Theatre Company which was then in residence at Boston University in the winter 2016.

The Pulitzer Prize winning play and gripping Broadway hit is directed by Gordon Edelstein and written by screenwriter and playwright Ayad Akhtar. A graduate of Brown and Columbia Universities, Akhtar was born in New York City and raised in Milwaukee, Wisconsin. As a screen writer, he was nominated for an Independent Spirit Award for Best Screenplay for "The War Within." Similar to the main character in his play, Akhtar is American born with Muslim roots and the play dramatizes and personalizes the tension between these two dichotomies while simultaneously infusing the scant yet much needed comic relief.

This play is a pontification on the contemporary Muslim American identity but more specifically, it is about a New York lawyer striving to climb the echelons of the corporate ladder while diminishing his Muslim roots and emphasizing his Americanized identity. When it is revealed during a dinner party that he was implicated in the papers as being part of the defense team of a man purported to be raising money for terrorism, buried tensions begins to surface, accusations are hurled and true feelings are revealed about race, class, religion and marriage; all the things you're not supposed to talk about at a dinner table. It is unapologetically controversial and rightfully so. It is unsettling, emotional, uncomfortable, tense, and refreshingly NOT politically correct.

"There's a long history of the West defining…Muslim[s]…In a post- 9/11 world, where… Muslim[s]…continue… to be defined [negatively]…we are called to defend ourselves, to define ourselves in opposition to what some are saying about us," Akhtar stated regarding the play. Most of us are fully cognizant of the pejorative media portrayals of Muslims since 9/11 and the more recent political conflicts with ISIS or Islamic State. The play essentially serves as an educational and more importantly personal point of reference to which non-Muslims can articulate better informed opinions on actual Muslim religious beliefs, practices and sociopolitical point of view. Disgraced reaches a pivotal controversial boiling point when Amir roars about feeling "pride" the day of the 9/11 terrorist attacks on the U.S. and referring to Muslims as being attributed the moniker of "The New Nigger"; all combine to make this play the more jarring; providing inarguably lively "water cooler", "armchair" and "social media" conversational topics. "The play exposes the ways people think and their prejudices without casting judgement or forcing a simple point. It exposes, it does not preach," said audience member Logan Nash in a post-show conversation.

"The conversation about Muslims in America is constantly evolving in tandem with the negative media portrayal of Muslims around the world," this from an article by Lisa Timmel and Phaedra Scott. They go on to say, "In the aftermath of 9/11 hate crimes against Muslims in the US jumped from around 30 per year to 500." Proving all the more reasons why the non-Muslim public, young and old need to be more aware of what it means to be Muslim in America. But

Amir, the play's protagonist, is not oblivious to what it means to take a stand in American politics, "If you're young and not a liberal, you've got no heart, if you're old and not a conservative, you've got no grain." Well whether you're got grain, heart or both, it would be a disgrace NOT to see Disgraced if it comes to a theatrical terrace near you. I gave it a 5 out of 5 stars.

The Theatrical Comedy "A Confederacy of Dunces" Combines Politics, Race and Jazz to Find the Funny in Life's Absurdities

"No wonder you've turned on me so savagely. I suspect that you are using me as a scapegoat for your own feelings of guilt."

— John Kennedy Toole, A Confederacy of Dunces

"I intend to challenge the way you think," asserts Nick Offerman as Ignatius J. Reilly, the principal character from A Confederacy of Dunces, which showed at the Avenue of the Arts' Huntington Theatre Company which was then in residence at Boston University, during the winter of 2015 and was extended due to popular demand.

Offerman, whom you may know from his role on NBC's "Parks and Recreation," effectively and with meticulous yet seemingly nonchalant accuracy, ignites the brash and corpulent Ignatius character as it was originally written by John Kennedy Toole in his Pulitzer Prize winning novel of the same title in 1981; adapted for the stage by playwright Jefferey Hatcher and directed by David Esbjornson, who coincidentally directed Guess Who's Coming to Dinner with Malcom Jamal Warner of The Cosby Show. Also working behind the scenes as part of the developmental team is Oscar Winning director Steven Soderbergh.

Confederacy of Dunces is a about an enigmatic and lovably conceited character relatively akin to the Kelsey Grammar character on the TV show "Frasier." Nick Offerman stars as the all-consuming character Ignatius J. Reilly, brash, weighty, egotistical, unconventional and still living with his mommy in 1960s New Orleans. He goes on a series of misadventures in the vibrant city which is infused with shady dealings, prostitution and of course jazz music.

He meets a cast of characters each more peculiar than the next in search of ideals of justice and freedom from his inferred fears. He is an optimist with an intellectual bent. His favorite book is A Constellation of Philosophy and he looks down on everything and everyone around him, most notably his supportive and devoted mother who financed the education that he uses as a weapon to subjugate her.

"Anything you have to say to me you can say it in front of my mother. She will not understand…" His probity is consistent and readily apparent. After an accident that resulted in strained finances, his mother beseeches him to get a job and when he did, he galvanized what he perceived to be suppressed fellow workers to start a workers revolution against racial and economic injustice and inequity; a thematic ideology that continues to plague contemporary society. He declares: "Had I been a Negro, I would have been a terrifying one." The play also examines unfair policing of minorities, another modern day challenge impeding social progress and equality for all. Much like the author of the novel turned play, Ignatius seems to titter on the edge of madness, and when his mother threaten to institutionalize him, he runs away with his girlfriend.

"The title of the book comes from a famous Jonathan Swift quote: 'When a true genius appears, you can know him by this sign: that all the dunces are in a confederacy against him'", writes Charles Haugland in an article about the play. The word "dunce" was adapted in 1570 according to Merriam-Webster dictionary to mean "…a slow-witted or stupid person." It was inspired by John Duns Scotus, whose once accepted writings were ridiculed in the 16th century. Basically Confederacy of Dunces translates to "Conspiracy of Idiots."

Offerman portrays Ignatius tethered with the often complex dualities of humanity: Ignatius is lovable and insufferable, liberal and conservative, logical and irrational and so on. The play is a prima facie comedy, however it harbors a plethora of socio-political and intellectual subtext which indeed has the potential to "…challenge" the way we think about mental illness, economic disparity, classism, and race relations. The murmurings of social dissidence are its conduit. Also present are grandiose utopian ideologies and palpable tensions between law enforcement and civilians all unified to make this play current and relatable. Written at the cusp of the civil rights era, the way in which it captures imminent social upheaval is jarringly prophetic; especially in the face of societal discordance currently in our midst in the form of capricious policing, terrorism and class warfare.

Confederacy of Dunces exemplifies the recurring revolutions ignited by social unease, dissatisfaction and the need for civil disobedience that are the arguable dogmata leading to the American Revolution. The play reminds us that as long as we continue to oppress one another, there will continue to be defiant archetypes like Ignatius P. Riley along with his philosophical "constellations" of human evolution and spurred rebellions against the status quo.

This play is a blatant, caustic, atmospheric, satiric and unusually comical dramatization of serious themes. Confederacy gets to the heart of the matter but not without side spitting laughter.

I once heard a dramaturge profess that the theatre is life, film is art and television is furniture. This play effectively reminds us of our protracted love affair with the theatre and essentially with life. I gave it 5 out 5 stars.

In the Age of Political Chaos and Rampant Technology, Longing & Nostalgia Plague the Characters in Durang's Broadway Play

"Anyone who wears a tiara and sequins is always going to be the winner."

— Christopher Durang, Vanya and Sonia and Masha and Spike

Theatre Hall of Famer and Tony Award-winning playwright Christopher Durang of the comedy

"Vanya and Sonia and Masha and Spike",which debuted at the Huntington Theatre Company in the winter of 2015, speaks to the heart of us all in his play replete with pathos and eye-watering humor when he tackles loss, sexuality, intergenerational dating, unrequited love, longing and the neo-technological challenge to seemingly antiquating family values. The Play is in actuality a timely social commentary regarding the state of humanity in the age of technology; which tends to create an illusion of unity, while many of us are aggrieved with a sense of loss, isolation and yearning for something more; much like the characters in Durang's play.

The play's characters and more visibly their names are based on the characters created by the Russian writer and playwright Anton Chekhov whose works Durang studied extensively at

Harvard University in addition to earning his Masters of Fine Arts in play writing from Yale University. But Chekhov's underlying themes of loss and longing is at the core of "Vanya and Sonya…" and as a Chekhov reader myself, I can certainly attain to that premise.

"This house feels a lot like a house in [one of] Chekhov['s plays.]" says Durang in a phone interview with Boston Globe correspondent Patti Hartigan, referring the characters in "Vanya and Sonia…" The play begins with Vanya (Martin Moran) and Sonia (Marcia Debonis), making a big fuss over coffee with Sonia ending up smashing a cup of coffee on the floor contradicting her prima facie benevolent appearance which conceals her passive aggressive tendencies while symbolizing an imminent change which came in the form of their sister Masha (Candy Buckley) and her younger boyfriend Spike (Tyler Lansing Weaks).

Soon after, deep seated resentments, angst and emotions are revealed as Sonia, the adopted sister, confesses her feelings for Vanya and Vanya has a melt down over a "texting" incident, a transgression executed by the much younger Spike, while reading from a play he wrote. He then goes on a tirade about how things used to be and how "we used to do things together" as a people like watching the now timeworn TV shows and licking postage stamps; which all has become antiquated.

And just when I thought I was going to love everything about this play, out of nowhere appeared this neo-aunt jamima: the stereotypical sassy Black maid, whose character name I can't or perhaps subconsciously choose not to remember, played by Haneefah Wood, a minority playing a minor role. While her character can at times spur genuine laughter from the audience, her acting at times comes off, nervous, frenzied and cartoonish and like me, the audience did not warm up to her right away as they did the major characters. She goes on and on quoting literary tragedies and mythology while producing morose psychic predictions and voodoo practices involving the unavoidable voodoo emblem, yes...the voodoo doll; which had me somewhat entertained but mostly just squirming in my seat. She is not "typical" in that she is inexplicably educated, perhaps she is a student/maid—or even more farfetched—an idiot savant of Greek mythology and Shakespearian tragedies. There were times I felt the audience was laughing with her and sometimes at her. She is the personification of the trendy ideology of the quasi-angry black woman, though it is not clear as to why she is angry; that is left to conjecture and supposition.

The most sympathetic character is Sonia who says things like "I hate my life!" and is the most bitter and melancholy of all the characters plagued by bucolic isolation, regret and self-reflection regarding the decisions they made earlier in life that brought them to this point. The audience clearly rooted more for Sonia and example of this was when she turns down an invitation from a possible suitor, which she complains of wanting so much, there was a collective sign of regret until she changes her mind and you could almost hear the audience letting out a sigh of relief.

At the play's end, we can descry a hopeful future for these characters; that their lives have already began to change for the better. If you, like the characters in "Vanya and Sonia and Masha and Spike," are at a crossroads with the state of your life within this neo-technological world and yearn for something more, then see this play if you ever comes your way and perhaps you will see yourself and be inspired to change your life. I gave it 4.5 out 5 stars.

Company One Theatre presents "VIETGONE": A Play about the Vietnam War that is Not Really about the Vietnam War

"Our purpose in Vietnam is to prevent the success of aggression. It is not conquest, it is not empire, it is not foreign bases, it is not domination. It is, simply put, just to prevent the forceful conquest of South Vietnam by North Vietnam."

--Lyndon B. Johnson

[True in part but mostly the war was unduly prolonged to preserve America's HUGE ego and grandiose self-image which cringed at the thought of having to admit "losing a war" according to the depiction in the movie: *The Post* with Tom Hanks and Meryl Streep...]

In the midst of Asian & Pacific American Heritage Month in these our troubled and divisive times, Company One proffers a spit-fire zinger of a disturbingly delicious Asian-American remedy in the form of Qui Nguyen's VIETGONE, which played in the spring of 2019 at the | Plaza Theatre at the Boston Center for the Arts."

"In this road-trip-meets-sex-comedy, motorbikes and ninjas and Marvin Gaye juxtapose themselves against the backdrop of war-torn Vietnam and the sterile barracks of Fort Chaffee," writes Ilana M. Brownstein, director of New Work at Company One.

"When Saigon fell in 1975, citizens fled the city by any means necessary, headed anywhere 'safe.' Thousands ended up in military bases-turned-refugee-camps scattered across America, where things were not exactly like the travel brochures....But this isn't really a story about war — it's about the messy, conflicted, joyful, dirty ways humans fall in love, even when the world seems to be falling apart. It's also about what happens when a playwright takes control of his own inconvenient history, weaving together truth and fantasy and everything in between," Brownstein explained.

Nguyen's parents informed him that they "fell in love at first sight," but in reality, it was just a hook up in a refugee camp in Arkansas after the fall of Saigon! Set in the backdrop of the Vietnam War during the 1960s and 70s, this play is essentially a politically incorrect, facetious, raunchy, psychedelic spectacle of war, love, sex, rock & roll, kung fu fighting and ninjas! Be prepared to bear witness to muscular male bodies, two piece bikinis, an omnipresent bed coupled with Marvin Gayes's "Let's Get It On..." which is sure to have you come close to edging on your seat.

Yet it is also filled with intelligent observation and assertions, evoking both empathy and inciting need for action against socially constructed ills of our society such as racial injustice, scapegoating, stereotyping and bemused condescending sense of complacency, disparagement and indifference from a surplus of the the white majority towards most often aggrieved and marginalized minorities. It attempts and to a large extant succeeds in exploring the Vietnam war through the lens of the playwright's father, particularly the point of contention that some Americans felt that the war was futile and that America should have not been there to begin with.

VIETGONE is a vibrant colorful blast with effective and inventive quick change staging, political messaging, witty and informative dialogue, funky contemporary music and plenty of eroticism to keep both your ears and eyes vigilant. It speaks to current political issues such as racism, the immigrant experience and intolerance but renders a production infused with levity, laughter and hope for an increasingly multicultural-multiracial America.

It might help to remind us that, within the context of immigrant contributions to the U.S., that

Asian American migrants have made valuable benefactions to the economic bastion that is the United States of America. Just before the Civil War, during the building of the transcontinental railroad that would unite the east with the American west, the Central Pacific railroad experienced a labor shortage in the scantily settled west. There simply wasn't enough white people. It enlisted Cantonese workers in China who did monumental work in constructing the line over and through the Sierra Nevada mountains and then across Nevada to their meeting in northern Utah; thus in part made possible a continuous rail line trussing locations on the U.S. pacific coast with one or more of those on the eastern trunk rail systems that would be known as the United States transcontinental railroad. This would help boost trade, commerce and travel and yielded large regions in the North American heartlands for settlement; this made possible in part by Asian immigrants.

This play serves as a reminder that all of us, who are not indigenous Native Americans, are either migrants or American born descendants of migrant groups who came to America from somewhere else and that our prima facie differences, our disparate cultural ingredients are what constitutes our unique American flavor and identity; that which should unite not divide us. Whether it was on the Mayflower or on Ellis Island on the New York harbor; our families knelt at the foot of the statue of liberty in search for something better than where they came from. All of us, in some way shape or form, contribute to what constitutes America or land of immigrants!

"The best two hours of my life!" Exclaimed one audience member. See it should it wonder into your neck of the woods and *you* be the judge. I give VIETGONE 5 out of 5 stars!

Doctor and Artist Mia Champion Gives Us Something Artfully Scientific

When Mia Champion was asked what she wanted to be when she grows-up, even at the tender age of six, she boldly stated "a part-time doctor and a part-time artist." Today, she has proven that dreams can come true because she is both a doctor and an artist living in the Somerville area.

Mia's empirical excursions as a scientific researcher and editor have afforded her with a distinctive comprehension of the various fields of biological research that are illustrated in her exceptional paintings. The molecular processes that are causal to an assortment of diseases, and in some paintings the survivors of these afflictions, are represented in this collection. Her works possess a generous amount of veracity and wonderment.

She has made her mark as a trailblazer proving that brains and beauty can co-exist harmoniously through the bright language of her innate creativity. She possesses an elegant yet keen artistic and scientific voice. Her paintings are rich in color and her desires to both educate and entertain are readily apparent. Her works proffers a fluid language that effortlessly traces the lilt and flow of her artistry, which softly invites us to come along on her imaginative and scientific journey. Her talent is likened to a Quasar from a distant galaxy whose light is so powerful it permeates the darkness of the cosmos and become embedded in the minds of all who are fortunate enough to view its luminosity. Much like the morning, her light filters through our window, and we are the better for it. I was able to catch-up with her during her current show, "All That She Sees", at the Out of the Blue Gallery and asked her some questions:

Jf: When, where and why did you start painting?

Mia: When I was six-years-old and adults asked me what I wanted to be when I grew-up, they were always slightly shocked when I replied with absolute certainty a "part-time doctor and a part-time artist", especially since there are not any medical researchers or professional artists in my family. Back then; girls were not encouraged to pursue science and math. Although I routinely sketched and painted as a child, I didn't do it seriously. One afternoon, after a 5-hour college chemistry lab class, I was walking pass a bookstore that had art paper and charcoal sets for sale and the artist in me woke-up! I am mainly a self-taught artist and started drawing faces and form with charcoal and switched to painting. Now most of my pieces are oil paintings, however I have a small collection that are mixed-media works with pencil, charcoal, acrylic, paper collage, and digital software.

Jf: Where do get your inspiration?

Mia: The unique languages of science intrigued me. I found that focusing on 'the big picture' by visualizing the concepts made it easier for me to absorb all the necessary information. I realized that this was a useful way of learning and could be a tool for communicating [complex] scientific concepts to the general public. I received my PhD in genetics from UC Davis. While in Kansas City, I met a group of designers and trying to communicate my work to them and my family inspired me to complete my first science art pieces. Over the years, I have been inspired by a diverse collection of master artists. I feel that my art has been most influenced by Renaissance artists, such as Michelangelo and Leonardo Da Vinci, who highly valued the synthesis of science, art, geometry and nature. Fortunately, I have also been influenced by my travels. The most memorable was a bike trip from Vienna to Prague, that enabled me to stop at numerous, and remote monasteries and castles that houses rare collections of art.

Jf: How does your art connects to the community?

Mia: I am dedicated to educating the general public and inspiring an awareness of scientific discoveries in order to facilitate an understanding of bedside applications. I feel that this will empower us as a community so that we can make informed decisions today so to ensure a better tomorrow for our society.

Jf: Where do you see your work going in 5 years?

Mia: I hope that my work continues to evolve in order to communicate the scientific discoveries and medical issues of our times in an effort to inspire education, discussion and voter participation. I also plan to continue donating a percentage of all my profits from art sales to different organizations, like The Children with Diabetes Foundation, dedicated to helping those members of our community who are suffering from illness.

To view samples of Mia Champion's artwork, visit: www.twistedhelixdesigns.com.

Jon Heinrich Photography: Sky Energy to Earth

Jon Heinrich got his first Nikon for graduation from Colorado State University in 1998, just at the cusp of life when things begin to happen. Since then he's been experiencing the world for what it is and capturing his most beautiful experiences to share with his fellow beings.

Through film and digital photography, Heinrich captures the natural mystic energy that permeates all human experience. The essence of light, energy and earth reflect Heinrich's philosophy that the more you intentionally direct your life towards making the world a better place, the more beautiful it becomes. Human revolution begins with the individual.

Music photography combines Heinrich's passion for seeing new places and collaborating with artists. Together, the two yield telling images of those driven souls who have made the most of what life has to offer. In addition to shooting live improvisational performances all over the country, there is nothing like the local art scene in Boston. As the epicenter of jazz emanates creative vibrations, Boston's visual art community is also strongest of anywhere in the motherland with more open studios than any other city in the nation. Heinrich has spent the last three years documenting this Cultural Revolution as staff photographer for Meniscus Magazine.

In addition to freelance portrait photography and documenting live events, Jon's penchant for catching living motion and light is at the core of his fine art photography.

On top of freelance assignments and Meniscus Magazine, Jon is working on the Translation project with fellow artists Rachael Wilcox (starvingartistgallery.org) and Andreas Gmür (andreasgmur.com). Exploring an artistic dialogue between different media, the project communicates the portrait of a human being from photography to ceramic relief mask to oil painting. "A single human expression will be transported and translated through photography, sculpture, and then painting, creating an evolution of understanding between both ourselves and the different mediums," explains project founder, Rachael Wilcox.

On the other side of the brain, Heinrich works on executive-level corporate communications programs at CXO Media, publishers of CIO and CSO magazines. As a project manager, he leads international marketing campaigns consisting of nearly every type of media from print to webcast, and is practiced in getting high-quality creativity out the door within tight schedule constraints. You can visit him at: www.meniscusmagazine.com

"Pedagogy of the Oppressed": Teaching, Learning and the Immigrant Experience

"Knowledge emerges only through invention and re-invention, through the restless, impatient, continuing, hopeful inquiry human beings pursue in the world, with the world, and with each other."

–Paulo Freire

In a previous pre-blog age article which does not appear in this book, I compared my experiences as a student at a Catholic school for boys in Port-au-Prince, Haiti, to the teaching ideology critiqued in Paulo Freire's groundbreaking book: Pedagogy of the Oppressed. In that book, Freire criticizes the traditional model of schooling in which the teacher treats the student as a submissive, unintelligible mind in which to "deposit" knowledge, and in which the student receives information without question.

One of the methods in which I was taught in Haiti was through the use of dictation; the teacher would read from a textbook in a sonorous voice while using unnecessary verbosity. The students were resigned to cognitive submission, merely bowing their heads and recording the teacher's lesson without question.

Freire refers to this educational model as "the banking system of education," a system in which the teacher is the "depositor" and the student the "depository." Another method used was bleak memorization of ample amounts of text to be stored in the student's memory bank for later use.

During testing, the student recalls the knowledge that has been "deposited" in his memory bank, and parrots back the information upon request.

Upon arriving in the United States, my academic skills, or should I say my "memorizing" skills, were so advanced that I was allowed to spend only a half-year in the eighth grade. In high school, I was able to excel once again, winning all types of academic awards. However, there was only one problem with all my achievement as a learner: I understood practically nothing; all I did was "memorize" all that was taught to me, just as I did back in Haiti. I found myself asking: how did all of this fit into my immediate reality? I did not see a purpose for what I was learning; I just knew that I had to learn it since that was what was expected of me.

At the same time, I was confronting the challenges of the immigrant dilemma, the culture shock of being in America and attempting to assimilate to an intimidating, and at times unsympathetic, reality, in part resulting from not being able to speak English. One of the first things that brightened the shades of my anxiety as a new arrival to this country was discovering there were no punitive consequences for not learning or not learning quickly enough. It was such a welcomed relief that it brought my thirst for knowledge to a new level. Having eliminated the fear and anxiety of possible failure and the violent repercussions that would come after, learning became an exciting panorama. However, I still did not understand how to learn without conjuring up old habits of deliberate memorization.

The Haitian kids referred to me not by my birth name, but by the way I learned. My new nickname was "par Coeur," or "by heart" in English. When the teacher would ask a question, naturally, I would have my hand up, and all the kids would roll their eyes and sigh in anticipation of my protracted recitation of meaningless text. The teachers never took me aside and explained to me that complete memorization was not always necessary, and that sometimes understanding the relevance of the material was more important. I did not understand this concept, until one of the more practical students explained to me the inherent impracticality of absolute memorization without having an understanding of reason and purpose. Mind you, this was a student who received mostly C's to my consistent A's; when he would ask me a question regarding the "meaning" of the text that I had just memorized, I could not answer him other than to recite the text over again like a programmed automaton. Although I vaguely understood the student's earnest explanation of conceptual understanding rather than literal memorization, I was not yet ready to accept this new way of learning and understanding.

In my senior year at Boston English High School, after I had been transferred from the bilingual program to a mainstream education program, I began to learn the academically enlightening practice of "critical thinking." It was then that I was taught to use my analytical muscle to deconstruct meaning from classic works of literature such as William Shakespeare's "Julius Caesar." It was then that I finally began to feel mentally awake as a student.

The new challenge for me then was adapting to a new pedagogical model, while ridding myself of my old academic habits of simply recording and memorizing information without question.

It wasn't until I attended college for nursing that I began to understand the "proper" use of memorization and the constitutional meanings of learning materials. I went from passively consuming to actively participating in the learning process. What made this transition easier was that I knew that I had to apply what I had learned shortly after class in the nursing lab! And once I had learned it in lab, the teacher would eagerly appeal to students to ask questions, to open the gates of knowledge in a non-intimidating fashion. The next day, we would all attend the clinical rotation area, where we would work with actual patients and implement classroom teachings in real-life situations. In the clinical setting in nursing school, I opted to apply old and new learning methods by combining memorization with practical dexterity with grace and confidence, and that made all the difference.

So far, I explored the teaching techniques and ideologies in Paulo Freire's book: "Pedagogy of the Oppressed," a text celebrated for its influence on education worldwide. Freire's book focuses on the idea of the classroom experience wherein the teacher is omnipresent and dominant and the student is trivial and passive. I recalled my years in an all-boy Catholic school in Haiti and how the teachers dictated sonorous text to the students, who then simply recorded the information without question. I mentioned the idea of deliberate forms of memorization as a way to demonstrate basic comprehension of the material taught to the students. I compared my educational experiences in Haiti to my experiences in American schools, and described how I began to learn critical thinking skills at my American high school and college. I also discussed my method of combining the memorization model I learned in Haitian schools with the more practical model I was exposed to in America, whereby I came to understand the real-life critical implications of the memorized text.

Having learned how to learn by combining memorization and application while assimilating U.S. customs, now I was faced with other learning influences. At the very core of it were social influences. The social factor did not affect me much at all in high school, but once it came time for college, things changed for the better; hence another type of learning began. Instead of textual learning, it was contextual learning within the social framework of the times. Sometimes, I would walk into a college classroom, and there would be nothing but Caucasians, including the professor. They would just sit there, staring at me, their eyes at times menacing and challenging as if waiting for me to prove myself as a black, foreign-born student. I perceived them to be thinking, "I have seen all I need to know about your kind in the evening news, so now it's up to you to change my mind."

But what they did not realize was that they had a limited view of people of my ethnicity. They didn't realize the magnitude of their ignorance. I think that opportunities are always available for people to learn about other cultures. However, people have to make that choice, to learn about others or to remain ignorant and complacent in this great American land of freedom and opportunity. I've made an effort to learn about the American culture — is it too much to ask for the same from you, regarding my Haitian culture or the multitude of cultures living here in the U.S.? Hence, I had to learn to cope with prejudice and racism in both academia and in the wider social sphere. Some people here in America, minorities included, prefer to go on being ignorant, so that they can continue to feel socially superior to others. And the thought of being deemed inferior to anyone incited me to achieve and excel beyond my perceived limitations, through tireless study both independent and formal.

At first, I was timid about being an overachiever. Why stand out even more? Why not fly under the radar? I believe that life burns brightly, like a firefly, but only for a short time. Therefore, why not shine as bright as you can, while you still can? Why not excel to the fullest? I was fearful of repercussions, such as other people's jealousy and envy. But I decided not to let that be a hindrance to my thirst for knowledge. My hard work eventually paid off when I was nominated as one of the top three finalists for class valedictorian in college, and was consequently inducted into the international honor society and made the national dean's list.

During my time here in the U.S., I have unfortunately come to realize that blacks and foreigners are perceived to be less intelligent than whites, but I believe that everyone has their own unique brand of intelligence. I worked as a tutor in college, and the majority of the influx of students who were seeking help were white. I would greet them and offer assistance, at which point the white students would excuse themselves and essentially never return. The stress of being discriminated against for being a black immigrant and being perceived as dumb could have hindered my learning experience, but it did not; it only compelled me to work that much harder. However, I won't ignore the fact that it did influence my own development as a student.

I had to draw on spiritual as well as ancestral strength in order to learn to develop as an educated person. Many obstacles may come my way, but if I can see them as part of the learning process and not as a deterrence to it, I will reap the maximum benefits of what life has to teach. I no longer feel intimidated by the idea of not being able to "memorize" the lessons as I did in Haiti. Nor do I feel insecure in the social learning environment, where my capabilities might be questioned. Having learned to be more practical, I have now put it all together. The collective experiences of Haitian Catholic schools and American public schools, all having their own brands of social and cultural influences, have contributed to or have influenced my development as a student.

Having familiarized myself with Paulo Freire's "Pedagogy of the Oppressed," I now have renewed academic energy and a restless curiosity about the world in which I live, while learning from the practical interactions and intellectual collusions with my fellow human dwellers. I now know that combining memorization of facts along with critical inquiry — in order to draw practical real-life conclusions — proves to be the most effective form of pedagogy for me, and for the betterment of humanity in my opinion; that is, if we expect to actively shape our society rather than just passively live in it.

Health Watch: Why Your Teeth Could Be Killing You

"I told my dentist my teeth are going yellow. He told me to wear a brown tie."

Rodney Dangerfield

My motivation for writing this article is simple: to alert people about the correlation between poor dental hygiene and systemic pathology like Coronary Heart Disease (CHD) and what you can do to protect yourself.

First and foremost, I do not profess to be a medical doctor (that honorific belongs to my brother Dr. Guy Claude Fleury) nor am I a health and wellness expert; however I do have access to medical diagnostic books as well as a medical background, understanding and personal experiences that I think are applicable to the subject matter of which I will attempt to write about. I have taken science courses as part of a nursing program and liberals arts degree program which included Fundamentals of Nursing, Biology I & II, Anatomy and Physiology I, & II, Pharmacology, Nutrition, Microbiology and Medical Terminology just to name a few.

The other criteria of which I think is of critical importance in writing this article is that a male family member recently died of CHD and his doctors concluded that there was an undeniable connection between his heart disease and his poor dental hygiene. This family member—who was a professional man with his own business—neglected to take care of his teeth for years. Even as one spoke to him, one could see the debris of bacteria nesting like yellow swirls in his teeth and gums but no one dared to tell him about it; that is until it was too late.

Based on my own personal experience I've noticed that a lot of people here in America do not consider going to the dentist or dental hygienist on a regular basis. People are often leery of the dentist with their dreadful drills that triggers shivers of fear and anxiety in their patients. I've seen some of my acquaintances; friends and even family members lose some of their teeth due to poor dental care. To prove my point, even health insurance providers like Mass Health who offers medical coverage to the disabled and families with dependent children only recently offered dental coverage to their participants. I suppose they did not consider "dental care" as a necessary part of the general physical and preventive health maintenance ideology. Mass Health have narrowed their dental coverage to only include mostly preventive care such as but not limited to regular cleanings and check-ups.

I would not be writing about this subject had I not been able to relate it to myself. I have been maintaining regular dental hygiene appointments for years now, every six months to be exact. Even more diligently since I've lost my dad to heart disease back in 2005.

According to the consumer handbook *Bottom Line Year Book 2018*, "In a study of the records of more than 26,000 people, those who never saw a dentist were 86% more likely to get bacterial pneumonia than those who had dental checkups twice a year. Regular dental cleanings can reduce levels of bacteria that cause lung infection." Declared Dr. Michelle E. Doll, MD, assistant professor in the division of infectious diseases [at] Virginia Commonwealth University School of Medicine, [in] Richmond.

"Over the past decade, an increasing amount of research have been conducted that supports the association between periodontal diseases and systemic disease, "declares Mea A. Weinberg, DMD, MSD, RPH, a clinical associate professor of Periodontology and Implant Dentistry at New York University in her article, "The Fire Within: The Link between Oral Inflammation and Systemic Health has Signaled a Paradigm Shift in Treating the Periodontal Patient." She goes on to say that, "The role that inflammation plays as a pathway to the rest of the body is becoming much better understood, making the control and prevention of gingivitis and periodontitis a critical part of optimal patient care." Because new research have come to light to illuminate these silent potential killers known as gingivitis and periodontitis (which in laymen's terms means inflammation of the gum tissue surrounding the teeth), more people are becoming aware and paying more attention to their own esoteric practice of dental hygiene. One of my male friends has recently told me that he too have known about the dental/heart connection since high school and his only 34 years old. He said that he had known that flossing was imperative to good dental care and have been doing it regularly since then. "The oral cavity is the portal to the rest of the body," states Weinberg, "…an emerging body of evidence has linked oral infections—primarily chronic inflammatory periodontitis—to systemic conditions including atherosclerosis…"

Dr. Dan Peterson of Family Dental Care in his article, "Oral Health and Your Heart" concurs with Weinberg by promulgating that, "Periodontitis seems to influence the occurrence and the severity of coronary artery disease and increases the risk of heart attack or stroke, and the study proposes two hypotheses for this occurrence. One hypothesis is that periodontal pathogens could enter the blood stream, invade the blood vessel walls and ultimately cause atherosclerosis. (Atherosclerosis is a multistage process set in motion when cells lining the arteries are damaged as a result of high blood pressure, smoking, toxic substances, and other agents.)" Dr. Peterson also highlights the astounding fact that the correlation between gum disease and heart attacks is considerably higher than the association between high cholesterol and heart attacks. He says that, "New studies suggest that people who have gum disease seem to be at higher risk for heart attacks, although no one knows how this relationship works. Your oral health affects your overall health, but the studies that will find exactly why these problems are linked are still underway."

Peterson also emphasizes the point that flossing is imperative and integral to your dental and essentially systemic health. How can gum disease affect your overall health? Well, according to Peterson, "…bacteria present in infected gums can come loose and move throughout the body. The same bacteria that cause gum disease and irritate our gums might travel to your arteries."

So although the research showing the connection between poor dental hygiene and heart disease is inconclusive, it is imperative that you keep your mouth healthy and see your dentist and/or dental hygienist regularly or at least twice yearly. My dental hygienist recommended that I brush my teeth with the electronic tooth brush Sonic Care, she also related to me that the sound that it makes as you are brushing have a germ killing affect. Sonic Care can be expensive; a more affordable alternative is Spin Brush Pro Clean Sonic which essentially is just as effective. Another dental health tip that my hygienist informed me of is that flossing is even more critically important than brushing. I have personally found that when I went to see my hygienist, I discovered that my teeth had more plaque (a bacteria-containing film on a tooth) and my gums used to be more inflamed before I started flossing regularly.

"Infected gums bleed, making it easier for bacteria to enter your bloodstream," professes Dr. Peterson. "If bacteria become dislodged, the bacteria enter through cuts or sores in your mouth and travel to other parts of your body through your bloodstream…This can cause arterial plaque to accumulate in the arteries; which can cause hardening and affect blood-flow. Compromised blood-flow to your heart can cause a heart attack." Peterson also reminds us that gum disease is most definitely the result of plaque buildup. So to minimize your chances of getting gum disease which can compromise the homeostasis of your heart, remember to brush, floss, floss and floss some more on a regular basis and preferably after each meal and most definitely before you go to bed; so then you won't have to worry your head about the health of your heart.

The Spiritual Life: An Alternative Way of Healing Mind, Body, Spirit

"You are your only master, who else? Subdue yourself, and discover your master."

--The Buddha

In a previous pre-blog article not appearing in this book, I discussed how I came to Reiki, my initial skepticism nagging curiosity about the practice, the disputed founder Dr. Mikao Usui and his Reiki principles of "do not worry, do not anger, honor your parent, teacher and elders and show gratitude to everything." Now I will continue by going more in depth about Dr. Usui's background and how he was said to have founded Reiki.

After being challenged by one of the students regarding healing and the Bible at the Christian school where Dr. Usui is said to have taught, he became frustrated with his inability to provide the answers to questions about faith and healing. He was in want of something more concrete than the blind faith that he practiced at the time, so he went on a spiritual expedition. In his devotion to finding spiritual truths, Dr. Usui travelled to the U.S. before uncovering some truths in Japan. He found an old Indic version of the Sanskrit language, penned by the disciples of Guatama Buddha. In these sutras, or scripts, there was a description of the methods, symbols and formulas the holy man used to heal. According to Lubeck's story, these symbols play an integral part in the healing practice of Reiki.

In his book, "Way of the Heart," Lubeck continues to tell Dr. Usui's story. Even after discovering the Sanskrit sutras, he writes, Dr. Usui was not satisfied. He felt that "he was still missing one thing!" He had the desire to directly heal people using "the laying of the hands" model. He was told by a monk in the monastery to visit "the holy mountain of Kurayama…in order to meditate and fast in a special manner." The monk also told him to trust in God to bestow upon him access to the healing power. "Dr. Usui then went to this mountain for 21 days, and just as he had hoped, on his last day…a bright ray of light came down to him from heaven, struck his forehead and filled him with strength and vitality." I know, I know, but I'm not making this stuff up. Hang in there I promise you it'll pay off in the end. After he had been struck by the light, the symbols he formerly greeted in the ancient Sanskrit text were "shrouded in shining energy bubbles." He knew then that he had "access" to Reiki: the universal life energy.

In sharp contrast to Lubeck's recount of Dr. Usui's beginnings, Frank Arjava Petter offers the idea that Dr. Usui, until this day, is considered to be "a fabled creature shrouded in mystic fog." One thing that is for sure is that he was human just as we are. But he admits that not much else is known about the man. First of all, Petter essentially disarms Lubeck in remarking that Usui was Christian despite his spiritual searching. Rather than constructing a fable-like account of Dr. Usui and how he invented the discipline now known as Reiki, as Lubeck does,

Petter offers more demographic type information, as well as some of the philosophies behind Usui's life process and beliefs. He states that Usui's main learning process in …reaching an internal source of wisdom, as well as an internal understanding that one can only get when you follow your own instincts gained from living your life and following your own will. And that was in part fundamental in connection with his Reiki ideologies.

Speaking of will, let's take this time to define free will, soul, and spirit; all three correlate in some way to Reiki and its philosophies. "Free will" is defined as choice and power and it happens in the present. "Soul" means purpose and direction; it's what gives us our spirit. And "spirit" allows us to see our higher consciousness, motivates our dynamics of being. Now I must confess that these definitions are borrowed from Professor Ferguson of UMass Boston, whom I mentioned earlier. I took his class on the mind-body-spirit connection. I found him to be very inspirational and to possess a quiet but penetrating intelligence.

One of Ferguson's often repeated lessons was to "never give energy to what you don't want." He calls it the "law of neutrality." Don't be for or against, just be. And then truth will come to you.

I discovered in my research that Reiki has its roots in Buddhism. In Jack Maguire's book Essential Buddhism, he elucidates the interrelatedness between Reiki and Buddhism. He avowed that it might be helpful to mention that the founder of Reiki, Dr. Usui, was a Buddhist. Hence to understand the origins of Reiki, it's logical and imperative to understand the origins of Buddhism. Buddhism is considered to be of one the top five most popular religions in the entire world, the others being Christianity, Judaism, Islam and Hinduism. Buddhism has existed for 2500 years. It has been far more ubiquitous beyond its homeland of India than any of the other world religions. That's why some experts consider Buddhism to be "the oldest world religion."

Maguire defines the word "Buddha" to mean "the awakened one." It derives from a Sanskrit word from the "Indo-European root that gives us the English word bud." He adds that the

Buddha managed to "bud" and then "bloom" into total consciousness…;" he became enlightened. Then Maguire offers that "the amazing truth of the matter is that we are all potential Buddhas, perfect and complete right at this moment, but very few of us realize it.

"I used to eat feelings of incompletion and restlessness for breakfast. Then one day, I made a conscious choice to grab my feelings by the shoulders and shook them, just hard enough for them to fall out of place, so that they then could fall back into place. And in order for that to happen, I knew that I would have to command myself to do some deeply spiritual soul searching. I knew that I wouldn't be able to stand on the side lines and be directed by the ray of light. Besides, I haven't even opened any one of the windows in my heart for it to get in and permeate my being. Consequently, I also knew that I had to eventually assume some control over myself, over my life, over my light."

In describing Buddhism, Maguire declares that Buddhism is not like Christianity, Judaism and Islam, religions of the book or the revealed word. Let me briefly describe Zen meditation, since it is our next topic of discussion. According to Random House Dictionary, Zen is defined as a Buddhism movement that emphasizes enlightenment by means of meditation and direct intuitive insight. Maguire quotes Vietnamese Zen teacher Thich Nhat Hanh, who in his own wisdom said that "our own life" is the instrument in which we experiment with truth. In other words, eventually we release what we put into our bodies. If we simply stared at our meals instead of eating them, we would feel empty inside. I can study Reiki all I want, but if I don't live it, I might as well have not even opened up a book to study it. So I will be my own master, in that I will set myself free of my perceived limitations and embrace the grandeur that is the Reiki light, love and joy!

The right road disappears beneath our feet.
– Alice Walker

So far, I have discussed how I came to Reiki, my initial skepticism and nagging curiosity about the practice, and the disputed founder Dr. Mikao Usui's Reiki principles of "do not worry, do not anger, honor your parent, teacher and elders and show gratitude to everything." Now I will explore Dr. Usui's background and how he is said to have founded Reiki. Dr. Usui was not wholly satisfied with just book knowledge of Reiki; he had a desire to heal using the laying of the hand method. He went to the holy mountain of Kurayama for 21 days where he was struck by light on the last day and became enlightened.

In his book, "Reiki, Way of the Heart," Walter Lubeck discusses why people come to the Reiki path. He asserts that people are intrigued by why so many practitioners are inspired by Reiki and ache to "know" Reiki themselves. He also states that, "Some people come to Reiki because they experience firsthand its healing powers often being treated for an injury and were fascinated by how fast it heals wounds."

How did I come to Reiki? Well, I met this individual and we started dating. We ended up living on a lake in Lakeville, Massachusetts. Then I found out that this person was a level I Reiki practitioner and started performing Reiki on me. At one point I think I started to cry. The sessions usually lasted 45 minutes to one hour. At that point, I had no prior knowledge of the field of Reiki, but it touched me all the same. The experience reminds me of a short poem from the book A Poem Travelled Down My Arm by Alice Walker, it goes: "Because you stroke my shoulders last night / a poem travelled down my arm." You see, I'm a poet, and when my companion stroked my shoulders by performing Reiki on me, my tears of creativity started flowing. And I almost always seem to find myself near a body of water. So how did

I come to Reiki? I saw the letters on the wall, the light on the lake, so to speak. It was like Reiki came to me, because my heart, unbeknownst to me, was open to it.

Petter and Usui wrote about the three pillars of Reiki, the first pillar being "Gassho," which means "two hands coming together." Dr. Usui taught "Gassho meditation." This meditation is often used at the start of a Reiki workshop or meeting. It's supposed to be done for 20-30 minutes each session, once in the morning, and again before bed. To perform this meditation, sit down and keep your eyes closed, and palms touching each other facing your chest. You must focus your whole attention at the point where two middle fingers come together. Attempt to eliminate any thought that might get in the way. Should you start to fantasize about, say, lunch, or your favorite celebrity, acknowledge it and let it go.

According to Dr. Usui, the second pillar: "Reiji," quite literally means "indication of Reiki power" and "Ho" means "methods." "Fold your hands in front of your chest in the Gassho posture, close your eyes, and now connect with the Reiki power. Pray for recovery and health. Now hold your folded hands in front of your third eye and ask the Reiki power to guide your hands to where the energy is needed," instructs Dr. Usui.

The third pillar: "Chiryo," means "treatment" when translated literally into English. During "treatment," the patient lies on a table with the practitioner standing next to the patient. The practitioner then places his or her dominant hand on top of the patient's head or "crown" (located at the center of the skull) and waits for the impulse or inspiration that will surely come through. At the time of the treatment, the practitioner allows his or her hands to move about the body, hitting all the areas that hurt until they hurt no more.

We all have the power of touch, as Alice Walker demonstrates in her poem. Has someone ever touched you while speaking to you? Did it seem to open you up a bit, your ears, your eyes, and your heart? I have worked in a hospice, and touch was as elementary as breakfast in the morning. At the hospice, we always seemed to have the Reiki energy, whether we knew it or not, to cast some light on the darkness of death and decay.

A medical professional informed me that insurance will not pay for a Reiki session. He qualified this by stating that although insurance won't pay for Reiki directly, it might be covered if it is masked as a more accepted form of therapy such as psychotherapy. But whether I end up paying for it myself or not, is irrelevant. I already know that it will be worth my energy, since Reiki has already has proven its worth in my prior sessions. I hope that you, too, are finding light, love and joy in your life, either with Reiki, or some other form of spiritual or religious practice.

Talking Back: A Critical Dialogue on Spirituality

"Just for today, do not worry
Just for today, do not anger,
Honor your parents, teachers and elders.
Earn your living honestly.
Show gratitude to everything".

—Dr. Mikao Usui

In a previous pre-blog article not appearing in this book, I wrote about how my mother helped to create my own reality, hence my own identity. Now I will write about the need to create my own existence outside of my mother, whom I consider my primary spiritual mentor.

"The healers' job is to get out of the way, to keep the healing space open, and to watch and listen for signs of what to do next." As it is written on The Reiki Page

The latter quote from the article "What Is Reiki" found on the Reiki website

http://reiki.7gen.com/index.html and focuses on the relationship between healer and seeker. They must separate in order for "something to happen" between their "healing space."

My mom and I often seem like we are joined at the hip. Sure, I understand our closeness has to do with the fact that she's not that much older than me, and also I was her only child for 13 years before my sister was born. She made it her mission to mold and shape my cognitive demeanor and profile, ensuring that they don't get too fragile. But by being so protective of my persona, she failed to realize that while I was strong in one area (her world), I was lacking in the other (the outer world).

After looking at myself through the eyes of those outside of my mother's clutching womb, I started to experience myself as an evolving, well generated black man. I combined my mother's well intentioned doctrinaire, with the knowledge gained through the wisdom of the eclectic external world. Mother had to "get out of [my] way," but at the same time be sure to stick around "to keep the [nurturing] space open." And while I was on my search, I often felt like wax, melting at the bottom of a candle, and with valiant hands reaching out for the light above!

It was during those times that I needed my mother--my spiritual advisor—the most. As the quote offers, I needed her to "…watch and listen for [my] signs of [need and tell me] what [I should] do next." But I reached for something deeper, something even my mother didn't have access to, my own inner strength, minus my perceived limitations.

Breaking through some spiritual limitations with my mother only left me to wonder, what else is out there? What other spiritual wonders have I kept myself from, by being too uncertain of who I was to cut the umbilical cord, forever tying me to my mother? Reiki is only limited by one's "old ways" of being, that one must challenge "old patterns" of behavior in order to "accept healing." I used to only believe that what you see is what you get, that is "if it can't be proven, it's not real!" However I have since reconsidered my new wisdom that "what you see, isn't always what you get." As trite as it may sound, for me, it's true. I have since decided to think outside of my enclosed box of suffocating limitations that reads "Do Not Open until I'm dead!"

Subsequently forsaking my own warning, I decided to open the box and dawned upon Reiki. I feel that Reiki, its inherent meaning being "Universal Life Force Energy," was and has always been a part of me. I just could never see the energy because I had not yet "earned" a "critical eye." Now that I have opened the box, so that dawn can charm the morning fog right off my squinting eyes, I intend to investigate both past and present limitations I have had infringed on me.

The article also purports that "The way we acquire deviations from our ideal form, is to accept [limitations] in our life [sic]." For instance, there had been a plethora of negative connotations associated with "mouthy" children in Haiti. You were not allowed to "speak up" during "adult" conversation. If and when you did, you were given a "silenced" glare, namely "the look of death," to foreshadow your punishment. In other words, "Ya gonna hav' 'ta deal wit me later mouth!" The article agrees in that it discerns the latter by introducing the idea that "A limitation maybe a parent yelling 'be quiet' enough that the child learns not to speak."

Growing up in Haiti, I was constantly told, "A child should be seen and not heard." So I learned to shut up. Still in present times, I find it quite uncomfortable to speak up within a forum, where people express ideas deliberately and freely. I fear sounding unintelligible, like a deaf person, mouthing off the words he/she have never even heard.

The article also suggests, "In any healing, the goal is to find the limitation, recognize the pattern, recognize where it came from, and let it go." So I am presently deconstructing what I've been taught, and relearning a new more enlightened set of wisdom. I am licking my wounds and stepping up to the podium. And the dust I find there, to me, represents the "old knowledge." I see the dust as scattered powder of self-loathing, self-deprecation, and self-indignations and last but not least, self-limitations! So I decided to blow it all off! All this gray stuff that was shielding my eyes! If I must have clouds in my life, I will have them be transparent, so that I can see the blue skies on the other side! All to make room for "new" information. I will use "old" information as a building block, and not a stumbling block towards the path to my "new" enlightenment.

"I'm mad as hell, and I'm not gonna take it anymore," as from that movie "Network." I have reclaimed my "ideal form" and "rejected" having the limitations placed on me. I am becoming free from myself and others in every way. I can only hope that you, the reader, can be just as motivated to continue to change your life, making each New Year a new you. Roll around in the colored leaves of autumn, or rejuvenate yourself in the silken youthful hands of spring. Then go out and rent the movie "Life is Beautiful!"

Affirmation:

"I invoke the healing Buddha and the master spirits of Reiki.

I ask that my channel be pure and clean, without fear, and with honor and love for all."

--The Reiki Page

The Spiritual Life: Looking for Love in All the Wrong Places

Do you yearn for unconditional love in your life? Do you find yourself looking for love in all the wrong places? Well, I can empathize, because I have also looked for love where I should not have.

We all want unconditional love and acceptance in our lives in order to reach our most basic goal: happiness. In my life, I have sought the often-conditional love of humanity and have also sought succor within the deceiving and confining walls of material superficiality to make me feel worthy. In today's society many people, like myself, seek self-worth outside of themselves, thus creating the illusion that they are happy and are worthy of being loved. However, this inept concept has recurrently been proven to be a fallacy. The question then is, "Where do we go to find the warm embrace of unconditional love and acceptance as we seek shelter from our highly mechanized society?

While participating in the often-mundane tasks of daily living hoping to find something to get excited about, I came an invigorating and refreshing book called Life of the Beloved:

SPIRITUAL LIVING IN A SECULAR WORLD by Henry Nouwen. This book has helped bring

me the closest I ever have to feelings of self-actualization by achieving the highest accomplishment: the acceptance of myself and my fellow human travelers, and with this acceptance boundless love!

I once heard that if you want to change the world, do what makes you come a-live!

Coincidentally, Nouwen writes to a friend who was sleep walking through life and experiencing a crisis of faith, which caused him to put his dreams aside and live an unfulfilling spiritless and loveless life. Nouwen explains how we often get in our own way by contending, "...the greatest trap in our life is not success, popularity or power but self-rejection". He goes on to say that "self-rejection is the greatest enemy of the spiritual life because it contradicts the sacred voice that calls us the 'Beloved'."

I couldn't quite understand what Nouwen meant by the idea of being the "Beloved." I know that at certain points in my life, I have felt loved if only for a short delicious moment based on something I've done to deserve it. Yet, as I kept reading through Life of the Beloved, it occurred to me that what Nouwen is saying is that to be the "Beloved" is to be loved unconditionally by something greater than mere humanity.

In recalling the defining moments of my own life, there have been times when I kept myself from being and becoming the Beloved by comparing myself to other people. Essentially, I surrendered to feelings of envy, jealousy, hatred, anger, and vengefulness. I felt unworthy and inadequate for who I am and ultimately for who I felt I should be. This then brings me to Nouwen's idea of being "chosen."

Being a black male from Haiti, I have always felt that I have to "prove" myself. I never felt "chosen" for my own unique set of gifts—that there was no one else like me in the entire world. For example, you may be chosen to be a better speaker, whereas I am chosen to be a better writer and so forth. We are all gifted in some way, and essentially there is room for all our gifts to grow and blossom on this earth. However, I did not know that then, and so I eventually bowed to the opinions of others for validation.

People look at me and at least at first glance judge me. First, because I'm Black, second, because I'm from Haiti. On being Black, they attribute to me all the stereotypes of a typical "homeboy" from the Ghetto. On being from Haiti, they bury me in poverty-stricken ideologies ascribed to third world countries. Naturally, because of this societal and self-imposed feelings of inferiority, I allowed these fallacious assumptions to make me question who I am by constantly being on the defense. It was like venting the flames of the never-justifiable self-doubt that coincidentally co-existed with self-hate. Fittingly I started to hear the haunting and bitter voices of scorn in my head hissing words like "prove that you are worth something; do something relevant, spectacular, or powerful. [Only] then you will earn the love you so desire." When in reality, I can just "be" without having to prove anything to anyone!

But, I began to look for love in all the wrong places: in the gym to build that perfect body, at college to hone my intellectual capacity, in a career to pay for that apartment in the city and in a relationship with the right "lover" who would make me the source of everyone's envy. Naturally, none of it made me feel loved or worthy of being loved. I soon realized that I was chasing an illusion! In reality, there is always someone with a better body, education, job, apartment and lover to make him/her the source of my envy.

Eventually, I fell into a deep depression, mostly due to dissatisfaction, and the loss of all the things I thought would make me not break me. As was necessary, I had an epiphany to rebuild my life and reality in its truest sense and initiated the process of coming closer to my most authentic and fabulously lovable self! Now I will spend the rest of my life getting out of my own way by undoing both my self-injurious behavior and what I previously thought to be the insurmountable negative and effects of a prejudiced society.

The road to love can be paved with disappointments and disillusionments, mainly because we fail to recognize love's tender and empathetic offerings when we see it. Essentially, we need to understand that love can often come from someone of whom we least expected it.

Love is not boastful, selfish, nor conditional. We can spend the rest of our lives waiting to love ourselves and for others to love us, or we can choose to claim our belovedness; that we are loved, respected and accepted because of who we are and not in spite of it. Only then will we know the ultimate love: the unconditional love of God.

A Light in the Woods: My Spiritual Journey

"...The woods are lovely, dark and deep,
But I have promises to keep,
And miles to go before I sleep,
And miles to go before I sleep."

From: "Stopping by the Woods on a Snowy Evening"
By American Poet Robert Frost

"There is pleasure in the pathless woods/There is rapture on the lonely shore/There is society where none intrudes/By the deep sea and music in its roar/I love not man the less/ But Nature more..." muses the philosopher Lord Byron about the importance of connecting with our natural world and I couldn't agree more.

I left on a quest for self-discovery, to find meaning in what I previously thought was meaningless. I did this because I felt that I had reached a spiritual impasse and was therefore unable to continue to offer you my humble wisdom. Well, after taking profound internal stock of myself and my life thus far while vacationing both emotionally and physically, I have returned to you with new insights that I think you will most likely find both engaging and thought provoking. I took two vacations, one on the cape in Hyannis and the other in Meredith New Hampshire while participating in a spiritual retreat at the Geneva Point Center.

My first vacation in Hyannis provided me with an opportunity to see life at a much slower pace. I was quite enchanted with all the colorful characters I meant while staying at the Heritage House Hotel, which is right in the center of town next to the JFK Museum with a plethora of restaurants, art galleries, souvenir shops, an eclectic coffee house/bar called "The Spot" for the alternative crowd, The Brazilian Grill with its fabulous buffet which includes seafood and authentic live Brazilian music and many night clubs offering anything from reggae, to top 40 dance and Techno at the local and only gay bar The Mallory Dock, to Hip Hop at Portabellies with four dance floors during the summer season. Portabellies has the most outrageous crowd of all. With ages ranging from 21 to 51, the most motley racial mix in town from Asian, Black, Caucasian, to Latino etc... all in the middle of nowhere. Who would have guessed? I took the cape escape package just before the season began the first week of April, which included a four-day three night stay with three meals and entertainment included all for under $300 dollars.

My other vacation in New Hampshire was with my prayer group "House of All Faiths Prayer Group" which meets at three thirty p.m. Tuesdays at the St. Mary's Church on Norfolk Street in Central Square and retreats annually in late June. All welcomed. It was at that retreat my spiritual journey began to deepen while walking through the woods, coming face to face with a deer and face to face with myself. There I experienced a wedding ceremony in a barn full of bats, found my inner child by hanging out with a group of youths doing things like playing musical instruments, telling scary stories etc… and rediscovering my love for God, myself and all of humanity. And then there was the emotional journey during which point I, like a flower, recoiled to try to make sense of it all.

I want to tell my readers that I decided to venture on this journey both for my sake and yours. You, by having related to me how my writing have touched you, enthused me to rise up to the challenge of becoming a better person, of seeking and finding more meaning in everyday living. As you know, I fervently practice what I preach. In the past I have infallibly shared with you both my struggles and my successes and this time won't be any different. Nonetheless, what will be different is my focus.

My previous column "Life, Love and Politics" was in retrospect a bit broad but it served my purpose at the time. Now, I intend to narrow my focus to what I feel most comfortable with: spirituality and the presence of God in each and every one of us and in each and every thing that we do on this good earth. I have never felt completely comfortable writing or talking about politics, at least not directly. Being from Haiti, where artists and intellectuals who dared to traverse such terrains were either killed or sent into exile, categorically dictates my uneasiness with this process. Besides, I think that Spare Change columnist James Shearer, of whom I am a fan, does a stupendous job by always being on the pulse of current politics.

Although I rarely feel contented when making blatant political statements as a columnist, I do feel quite congenial to the idea of making political statements in the poetic and fictional genres. For example, in a recent Spare Change News/Whats Up Magazine issue (July 2-July 16), I published a fictitious piece titled "Midnight in Paradise" (published in my book It's Always Sunrise Somewhere and Other Stories) where I delved into such political topics as homosexuality, transcending stereotypes and ultimately the often-shifting politics of finding true love. But now, my new focal point will be to explore spirituality in our lives, however grand or minute depending on individual judgments and perceptions. I will strive to bring to you insights, analysis and conjecture based on knowledge gained from extensive study and personal experiences, that of myself and of others. I intend to motivate, inspire, renovate and transpire daily miracles that may otherwise go unnoticed. Are you willing to come along for the ride? I know I am.

When Angels Cry: Death of an Addict and Rebirth of a Man

"Hi, my name is "John Doe" (for the purpose of anonymity). I'm an alcoholic, and drug addict. I had my last drink and drug September 13, 2005 and have taken my recovery one day at a time since."

So begins "John's" story of his laborious awakening, his journey out of the gaping maw of drug and alcohol addiction to the succoring angelic wings of hope and the often-shifting boat of recovery.

John knows all too well about the trap and madness that encompasses drug and alcohol addiction. He has quite literally been to hell and back. Now stronger than ever, he has re-emerged with seemingly effortless poise and grace, the likes of an Olympic contender determined to take home the medal that would symbolize his one-year sobriety thus far. He is a bright light around the Cambridge community and if you look close enough, you can see the morning sun rising in his eyes.

He is currently participating in the Carey Program, a 9 month program to help man with mental illness and/or substance abuse problems take back control of their lives, return to mainstream society and become healthy contributing members to their community. The program's foundation is helping people to help themselves. It operates out of the Multi-Service Center on Brookline St. in Cambridge and Steven Johnson is the program coordinator.

John's story is unique but is still easily relatable to others who have had similar paths of addiction and experienced the tumultuous waves of recovery. However, John's past has not only been marred by the perils of addiction.

He was an all-American gymnast, participated in the 1980 Olympic Trials, a Veteran of the Coast Guard and he once owned his own Gymnastic School. He confesses that drugs and alcohol have always been a part of his life but became more prevalent when a young gymnast under his coaching injured himself and became a quadriplegic. The same week, he also had two of his boys qualify for the Junior National Teams in gymnastics, which to him was a bittersweet contrast of success and failure, heartache and joy. In that instance, he eventually began to sink deeper and deeper into the dark corners of the human psyche that would eventually threaten his very existence!

He did not understand why God would let something like that happen. He recalls looking up into the sky one day and proclaimed "God, I renounce you." So began his path down a very ugly road, a road to self-inflicted agony. He became what he calls a "functioning drug and alcohol addict" for over 30 years. He delved into all kinds of mind-altering chemicals like alcohol, marijuana, and cocaine. He even tried to escape from himself by moving as frequently as the shifting climate of New England. However he soon realized that relocating did not change his situation. "I could not run away from myself as hard as I tried." Because for all intents and purposes, where ever you go, there you are.

When asked about hitting bottom, he responded that he had a heart attack back in 2004. But that did not stop him from continuing to use for another thirteen months. Meanwhile, he also started praying to stop using. He began what he calls "a process out of darkness." His prayers were seemingly answered when he was arrested for possession of a firearm and cocaine with intent to distribute. He plead guilty and could have easily received six to ten years but he lucked out because he went before a sympathetic judge who was all about helping those who want to help themselves. So he only spent 63 days in jail. All in all, he was arrested about four times for drug offenses.

Eventually, he ended up in Albany Street Shelter for two and one half months and in CASPAR for six months (Cambridge and Somerville Program for Addiction and Rehabilitation), which coincidentally runs ACCESS, which runs out of 240 Albany Street, a wet shelter where "Sober" addicts help other addicts. John states that five out of the ten "sober" addicts are using drugs themselves even though they are supposed to be helping their peers. He also asserts that according to his experience "more people relapse than stay sober." He goes on to say "people relapse 8 or 9 times before they get it right." But admits that statistics can be misleading and that staying sober is an individual choice. He maintains that relapsing usually means chance of death, arrests, homelessness or hospitalization in Bridge Water State Mental Health Facility. He declares, "I have never relapsed because my whole life was a relapse. If I use drugs again, I'll be dead sooner than later. I was in hell for 35 years. I don't want to go back there!"

He admits that utilizing drugs and alcohol caused him to treat people poorly, blocking the much-needed spirit of good will towards man. He has renewed his relationship with God, with himself and others around him by contending, "God is in my life [again] and that gives me strength to protect myself." Although he is a college graduate, he hopes to go back to school to study Theology. "I want my way of helping people to be God driven." He believes that if he relapses, that would equate with death to him. "I am at crosswords where it's life or death. There's no more 'I have one more drink in me' because I think I can still deal with it." He believes that this fatalistic ideology keeps him sober. Because of his newfound faith, he expresses a desire to escape the seemingly infinite and futile cycle of use-guilt-shame-use- -guilt-shame…. "For every year you've used, it's like walking into the woods and getting lost. I've been lost in the woods for 35 years and I want to twelve step out."

He is maintaining his sobriety by following a strict and structured regimen of work, exercise, twelve step recovery meetings and a daily dosage of prayer to his higher power. He realizes that his mind is not what it used to be due to his substance abuse. "Once a cucumber becomes a pickle, it can never be a cucumber again." But yet he still wants to be a source of inspiration and hope to others. He wants to take a dark path and turn it into light. He wants to believe that the addict in him is dead! He is in the process of fervently re-inventing himself. He professes, "By changing the way you look at things, the things you look at begin to change." And he is changing the way he looks at living life with the perpetual but not insurmountable cloud of addiction. He is constantly yearning for salvation. "Each day I receive a reprieve and I try to use it to the fullest."

Today John wears many hats. He is a self-identified Green Peace member, a D.A.R.E (a drug prevention program) contributor, participating in community service at M.I.T. as a gymnastics instructor, volunteer at 240 Albany Street Shelter, a sexton (custodian) at First Congressional Church in Cambridge, and an in-house recovery group leader at the YMCA. He looks ahead to a future full of promise.

"My goals continue to expand as I'm working toward becoming a grant writer for Spare Change News and starting my own local Television and Internet show at Cambridge Community Television on the subjects of mental illness, homelessness and recovery from drug and alcohol abuse. And to his fellow addicts he offers this advice "If you should have a relapse, forgive yourself and get back into a program. Find someone to talk to: social worker, sponsor, friend or family member. Massachusetts is a wonderful state for recovery." Since John's addiction has been slowly dying, his true essence and hope of a new beginning has been rapidly growing. The angels are smiling and so is John.

Stigmatized: Trump and the Media Combine to Bring Attention to the Crisis of Mental Health and Wellness in America

"Almost invisible, we people the city
Living in the shadows, we shine out,
Moving, breathing heart of life
We may be forgotten, ignored,
But we stand in your midst,
Questions to be answered, Lives to be affirmed."

--Christopher Swan
Quoted In: Spare Change News
On behalf of the marginalized
And forgotten members of society

Mental illness was once, and to some extent still is, a taboo subject that most people feel uncomfortable talking about within familial or societal spheres. However, because of the superfluity of president Donald Trump's questionable antics which has psychologists questioning his mental health, his blame of gun violence on mental illness, the ensuing media coverage and cinematic portrayals of people afflicted with mental illness, it has gone from private whispers behind closed doors to public dialogues. However, the one issue that has not dissipated is the stigmatization of persons afflicted with mental disorders, particularly marginalized groups like the poor and the homeless.

According to Merriam-Webster.com, the word 'stigma' comes from the Greek word 'stizen' which means to tattoo or to brand. As a black man in America, I can most definitely identify with the whole idea of being "branded", for no reason other than the melanin in my skin.

In the Haitian American community, admitting to having any type of mental disorder is extremely taboo. And in society in general, it is still perceived that disclosing to having a mental disability is analogous to admitting to having a severe weakness as a human being, but particularly as a man and even more so a black man.

Even I find myself judging others based on their disclosure of having a mental illness. I don't do it intentionally; it's more like a visceral reaction due to preconceived societal programming and negative conditioning than anything else. Once I know of someone else's mental incapacity, my reactive brain begins to immediately wonder about how "crazy", dangerous or unpredictable that person's behavior may be. When I catch myself doing that, I think to myself: "They may have mental illness, but mental illness doesn't necessarily have them."

"Labeling theory proponents and the theory's critics have different views on stigma and thus differ on the consequences of labeling for people with mental illnesses," says Sarah Rosenfield of Rutgers University in her article published by the American Sociological Review, Labeling Mental Illness: The Effects of Received Services and Perceived Stigma of Life Satisfaction. She goes on to say that, "The labeling perspective posits that because of stigma, official labeling through treatment contact has negative consequences for mental patients, like being turned down for a job or being rejected by a potential intimate partner upon disclosure.

"In contrast, critics of the labeling theory claim that stigma is relatively inconsequential. Instead they argue that because labeling results in receiving needed services, it provides significant benefits for mental patients," says Rosenfield. She elaborates that, "Labeling theorists examine that mental illness as a form of deviance: the label rather than the behavior per se shapes the fate of mentally ill persons…by compromising the life chances of those so labeled." For example once officially diagnosed or "labeled", the individual may immediately begin to think of his or her limitations and perceived disabilities. They may start to think of the possibility that they might never be able to fulfill their dreams. Attaining success can often be principally traced to a family member's steadfast support as well as from members of his or her community.

However, I am glaringly aware of the sad fact that not many people are as lucky in receiving that kind of support. Many with mental illness, particularly the homeless, are abandoned or neglected by their families and ultimately by society at large. Many have dual diagnoses in the form of mental illness and substance abuse.

"One of the tragic consequences of stigma is the possibility that it engenders a significant loss of self-esteem—specifically that the stigma of mental illness leads to a substantial proportion of people who develop such illnesses to conclude that they are failures or that they have little to be proud of," says Bruce G. Link, Ph.D. et al. in the article Stigma as a Barrier to Recovery: The Consequences of "Stigma for the Self-Esteem of People With Mental Illnesses," published by the American Psychiatry Association.

"According to the stigma theory…people develop conceptions of mental illness early in life from family lore, personal experiences, peer relations and the media's portrayal of people with mental illnesses." How many times have you heard someone in your family or circle of friends talk negatively about those afflicted with mental illness, maybe even refer to them as "crazy people"? How many times have you found yourself perpetuating the same act, in spite of the fact that you may or may not have a mental illness yourself? How many times have you seen the news featuring a sensational story about a person with mental illness committing a violent act, which results in inducing fear in the general public? Even president Donald Trump tried to deflect gun violence in America (which has the most gun related deaths in the world) by blaming it simply on the mentally ill, while paradoxically cutting funding to Medicaid programs aimed at providing assistance to that very population of which he speaks.

Those afflicted with mental illness are not always easily identifiable at least on the prima facie level or based on aberrant behavior. It may help to point out that very famous people, like Janet Jackson, Robin Williams, Roseanne Barr, and more recently, Mariah Carey and Demi Lovato admitted to having mental illnesses, but you wouldn't know it just by looking at them.

In an article in the Treatment Advocacy Center entitled "Demi Lovato: Bipolar but Staying Strong" Lovato is quoted as saying: "Why not air all my secrets? Why not share my story because some people need to hear it?" She went on to say: "I didn't really realize I was sick…I thought that writing seven songs in one night was normal. I thought that staying up until 5:30 in the morning is normal. Last night, I stayed up until five in the morning. I just couldn't sleep. My mind was racing and it's an ongoing thing and I still learn how to cope with it." Ultimately she decided to disclose because she wanted to bring attention to this issue and possibly decrease the stigma of those afflicted with mental disorders. She said, "You know, I speak about a lot of serious issues, and I really hope to get awareness out there about the issues that I dealt with."

According to a Duke University study, 49 percent of U.S. Presidents suffered from mental illness and substance abuse. There was Richard Nixon's alcohol abuse, Calvin Coolidge's hypochondria, Ulysses S. Grant and Thomas Jefferson's social phobias. However, mental illness did not keep them from living fruitful lives filled with joy, dignity and accomplishments. Why should it impair anyone else for that matter?

So, how far have we come when it comes to mental illness and stigma? I suppose that depends on you, and your thoughts and reactions regarding either yourself as a person living with mental illness. And if you're not mentally ill, it will manifest in your reaction the next time you encounter a mentally ill person; whether your assessment of them will be based on their perceived limitations stemming from stereotypes or stigma often showcased in media or their actual realities based on their *abilities*, accomplishments and capacity to live a fulfilling and dignified life in spite of their psychopathology, whether real or perceived?

The True Meaning of Christmas: Defining the Accrued Philanthropic Acts that Constitute the Real Reasons We Celebrate the Holiday Season.

"Once again, we come to the Holiday Season, a deeply religious time that each of us observes, in his [or her] own way, by going to the mall of his [or her] choice."

-- Dave Barry

Soon, the snow will cascade from the December sky, adorning trees that sparkle with shimmering lights on branches that seemingly spread like open arms as if to beckon blessings from above. And I, subdued with holiday cheer and even a little bit of jeer, recall memories of doves and wondering if the world will ever succumb to peace and love. So I began to ponder about what Christmas really means, at least to me.

I am not here to harangue you on the true meaning of Christmas, I am simply offering my understanding of this most wondrous time of year and you may or may not identify with me, but hopefully you will. You see, Christmas to me is about more than just ceremony. It is about more than the money we spend at the Mighty Malls of America to impress our loved ones. Christmas to me is about celebrating life, family, and community. It's about enjoying one another's company and appreciating each other's humanity. And by humanity, I mean both positive and negative characteristics that make us all who we are. Anyone can love someone who loves you back, but the real challenge is to love someone who hates your guts.

Some of us may not be aware of this, but often our love is conditional. And I include myself in this category. How many times have you find yourself falling out of love with someone because you suddenly discover that they are (taking a deep breath) "human" and therefore "broken?" We are all broken pearls along the road. We have all said or done things that intentionally or unintentionally hurt one another. We have all been cursed or blessed with being unequivocally HUMAN! After all, a common colloquialism during the colonial settlements in America was: "In Adams fall, we sinned all..."

In times of divisiveness, let us celebrate togetherness. I am learning to embrace this revelation of human imperfection to negate any prior illusions. I have since reasoned to look to someone greater than myself and my fellow human travelers for unrestricted love. It was at that time that I gleefully looked to a higher spiritual power for eternal and unconditional love. "I searched for God and found only myself. I searched for myself and found only God" as earnestly stated by the renowned Persian poet Rumi; to which I whole heartedly concur. When it comes to who we love, we ought not to limit ourselves to the contiguous few, only those who are closest to us like our families; that would perpetrate a fallacious notion of disconnectedness with each other; that my actions can't affect you and your actions can't affect me. However that is a fallacy with which I don't agree. You most likely heard the phrase "six degrees of separation"? or how about "if your neighbors bed is on fire, wet yours..." Essentially we all affect each other and we are someway somehow connected whether we are cognizant of it or not.

In times of divisiveness, let us celebrate togetherness. This ideology is further affirmed by Albert Einstein, who declared that, "A human being is a part of the whole called by us universe, a part limited in time and space. He experiences himself, his thoughts and feeling as something separated from the rest, a kind of optical delusion of his consciousness. This delusion is a kind of prison for us, restricting us to our personal desires and to affection for a few persons nearest to us. Our task must be to free ourselves from this prison by widening our circle of compassion to embrace all living creatures and the whole of nature in its beauty." In other words, we are all connected so let us all be united by this wise notion.

In times of divisiveness, let us celebrate togetherness. This brings me to speculating about the true meaning of Christmas. I truly believe that we can all find happiness with one another, granted that we do this one thing: learning to accept one another because of our humanity and not in spite of it; celebrate rather than castigate each other for our differences; recognize that we are all like the crayons in a child's Crayola box, each color brings its own vibrant gift to evoke a colorful image of the motley human art form.

In times of divisiveness, let us celebrate togetherness. Growing up partly in Haiti for the first decade of my life, in the middle city of Port-au-Prince, I remember when the government used to have Christmas for the kids in the Haitian White House. I remember the first time I heard of Santa Clause, except in Haiti, he is called "Papa Noel." I remember being in total awe of Papa Noel. I thought that he was this magical being who was going to rescue me from the growing pains of my childhood and enhance the moments of joy. But now, all these years later, I am trying to rekindle my fascination with the holiday season. As I walk around town at night, I bask in the glitter of the glimmering trees and exuberant smiles on the people's faces and I start thinking about what Christmas really means.

In times of divisiveness, let us celebrate togetherness. The true meaning of Christmas for me is essentially love yourself and one another as you are; knowing that you and your life are "perfect" in the eyes of God. In the words of the ubiquitous motivational speaker and spiritualist Wayne Dyer: "Everything is perfect in the universe, even our desire to change it." The true meaning of Christmas is not about out doing your neighbor's Christmas decorations, or buying the most expensive gift for your loved ones. At the threat of getting too syrupy, the true meaning of Christmas should be about lending a smile to someone who bears a frown, offering a hug to someone in tears, and providing food and shelter to someone in need. In my infinite quest for wisdom, I have learned that happiness requires two things: growth and generosity. You have to be willing to be malleable if you want to grow as an individual and you must also be willing to give of yourself, to service others for the betterment of society.

"Not everybody can be famous but everybody can be great, because greatness is determined by service." said Dr. Martin Luther King Jr.

The true meaning of Christmas is about seeing one another as family and not as enemies. Don't let the melanin in your neighbor's skin determine whether or not he/she is worthy of your respect. Don't let the size of your bank account or family breeding determine your worth or your neighbor's worth.

In times of divisiveness, let us celebrate togetherness. The true meaning of Christmas is seeing one another as one; as our nation's first president George Washington once said about the American colonies: "We are one." The true meaning of Christmas is about celebrating our legacies not deficiencies. It's about fraternity and diversity, not hostility and bigotry; collaboration not division; it's about being giving, joyful, and thankful for what we have and not being selfish, sour and ungrateful for what we don't have.

In times of divisiveness, let us celebrate togetherness. Even I struggle with these issues every day, so I speak from experience. I come face to face with anger and prejudice constantly, partly due to negative societal conditioning. I too am affected by my own fallible "humanity". But I constantly aim to eschew negative thought patterns to reflect a healthier approach. You may not always be able to dictate your thoughts but you can dictate your actions. Think good thoughts, say good words, do good deeds. You can CHOOSE to act on your "loving" thoughts rather than your "hateful" ones, especially during these times, the age of Trumpism, when hate crimes against racial and religious minorities (e.g. Blacks, Jewish and Muslims) have substantially increased by at least 30 percent according the latest statistical data. And to think that all these incidents have done is expose our ineptitude in the way that we treat each other as fellow human beings. These incidents have also identified and ferret out our inherent conscious and subconscious biases manifested in our lack of unity within our diversified country. What does this say about us as a society?

In the prophetic and wise words of Mahatma Gandhi, "Our ability to reach unity in diversity will be the beauty and the test of our civilization." I make my own contributions to the ideology of "unity" when I try to practice on a daily basis my own self-made mantra: "Be a source of love and light in the face of prejudice and hatred." Once you practice this yourself, perhaps then and only then will you finally learn the true meaning of Christmas. Joeux Noel et Bonne Anne a tous (Merry Christmas and Happy New Year to All)!

Trash Talking: The Tense Relationship between Man and Mother Nature

"There is pleasure in the pathless woods, there is rapture in the lonely shore, there is society where none intrudes, by the deep sea, and music in its roar; I love not Man the less, but Nature more."

--Lord Byron

Ah, this place called Earth. Stop for a minute. Look around you. Try to see your earthly surroundings as if through the eyes of a fascinated child. Bask in the majesty of the Great Smoky Mountains or stimulate and overwhelm your senses with the geologic colors and magnitude of the Grand Canyon; the lush splendor of a giant redwood; a 150 feet tall tulip, an ash, a sycamore or a weeping willow. Stop for a minute on your way to work and behold the morning sun rising over the lofty landscape; its light feeding the plants through photosynthesis and at dusk be still and behold the full moon.

Global environmental awareness and its proper care and protection is imperative to the thriving of our communal lives, despite the fact of **President Donald Trump** twit that, "The concept of global warming was created by and for the Chinese in order to make U.S. manufacturing non-competitive." Yes, I know. A "crazy" concept, right? It makes you wonder… what planet he's getting his "facts" from. But regardless of the president's "trumped-up" ideas about the environment, we all bear the responsibility of its proper maintenance.

Stop for a minute and think before you throw that empty plastic bottle in the river, on the city streets and sidewalks or in the public park, thus disparaging our environment. There are a number of things in this world that aggravates me, but none as pesky and infuriating as careless, indifferent and insolent litterers. Yes, you know who you are; the ones leaving your Dunkin Donuts cups behind on mail boxes, subways, and park benches or tossing their plastic beverage bottles audaciously on city streets in spite of the presence of onlookers. Perhaps it's because we live in a world where people are becoming increasingly rude and inconsiderate.

During my formative years growing up partly in Haiti, I received a social and familial education unlike the education I received in my catholic school in Port- au-Prince. My family and even my extended community of family friends and neighbors contributed to my upbringing. Proper manners were an integral part of my life on the island. My mother—Marie Evelyne—was an advent figure in my learning of proper manners and etiquette and one such behavioral teachings was to always "pick up after yourself" and to leave a place as clean as you found it. In Haiti, even the very poor adhere to a strict code of what is considered to be socially acceptable behavior. Hence once in America, I continued this tradition of being conscious in how I conduct myself in a public setting and one such conduct is not tossing my rubbish on public property. Now some may scowl reading this upon perceiving it as some type of a harangue about how they should conduct themselves but it's not meant to be. I hope to express the frustrations most likely felt by fellow pedestrians who too are probably fed up with straddling litter on the city streets. "America, we've got a problem," declares some state legislatures in an internet article titled "Toxic torpedoes." Apparently there has been an influx of truckers tossing bottles full of their urine out the window, littering our countryside. This further exemplifies the problem with people—who for esoteric reasons disregard the environment in which they live through blatant effrontery in disposing of their debris on public property.

"Littering is a mindset problem… we need to make it socially un-acceptable to throw rubbish on the streets, "asserts an anonymous person in a letter to the editor in Design Week titled "It'll take more than graphics to beat the litter problem." He goes on to say, "Offenders must appreciate the link between dropping litter and the cost of cleaning it up and realize that litter is never thrown 'away'—it's just moved elsewhere." This problem permeates apparently in other parts of the world, a number of people are ostensibly and collectively non- socially conscious when it comes to how they treat the environment. In Berlin, talking trash cans will soon thank people for not littering.

Another article in "The Science Teacher" promulgates that, "A 100-fold upsurge in human produced plastic garbage in the ocean is altering habitats in the marine environment." This is based on a new study titled "Environmental Accumulation of Plastic Expedition" (SEAPLEX), conducted by a graduate researcher at the Scripps Institution of Oceanography at UC San Diego. Apparently, in an area known as the "Great Garbage Patch", the journal "Biology Letters" evinces that plastic shards in the surrounding area has risen 100 times over the last 40 years causing detrimental shifts in the natural habitats of marine animals in particular.

Let's face it. The world is an ever evolving place. Now with the continuous dawning of the technological age, more and more "stuff" will continue to surface for us to dispose of. Now, I am cognizant of the possibility that not all of us were taught proper social behavior or etiquette, or if you were, you have forsaken your social manners and public etiquette over the years, but the cliché "It's never too late to learn" or in some cases "re-learn" social formalities rings true in this instance. So Stop for a minute, look around and find a trash receptacle and keep the earth green and clean. I'll close with these words of wisdom from world-renowned British theoretical physicist Stephen Hawking: "We are in danger of destroying ourselves by our greed and stupidity. We cannot remain looking inwards at ourselves on a small and increasingly polluted… planet."

Fiction

"If we are to make reality endurable, we must all nourish a fantasy or two."

Marcel Proust

The Skeleton in Madame Simote's Closet

"If you reveal your secrets to the wind, you should not blame the wind for revealing them to the trees."

Khalil Gibran

It remains a mystery as to how and why Madame Simote's husband actually died. Jean Herbie Simote was the handsome town doctor and was perceived to be a philanderer. He was rumored to have had affairs with a plethora of Madame Simote's female friends and even some of her relatives. In Haiti, the men are expected to cheat and their behavior is tolerated by their wives, because of fear of losing their financial security. The Simotes' lived in a rural part of Port-auPrince, Haiti's capital city. They never had any children.

During the early evening hours as the sun cooled and prepared to set, Madame Simote put out a number of rocking chairs on her front porch. She sat and fanned herself while enjoying the panoramic view of her neighborhood. Soon, she would be joined by some of the other women who lived nearby, once they too were done with the day's duties. She was surrounded by finely manicured lawns, rolling green hills, towering palm trees swaying and lavish homes with pious women constantly praying. In the near distance, Madame could see a large woman with an African head wrap and her hands on her hips, trudging up the hill with a gait analogous to a reluctant duck. She knew it was Madame Calamite, since she was usually the first to come.

"Oh, Madame Simote, bonjour. Hot day today, eh?," she said, with a wide white grin as she plopped down next to Madame without waiting to be asked to sit. "Please excuse me, but I've been so tired lately. My maid has taken ill and I've had to do most of the chores myself. The maids these days are not what they used to be; now they're all spoiled and lazy."

"I know, Ti Cheri. They think they should get paid even when they're laid up, too! So tell me, have you heard about Madame Madichon's son?" Madame Simote leaned towards Madame Calamite with raised eyebrows.

"No…what that boy up to now?"

"Well, the word going around is that he is an insatiable homosexual! His mother finally found out why he'd been spending so much time with the gardener and it's not because of his interest in horticulture." Madame Simote punctuated her point by bobbing her head in one grand up-anddown motion.

"Whatever do you mean?" Madame Calamite leaned further forward in her chair.

"Well, one particularly hot afternoon, Madame Madichon was looking for that boy but couldn't find him anywhere. So she ventured over to the gardener's quarters, seeing how he's always hanging 'round him and all. Well, as she entered the house and approached the bedroom, all she could hear was the sound of a bed squeaking and what appeared to be two male voices grunting and moaning. And girl, wouldn't you know it, she busted the door open and to her horror, there was her son sweaty and naked in bed with the gardener!"

"NO! Whatever did she do?" Madame Calamite asked, with her eyes wide open like she just saw a pig flying.

"Well, girl, her legs were knocked out right from under her. She fainted, girl! What would you do if you found out that your only kid was that way? That poor woman will never have any grandchildren. Hmmmm…" Madame Simote stared straight ahead as if looking at nothing in particular while Madame Calamite just sat there and shook her head in disbelief.

Soon, a younger woman with a slimmer build, her hair in a bun, climbed onto the porch, greeted the other ladies, and sat. "Madame Jeunes, where have you been keeping yourself?" Madam Simote asked with a polite grin.

"Well, you know, the usual, constantly spying on that cheating husband of mine. So what else is new?" The ladies shared the news about Madame Madichon's son. "Oh sweet Jesus, that boy is goin' straight ta hell. How could he do that to his poor mother? If I ever found out my son was … that way … I would tear up his birth certificate!" Madame Jeunes uttered, with fury in her eyes.

Soon, the ladies departed and Madame Simote was left to herself once again. The night's darkness was mitigated by the swelling moonlight and all she heard were crickets chirping. That day had been the anniversary of her husband's death.

She got up and headed back into the house. She walked over to the door of Mr. Simote's study. She stood and stared at the door before taking a deep breath and walking in. The door squeaked as she opened it. There was a letter in a locked box on the desk, just as she had left it. She opened the box, tilted her head back and closed her eyes. A single tear slid down her face. She regained her composure and prepared to read the letter once again. The first time she had read it was shortly after her husband's death. She sat at the desk and began:

My Dear Sweet Wife,

If you are reading this it means I am already dead. I could not go on with this charade any longer, nor would I allow you to continue to partake in it. We are living in a country burdened with social injustice, prejudice and small-mindedness. Because of this, I could not live my life just as I "really" am. You knew this before we got married, but being that we were childhood sweethearts and we genuinely love each other, I suppose that was enough reason to get married. But it killed me knowing that I could never be the man you deserve, it killed me to know that I could never give you any children and you would never experience being a grandmother. The only way I could keep living my secret other life and keep from being persecuted and possibly killed was to marry you, and for that I am truly sorry. Your devotion and loyalty ran deep, so deep that you deliberately spread rumors that I was a lothario, the biggest ladies' man in town, but we both know that is not the case. So I felt like I needed to rid both you and myself of this unconventionality. You deserve to be happy, and so I have taken rat poison to rid you of my abnormality. I know this will devastate you, but soon enough, you will find someone who can be to you what I could not. Farewell, my dear, and I will see you in the heavens.

With love,

Herbie

Madame Simote remained still for quite some time while looking out into the night and noticing the moonlight looking down at her through the half-open window above the bureau. Then, with a sudden sense of purpose, she placed the letter back into the box and locked it. She walked over to the mini closet in the far corner and placed the box on the top shelf, right next to Jean Herbies' ashes, before closing and locking up the closet door. She stuffed the key into her bra, looked around the room one last time, flicked off the light, and left.

The Snake and the Pauper

"The ignorant mind, with its infinite afflictions, passions, and evils, is rooted in the three poisons. Greed, anger, and delusion."

-- Bodhidharma

It was a beautiful sunny day in the forest of Carfou, a small town in the outskirts of Port-au-

Prince, Haiti's capital city. The birds were chirping and the trees were swaying in a sing-song sort of way.

Di Dim, a local farmer, strolled down the winding dirt road, occasionally stumbling onto the thick bulky tree roots. With his machete in hand, he swung and chopped the low-hanging branches in a whimsical way while whistling.

He had been a farmer all his life. He was part of five generations of farmers who had been slaves under the sovereignty and oppression of the French; that is, until the revolutionary war that rendered Haiti the first free Black nation in the world. He recently lost his farm because a white businessman robbed him of his land. In Haiti, the legal system is designed to protect the rich and, being a poor uneducated man, he was left with very little to no options to get his land back. Since then, he wandered the forest and lived off the land by chopping fruits hanging from the trees with his machete and hunting random animals with his rifle.

He soon came upon a dark cave and from inside the cave heard a hissing sound that sounded like "Pssssst. Psssssst. Pssssssst…" He looked around then bent down to look further into the cave and at that point, a white snake slithered out and said, "Hi there. My name is Sister Snake." Wow! A talking snake! His eyes lit up with excitement as he responded, "I am Brother Di Dim."

Sister snake looked him up and down and said, "I already know who you are, Brother Di Dim. I heard through these woods that you are a man of magic and so I have a proposition for you. Care to hear it?"

Brother Di Dim said, "Yeah…Yeah…" while bobbing his head up and down.

"I heard that you just lost your land and you are now a very poor man. I have always wanted to be a beautiful princess. If you use your magic to turn me into a beautiful princess I promise that I will marry you and you will become the Prince of Haiti and be a very wealthy man."

Brother Di Dim stroked his chin deep in thought. "Hmm," He uttered while looking down at Sister Snake. "Well I have always wanted to know what it would feel like to be a rich man…" Then suddenly he said,

"Ok! I will do it!" And Sister Snake said, "Good! Then we have a deal!" Then Brother Di Dim said to Sister Snake, "Ok, listen. While you go to bed tonight, I will work my magic and when you wake up tomorrow morning, you will be a beautiful princess."

Brother Di Dim went on his way and at midnight under the moonlight he made his magic. The next morning Sister Snake awoke and leaped with joy because she was now a beautiful princess. Her crown and shoes were made of diamonds and her dress was made of gold.

Brother Di Dim then came by to see Princess Snake and said, "I have honored my promise and made you a princess. Now will you marry me and make me the Prince of Haiti?" Princess Snake looked down at him and said, "Marry you? I can't marry you! You have bad teeth! When you have good teeth, I'll marry you."

Brother Di Dim went on his way and at midnight under the moon light he made his magic. The next morning, he woke up with good teeth and went to see Princess Snake and said, "I have honored my promise and gave myself good teeth. Now will you marry me and make me the Prince of Haiti?" Princess Snake looked down at him and said, "Marry you? I can't marry you! You have kinky black hair. When you have long blond beautiful hair, I will marry you."

So Brother Di Dim went on his way and at midnight under the moon light he made his magic.

The next morning he had long blond beautiful hair and went to see Princess Snake and said, "I have honored my promise and gave myself long blond beautiful hair. Now will you marry me and make me the Prince of Haiti?" Princess snake looked down at him and said, "Marry you? I can't marry you! You have ugly brown eyes. When you have beautiful blue eyes, I will marry you."

So Brother Di Dim went on his way and at midnight under the moonlight he made his magic.

The next morning he woke up with beautiful blue eyes and went to see Princess Snake and said, "I have honored my promise and gave myself beautiful blue eyes. Now will you marry me and make me the Prince of Haiti?" Princess Snake looked down at him and said, "Marry you? I can't marry you! You have dirty black skin. When you have pearly white skin, I'll marry you."

So Brother Di Dim went on his way and at midnight under the moon light he made his magic. The next morning he woke up with pearly white skin and went to see Princess Snake and said, "I have honored my promise and gave myself pearly white skin. Now will you marry me and make me the Prince of Haiti?" Princess snake looked down at him and said, "Marry you? I

135

can't marry you! You are a poor man. A prince must be a rich man. When you're a rich man, then I'll marry you."

But Brother Di Dim was told by the magic king that while he would be able to do all sorts of magic, the only magic he would not be able to do was make himself rich. Soon after he found out through the woods that Princess snake had married the rich white man who took away Brother Di Dim's land.

Brother Di Dim became furious and decided to expose Princess Snake's secret. On the day she was to marry, he turned her back into a white snake and all the villagers gasped in utter shock!

Sister Snake said to the crowd, "It was that negroid full of hemorrhoids Brother Di Dim that did this to me. If he did this to me, imagine what he could do to you! He is a dangerous man and must be put to death!" She then slid away back into her dark cave in the forest.

Once the King of Haiti heard this, he thought that Brother Di Dim sounded like a powerful man who could bring him and his country many riches. He sought him out and made him a Prince, and he was soon married to a beautiful princess. Brother Di Dim is finally happy, now that he has become the Prince of Haiti.

The Joy That Killed

"Mistaken identity, of course, has been the province of much postcolonial fiction. An important feature of this writing is the manner in which misrecognition has haunted all cognition."

-- Amitava Kumar

Mrs. Hannah Havnoklu, having had a night of nervous sleep, slowly sat up in bed and looked back at her husband, Hans. She smiled at him and got up to go to the bathroom. Today was going to be one of the most joyous days of their life together.

They'd been together since the beginning of high school, to their parents' dismay. Their parents had thought they were too young to be so in love and inseparable. Hans was two years older than Hannah and neither of them had ever dated anyone else. Then, the night of the high school prom, they went too far. They were at Mezaround Creek, a place where all the kids went to be with each other, and Hannah became pregnant with their first child. She was sixteen years old. Her parents didn't believe in abortion, so the plan was that she would carry the child to term and then give it up for adoption. For Hannah, those days were better off left forgotten. Her once docile and gentle family became quarrelsome, and the tension in her home forced her and Hans even closer together. Hans's family were open-minded hippies, and were more accepting of the situation. His parents had also met when they were very young and had Hans when they were teenagers.

When the day finally came for Hannah to turn the baby over to the adopting couple, she cried all day and night. "Darling, you're just too young," her mother had said. "You have your whole life ahead of you. Besides, what would people say? We are prominent people in this community and that makes us role models. I can't believe you've embarrassed us like this! These things do not happen to people like us." Then, with a lowered voice and furrowed brow, Hannah's mother practically hissed, "They happen to that Hans boy, maybe, since his parents are white-trash, marijuana smoking hippies who did the same thing you two are doing, ruining your lives by having kids when you're still kids yourselves." After she harangued Hannah, she came over to her and wiped her tears with her bare hands, all the while saying, "It's for the best, darling. You may not see it now, but you will later."

Hannah would never forget the orange sun setting in the view of her hospital room that day; everything was quiet and eerily threatening. Her mother had left with her first- born child, taking him to the adopting parents. Hannah had felt depleted, bewildered, confused and defeated. She'd simply stared out the window and watched the sun go down, as if it were the last time she would ever see a sunset.

When her parents forbade her to continue seeing Hans after she returned home from the hospital, Hannah had tried to kill herself by downing an entire box of sleeping pills. She'd been slouched down in her bed mumbling gibberish when her mother found her, and she woke up the next day in the hospital. She was allowed to see Hans again, but he wasn't allowed to come over to the house. After she graduated from high school, Hannah and Hans left Ohio and went to San Francisco to start a new life. Hans enrolled in college and worked as landscaper, and Hannah worked in a flower shop. A year later, their second son, Hans Jr., was born. Eventually, Hans became a dentist and Hannah became a schoolteacher.

Now, Hannah was forty-eight and Hans was fifty. Neither of them knew that their meticulously constructed world was about to self-destruct, leaving nothing but scandal, lies, and deceit. But for now, Hannah looked into the bathroom mirror. She noticed the crow's feet around her eyes, her droopy chin and neck and sagging breasts. She sighed and said, "Oooh time, the subtle thief of youth."

The sun was playing hide and seek behind overcast clouds hanging over the quiet suburb. Downstairs—while Hans was still in bed—Hannah commenced with preparations for the anticipated arrival of Hans Jr., who was coming for a visit. Outside her kitchen window, there were two crows in the garden, which was adorned with the spry blooming of spring. Hans Jr. had called just days earlier, to their surprise, since he mostly called on holidays and birthdays. They both wished that they had a closer relationship with their only son.

"Mom, put the phone on speaker and get Dad, I have an announcement," he had said. "Mom, Dad, I'm in love and I'm also engaged…" Both Hannah and Hans interrupted with bursts of joy and welcoming surprise. "Oh my… That's great honey!" exclaimed Hannah. "Yeah, son, that's great! So when do we get to meet this lucky gal?" asked Hans. Hans Jr. hesitated and said, "Well, I was hoping to bring Chris to meet you guys on Easter Sunday." Both his parents cried out "Sure, that will be fine, looking forward to it!" in unison, as they often did. And so it was set.

It was noon and Hans Jr. along with his new fiancé were expected any minute "Honey, can you help me pick out a tie to go with this black suit?" Hans called out to Hannah. "Oh, honey, why on God's earth would you wear a black suit on such a happy day? Why don't you wear the red tie to add some color to spruce up this funeral suit you're wearing?" Hans took her advice and that was that. As Hannah set a large plate of Easter eggs on the lavishly decorated table now teeming with an overabundance of food, the doorbell rang.

"Honey, I'm busy in here, can you get that?" Hans answered the door and appeared flabbergasted when he saw who Hans Jr. was with. "Chris" turned out to be a man, but not just any man. Hans recognized him as the same boy in the pictures that he had been receiving from the adoptive parents of their first child! He clutched his chest and fell dead to the floor. "Dad! Oh my God, Dad!" Hans Jr. rushed to his father and tried to revive him with no avail. "Mom, come here quick!" Hannah could be heard from the dining room, "What's all the commotion out there?" She ran to the front door and gasped when she saw the man standing over her husband on the floor. "Mom, what's wrong. Why do you look like that?" Hannah's skin turned to a pale bluish color and all the life quickly drained out of her as she too suddenly plopped to the floor.

"Oh my God, Chris, call 911!" It was too late.

***

Hannah and Hans Sr. were buried a few days later; both Hans Jr. and Chris were at the funeral. The truth about their relation to one another remained a mystery as they watched their parents' languid bodies being lowered into the ground. The men held hands as they left the cemetery grounds; they looked up together and saw two crows fluttering through the dismal sky, heading in their direction.

Kamikaze Moods: Based On a True Story

Kamikaze: of or pertaining to a suicidal attack by a Japanese airplane pilot in World War II.

— Webster's New World Dictionary,
Third College Edition

Seuqcaj woke up one morning in the year 2000 and felt the white walls in his apartment closing in on him.

At first, he thought he was in a hospital ward, as he had been many times before. The first time he had been hospitalized was for attempting suicide when he was 16 years old. He had faked his way out of the hospital. He'd outsmarted the staff by pretending to be mentally stable and socially well-adjusted, which he knew he wasn't. But he had been about to start his senior year that fall, and was determined to graduate in front of family and friends rather than being homeschooled in some group home.

He had tried to end his life. Actually, what he had really wanted to do was go to sleep for a while and take a break from all the hurt; at least, that's what he'd told himself at the time. He had taken an entire box of sleeping aids. He remembered feeling anxious afterwards, waiting for a wave of death to swoop him into the great beyond. But he had just become groggy and delusional. He recalled the white walls spinning around, as if in a dream. Then he'd seen a blurry image in white approaching. It was his mother in her nursing uniform. The next thing he knew, he'd woken up in the hospital. His mother was sitting beside his bed, crying. That's when he'd been placed in a group home for troubled kids.

A lot had happened to bring him to that horrible place, the group home in Salem, Massachusetts. He had been terribly abused at home; neglected by his mother and verbally and physically abused by his stepfather, who had also threatened his life. His stepmonster—a nickname he created himself—used to pace next to his bedside with a long iron bar every night, to the point where he hardly got any sleep. He had only been 13 years old. One night, fed up with the nightly routine of terror tactics, he had gotten up and gone after his stepfather with a knife. He had dared him to come at him and get it over with, yelling, "One of us is not coming out of this alive and it's not gonna be ME!" The monster stepfather had backed off then, and said that he was "only kidding," with a sinister smile on his zombie-like black face. He left Seuqcaj alone after that night, but the physical abuse towards Seuqcaj's mother and his psychological abuse towards them both would last another 10 years, before he and his mother packed up and abandoned the apartment before the monster returned home from work.

Years later, Seuqcaj had his own apartment and was in medical school studying to be a psychiatrist. Seuqcaj had experienced some sporadic periods of depression and hyperactivity over the years, which had caused him to drop in and out of college during his undergraduate years. He had never been formally diagnosed with any major mental illness per se, but he knew something was wrong; but because of his Haitian background, he slept night after restless night on the pillows of denial. One day, he woke up and felt the white walls closing in on him yet again. He felt an urgent need to find a way out; fear and anxiety were doing a sort of grotesque dance in his psyche, and he knew that no matter where he went, there would be no escaping his emotions. Just then, he remembered wearing a T-shirt in high school with the words "Kamikaze" emblazoned on it. During World War II, members of a special corps of Japanese air force pilots—kamikaze pilots—were charged with the suicide mission of crashing an aircraft on a target laden with explosives. How ironic that he had purchased that very shirt just months before his first suicide attempt. He wanted to take pills again, just escape for a while and "sleep it off," he thought to himself. But this time, he knew the danger of being alone and not being found in time. So he decided to check himself into the hospital.

By going to the hospital, he knew he was going against everything he'd been taught in Haiti about what a man should be. He was always extolled by his aunt for being "a good little boy" who never broke the rules, and when he did, took his beating without even making a sound; a "good boy" who never complained and kept his feelings to himself. But as he sat in the lobby of the hospital, years of repressed emotion welled up in him like a volcano that was well overdue to erupt. He had been told that he had mentally ill family members, but they were ostracized and never mentioned in conversations. Some of them eventually succumbed to suicide. He knew for a fact that he was the first in his family to admit to himself that he was indeed sick and also to get help. That day, he became an iconoclast against his family's taboo against mental illness.

***

After spending three months in the hospital, he was released to a shelter, since he had lost his home and was unable to continue medical school. He knew his life was forever changed. He knew that the habit of living for the future had a way of making the present elusive, so he decided to live in the moment and began to rebuild his life one day at a time. He was diagnosed with bipolar disorder (a.k.a. manic/depressive illness). As part of his treatment, he was encouraged to become an active member of his community. He became a peer educator and gave lectures to students preparing to enter the mental health field. While putting medical school on hold, he went around telling his story to help de-stigmatize mental illness, particularly in the Afro-Caribbean American community. He often shared a poem during his personal appearances:

Decorative calm tantrums scrolling psychopathic scenes; locked up in cerebral birthing grounds, learning to think thoughts of sanity. Adorned in hospital gowns and bedroom slippers, I stand: a "psychotic" example of sanity. Emotions ranging from blue to red, acrimonious examples, while massive muscles wearing moonlight colors safeguard society from my pathology.

Walls wearing white silk form a decorative calm; a ploy to procrastinate pandemonium on the ward. Milieu "counselors" tend to the task of sorting through the aberration; blacks and whites develop contact, copying scripted color stereotypes; my world is a roller coaster of stormy highs. Like overtures and summer sunset fires and acid lows. Like a crashing elevator from the horrific heights of the Hancock tower!!! Nurses in white worried uniforms bellowing "medication time!" Working doubles neglecting their homes and hobbies "medication time!" becomes their mantra.

Then, upon being released, having been deemed "safe" for society, I wander the streets decorated in death and debris, lurking around affluent trash cans looking for my lost life. Now doctors dictate that I suffer from a disease of ambiguity. Now, I find myself roving the streets in society's straightjacket.

Under the Cover of Night

"You must not lose faith in humanity. Humanity is an ocean; if a few drops of the ocean are dirty, the ocean does not become dirty."

--Mahatma Gandhi

The full moon permeates the darkened street where Chiro sprints to hide under the bridge, the rolling waves of the ocean muffling the footsteps trailing behind him. Exhausted from fear and the run itself, he leans against the wall to catch his breath as the hooligans pursuing him get close enough to hear his panting.

He thinks about how he got into this mess to begin with and longs for the life he once had with his wife and his two kids, a son and daughter, until his habits got the better of him. One night he came home and his wife, Zelda, began to scream at him. She told him that she couldn't "live like this anymore"— barely able to put food on the table even though she was working two jobs, while he sits on the couch, smoking pot and browsing internet porn sites while leaving the kids to fend for themselves. Things got really bad when he started doing harder drugs and took up gambling, and Zelda ended up doing what her own mother had done: sacrificing her own happiness to keep her family together. Her own mother had also looked the other way when she found out that her dad was having an affair. Zelda had sworn then that she that she would never allow herself to become her mother. But eventually her mother's fate crept up on Zelda and before she knew it, there she was with a cheating, drugging and emotionally unavailable husband.

Chiro knew that he was a deadbeat dad and he didn't seem to care. After all, he did model himself after his father, so he felt justified in his behavior. But now, as he cowers under the shadowy bridge fearing his life may end in a matter of minutes, he suddenly has an epiphany about wanting to become a better man for the sake of his family. He looks up to the starry skies and makes a plea with God. "God, please help me. I know these guys will kill me, like they've killed others who came before me. God, I promise if you sparc me, I will try my hardest to be there for my family. If I should fail to honor my promise to you, God, then you can take me. But tonight, God, please spare me, please ..."

"Chiro you rat, we know you're here somewhere. We can smell fear remember?" Dino, a big tall muscular guy with broad shoulders barks out in a baritone voice. "Yeah, that's right, ya might as well come on ouuut!" Lenny, the smaller guy says in a high pitched, almost cartoon-like voice. Chiro's heart starts to beat faster as the ruffians edge closer to his hiding spot. "What was that?" Dino asks Lenny. "What was what?" Lenny responds seeming incredulous. "There it is again!" At this point, realizing that Dino is on to him, Chiro decides to make a run for it. "There he is! Get him!" The men take off after Chiro and it is not long before they catch up to him.

"We've got you now! Where is my money?" Dino huffs with his huge hand around Chiro's neck. "I … don't … have it you big brute! Get your paws off of me!" Dino looks over to Lenny, "What are we gonna do with this fool, Lenny?" "Kill him, Dino. No one stiffs us and gets away with it!" Dino whips out his knife and holds it right up to Chiro's throat. "Now for the last time, where is my money?!" Chiro struggles to free himself from Dino's tight grip, "I'll get it to you tomorrow…"

"Nah…you said that yesterday. Now you've left me no other choice but to do what I gonna do…" He raises the knife above Chiro's chest and just as he brings it down, a voice hollers in the distance and the men look up to see flashlights bouncing in the darkness.

"Hey! What's going on here?" Both men then take off into the night to evade the cops.

***

Chiro's promise to God is soon tested when the temptations of old habits present themselves. But he is steadfast in his devotion to his family and his promise to God. He joins a drug and alcohol support group, to Zelda's relief. He sells his car, his most prized possession, to pay off the mobsters. He once gave the car more love and attention then he did his own family, but now it is all but a distant memory. He looks up into the sky and says, "I can live with that."

Serendipity

"Sometimes life drops blessings in your lap without your lifting a finger. Serendipity, they call it."

--Charlton Heston

Your alarm is going off and you roll over in your bed and turn your back to it all the while cursing it for being so obnoxiously loud and intrusive. It's 5:30 a.m. and you have to be at work by 8. When you occasionally open your eyes, you can see the sun rise over the nearby lake, hovering patiently waiting for you to wake up and take notice of it. But you went to bed late last night sorting out your bills at the kitchen table before you became totally exasperated, muttered "Fuck it" under your breath and went to bed at 1 a.m.

Once your still hyperactive brain decides to quiet down, you had that dream again. You were dressed in a white tuxedo standing in front of the clergy with your friends and family sitting behind you with seemingly permanent smiles in their faces like the joker. And then their smiles turned to discomfort, embarrassment and their faces express worry when Mark still hasn't shown up. You two have been together since high school and you've been waiting 10 years for this moment, the moment when you'll marry him and be together until the end of your times on earth. You glance down at your watch and it's almost 12 p.m. Mark was supposed to be there by 11 a.m. And then you look up into the sky and there is Mark, riding a white winged horse and he looks down at you and smiles, except there is something peculiar about his face. You look closer by squinting your eyes to realize that he has no eyes. His eye socket are dark and empty and consumed by a hazy rush of fear and distress, you bolt up in bed panting like you were being chased by some horrific looking creature in a sinister forest.

You have tried to figure out what the dream means since Mark has been deceased for about a year now. He died due to complications of pneumonia that went untreated unbeknown to both of you. You did not anticipate this and so there were things that went unspoken because he died so suddenly. And almost every night, you have the same reoccurring dream and you are feeling persecuted but yet don't feel like you have any control over what happens when you are no longer conscious. You resolve to talk this over with your therapist. You've been seeing him since Mark passed away, for a long time, you were unable to function. You refused to leave the house or get out of bed in the morning. Your sister had to come over and care for you and even helped with paying the bills since you lost your job due to excessive absence. But after 3 months had passed, with the help of your sister and therapy, you managed to get back on your feet, attained another job and started to slowly come out of your former zombie like state of existence. But your presence of mind is still unconsummated and these days, you are functioning on automatic pilot; just going through daily monotonous routines with no joy, optimism or passion. You've isolated yourself from your friends in spite of how hard they try to reach you by phone or email. You feel angry at Mark for leaving you and so you've decided to punish everyone around you, including yourself, because you don't understand why this had to happen to you. Your once benevolent, sunny disposition have soured into a bitter scowl and an impervious facial expression that conveys indifference.

It is now 6 a.m. and you've finally decided to get up. Outside, the sun is higher in the sky and your open your bedroom window, stick your head out, close your eyes and take a deep breath of your mountainous surroundings. The sound of the streaming lake uncoils your often convoluted and distorted thoughts and for the first time in months, your usually stoical face breaks into an apprehensive smile. But something in you wants to stay demure and unaffected, so you quickly reverse back to scowling. Yet you feel there is something dissimilar in the air, as if your usual routine is about to take a turn for the best, but you're not sure you're prepared for it or even want it.

You make your way into the bathroom and as usual, you avoid looking at yourself in the mirror while you shave and brush your teeth and as usual tears splices down your face. After you've downed your carnation instant breakfast, you head out to work at the Blue Blood Department Store, where you are Shift Supervisor.

You like your work, but you don't welcome the unwanted attention of your female co-workers, who all think you're a total "hotty", even though they all know you're gay since you use to bring Mark to company picnics and such. You ignore their excessive fawning and just go about your day. And then he walks in. A handsome guy of average height and weight who looks like he maybe from Brazil. You practically scurry over to ask him if he needs any assistance. He smiles and says yes and you can see a knowing twinkle in his eyes when he looks at you and as if you two are exchanging secrets codes with one another, you return a knowing smile back at him. And deep inside of you, you know something has changed. You look over his shoulders and outside, you can see the sun setting through the double glass doors seemingly staring at **you**, knowingly.

Sacred Hearts

"Vain are the thousand creeds that move men's hearts…worthless as withered weeds to awaken doubt in one."

--Emily Bronte

The sun rises up from the abyss of the earth like a giant orange over the rocky Sunny Meadows mountains this morning to awaken the locals to greet what promises to be yet another perfect day in their beloved town. The birds are chirping their esoteric songs. The honeysuckles bask in the morning dew and the bees are buzzing in a mad frenzy to pollinate the flowers.

It is the quintessential Middle America small town, replete with meadows, marshlands and spattering of wild life. Its population is barely two thousand with one school. The neighborhoods look dilapidated with old dirty broken down cars and mechanical junk in most of the driveways. The houses have paint that is peeling off, surrounded by un-mowed lawns and over grown trees. In the yards of some, there are rusty old swing sets and broken hammocks that have seen their hay days come and gone.

Father Uri Maher is the respected town priest towering over the only church in Sunny Meadows. On Sundays, the bulk of the town dress in their Sunday bests, get into their beat-up automobiles and make their way to the Sacred Hearts Catholic Church; which sits on top of a rural hillside and where the town gathers to catch up on the latest gossip, see old friends and break bread together during coffee hour. Father Maher is grateful to have a young apprentice priest under his charge and smiles when he sees the demonstrated gusto and exuberance of his young protégé; whom he hopes will prolong his legacy.

Sunny Meadows in the evening is the best part of Father Maher's day. During the night he ventures out to the woods contiguous to the rectory to clear his head. There in the still of the night, he can hear the caterwaul of katydids; stumbling onto a fawn as it tiptoes from the woods to the often dangerous human grounds; the rustling of leaves in the towering trees above his head; a doe rustling to life after a nap; mysterious eyes carved obsidian glaring at him. Yet he remains fearless. Perhaps it's his faith or perhaps it's something born of the nucleus of his being. He stands under the starry skies gazing into oblivion while rocking back and forth with his hands in his pockets and begins to whistle, competing with the supple blow of the night breeze weaving in and out of the dancing trees. He looks down to see a rabbit peeks its head from its burrow, he tries not to draw his breath too harshly less he frightens it back into its hole. While a conglomeration of broods chirp in their nests, Father Maher looks up, closes his eyes and contemplates his conundrum. He knows it can compromise his tenure in the Church as well as his life in Sunny Meadows. He adjusts the tight Priest collar around his neck in an attempt to free his breath. This thing inside of him, something he feels he must keep concealed, like a stain in his white Sunday service apparel.

Amidst his stealth he runs into Old Lady Granbouche, she is the town gossip. If she so much as catches you even peeing in public, she is sure to pass a note to the minister in the church collection plate stating your perceived "sin" to ensure your repentance. He tries to hide but just as he was about to turn the corner....

"Hey there Billy boy...where ya goin' in this murky evenin' weatha?" She said smiling.

"Oh, hi Ms. Granbouche...I'm just takin' a walk, nothin' exciting." He tries to seem nonchalant.

"Well, you be careful. God has eyes everywhere you know..." She said waving her bony fingers in a circular motion.

"Ooook, I will..." *You old batalac*, he says thinking out loud.

Just then, he hears a grunting sound. "Is someone there?" He asks in a monotone voice.

. "It's me Father," a male voice responds. "Oh, Billy my boy, what are you doing out here all alone?" Father Maher recognizes Billy's voice immediately. After all, he baptized him and has known him all his life.

"Father I must confess, I'm out here drinking. Well, actually I'm celebrating, I turned eighteen today!" He says in a high pitched voice.

"Oh, well...happy birthday my boy. But why are you here alone? Where are your chaps?" "Well Dilly and Scalli just left 'cause they had to get some chores done before bed." Billy pauses then with a sly grin asks, "What about you Father? What are you doing here all alone?" Father Maher is nonplused by young Billy's bemused and knowing tone. Is it possible that this young man knows something? Suspects something? His eyes twirl with wonder and paranoia.

"Well, I...I wanted to clear my head about some things..." he says trying to sound blasé. Billy pauses once more and with growing confidence and a twinkle in his eyes asks, "Well care to help me celebrate Father?" Father Maher's heart accelerates as he considers the invitation. What's the worst that could happen? He thought. He can sense inklings of sweat forming on his forehead in spite of the cool evening breeze. "S-sure Billy, why not?" He saunters over to Billy who is standing in the shadows under the glare of growing moonlight. Billy twists off a beer from the pack. "Here Father..." He hands him over the beer, its fizzle made more audible in the halcyon surroundings. Father Maher reaches over to grab the can, their fingers overlap and Billy runs his thumb over his and he can see Billy's moonlight colored grin along with a knowing smirk, reminiscent of Elvis Presley; who was Father Maher's first furtive enthrallment. Both eyes meet and are transfixed, as if speaking a covert language; like the cryptic mating calls of wild animals. They are drawn closer together as if by the orbiting electrons of the waters of the muses, with only the hard coldness of the beer can between them.

"Billy...I...I...don't think..."

"Shush..." Billy puts his index finger over the Father's lips, "I know. I've always known." "But...but...how could you possibly..." the Father mumbles incredulously.

"Father, I can't explain it...like, birds of a feather...like...you know?"

"I...I've loved you for a very long time Billy. But this isn't right. The Bible says..."

"Father... What does your heart says?"

"Billy, I'm a Priest. The bible is my spiritual conduit. I...can't...just..."

"You're a good man Father. Love of any kind isn't wrong like, you know?" But before Father Maher could say another word, Billy abruptly forces his lips upon his; which he instinctively resisted at first before he fully surrenders with the voracity of a predator for his prey, after a protracted famine. Both men are locked in a harried embrace fueled with reckless and intrepid desire on the part of Billy but fraught with feelings of guilt and fear on the part of Father Maher. Yet something besides culpability implodes inside Maher; his heart having been jolted awake from hibernation causes blood to blunder through its chambers and for the very first time, he knows the sheer joy of experiencing what Billy must be feeling at this moment: young, wild and carefree.

In the years to come, Maher continues a cautious relationship with Billy. To keep Billy close by, he hires him as the grounds keeper for the church and rectory. No one ever gives their relationship a second thought and Maher is vigilant as to how he conducts himself around the strapping young lad, careful to keep a tight lid on the boiling pot of their amalgamated hearts. On Sundays, when Maher preaches about sin, he looks directly at Billy, who bears a knowing smirk; reminiscent of Elvis Presley.

Poetry

"I was a victim of a stereotype. There were only two of us Negro kids in the whole class, and our English teacher was always stressing the importance of rhythm in poetry. Well, everybody knows… that all Negroes have rhythms, so they elected me class poet."

Langston Hughes

Where Am I From Originally?

Yeah, well the all-important vetting question, as if that alone
narrates the story of me, as if we all forgot that if you are not
Indigenous, then my story is your story in this country's
convoluted trajectory. All descendants of immigrants from
another country, all kneeled at the foot of the Statue of Liberty.

Where am I from originally?
It doesn't matter really... to most I am only a
BLACK AMERICAN CITIZEN
still waiting and hoping for the
American Constitutional Decree of Equality, regardless
of my birth country.

Where am I from originally?
Only sanctions yours snap judgment of me; it doesn't tell
you anything about my personality. It doesn't tell you
anything about America's main adversity, namely economic
disparity and racial disunity. It doesn't tell you anything
about why we still have a race problem in the 21st century.
Why does it matter where I'm from originally? After all, Africa is the birth
country of all of humanity, where scientists have back-traced the birthplace
of the human race, Africa was the ascension of human evolution and
eventual migration, our sapient ancestral diaspora in the parched deserts of
Sub-Saharan Africa!

Where am I from originally?
That question is better suited to a foreigner just visiting this country,
for I, like you, am an AMERICAN CITIZEN, abiding
metastatic racial disharmony,
proving that apart we are a cacophony of caterwauling disparity, touting
that together we can be a harmonious disparate symphony...

Where am I from originally?
Why don't you use this opportunity to see what makes me unique rather
than what makes me incomplete?

What makes us come alive through exuberant sharing rather
than through discordant sparring? If you want to know more
about my journey, then ask about what inspires me. If you

want to know more about my journey, then ask me about my
favorite color that is NOT skin color. If you want to know
more about my journey, then ask me about my lifelong hobby
and who I want to be in this diversely-amalgamated yet still
racially-divided country.
Where am I from originally?
Just take time to talk to me and you will see I am only a light from the womb of the human
galaxy, just like you actually...

Branded: Black as Means of Commodity

Modern day black commodity
A derivative market of slavery...
Black body;
Black culture;
Black branding;
Fetish objects of capitalism?!

Devalued laborers as fraught consumers,
Filling the coffers of their oppressors.
In history's vault...
As Cedric Robinson wrote in *Black Marxism*:
"To be black was to have
No civilization
No culture
No religion
No history
No place...
No humanity worthy of consideration."

In the cacophony of this capitalist county,
Black men were detained in their disparate
But imbricated roles,
Like a run of toppled dominoes...
Casted as commodified bodies,
Disparaged workers and
Thronging consumers looking to escape their shame,
By wearing labels bearing someone else's name...

Today that is their game;
Yet still they use their style and swagger
In protest and in search of a new maneuver,
As they watch the usurpation of their culture
Scattered along the margins of the
Society which excludes them;
Their humanity and masculinity
Secondary to their race in a capitalist society
Whose primary ideology is the working male body;
But black men's souls become darkest at the
Crossroads of patriarchal privilege and racial repudiation;

That is to say…a *real* man must work no matter what!
But *that* work is hard to come by especially when *that* man is black!

But as commodity they can "be like Mike"
Like professional athletes like Michael Jordan;
That is if their willing to see their remarkable ability
Commercialized…
Successful blacks used as tropes
To sedate and tantalize,
Elevate and emphasize,
The promise of success for those blacks
Who are on the marginalized…
But history manifested in our memory
Has taught us that tropes are in fact
Like the black characters in a horror movie…
They are usually the *first* to get the axe!

Blacks as commodity are referenced ideologies from
Jordanna Matlon's article aptly titled:
"Black Masculinity under Racial Capitalism";
Published in *The Boston Review.*
She was sure to point out that capitalism is
Comparable to "abolitionist politics";
We all benefit to be free from its antics…
While emphasizing that "A truly radical counter hegemony can only be
Realized by disassociating both blackness and manhood
From capitalist registers of worth."

Simply put black liberation is our
Collective *in*vestment
But as capitalist commodity it compels
Our collective *divestment*!
Blacks need not succumb to being *branded* as "worthy"
By capitalist elites who place no "worth" on their humanity.

Introduction

Message from: The Pastor

"Happy Holidays! I am constantly thankful for the amazing people who come to our church – and give of themselves in so many ways. It is often because of the holiday spirit that our ministry is able to share God's love, offer joy and inspire hope. A first-time attender to our church, Jacques Fleury, felt that spirit when he came to church recently, and led him to write the following poem. I thought it was perfect to share in celebration of the holiday season:"

To Be a Happy Man

Weary of being downtrodden,
Weary of being disenchanted,
I beseech the heavens
To singe me back to life;
To see the invisible before me,
To feel what seems to elude me,
To be awakened to wonders,
To transcend barriers,
To leap in ethereal bliss,
To bounce in majestic mists,
To see beyond a recoiled flower,
To receive spirit with power,
And in the midst of this self-imposed wretchedness,
To Ponder: How does one find happiness?

Is it to gather as much as one can?
No, for this notion has tried and failed.
Is it to boast as much as one can?
No, for this notion has tried and failed.
Is it to be as ambitious as one can?
No, for this notion has tried and failed.
Then to mitigate my frown,
These words came tumbling to the ground:
"To be a happy man, you must lend a helping hand."
Ah, ha! For happiness, I must take a stand;
After all, it has been said:

"You gonna give to grow."
Now I know what I should have known:

For happiness I must take a stand!
Give a helping hand,
To those standing in quick sand;
"To be a better man, you MUST lend a helping hand."

Time and Tides

I was lavishly infatuated
With the moment
True shades of blue hue
A tropical paradise
Dancing out to the shore
Anxious to return back to the sapphire sea
Then there he was in a Polynesian loincloth
And I became transfixed by his vibrant vision
In awe of the magnitude of his intricately
Shaped mount, the loveliest ever
Like an endless summer
Than just as he appeared disappeared
into the affluent weather
Perhaps it was the dark claw of
Intrigue and mystery
Perhaps it was the sand castle of distant memories
Enduring earthquakes
All interwoven to make me come awake!
Lying on a bed of teal sea
A crystalline lagoon like Bora Bora
My own private islet like
Tahiti and Motu Toopuca
I genuinely felt as elegant as palm trees
Like the summer smiles emanating
From camaraderie in the midst of
The pleasant rustling of haunted voices
Gathered around the camp fire
Ears adorned with the
crackling sounds of laughter
lighting up the night
evoking a longing for forever
but time has illogical rights
and the tides can not stand the test
and so I'm left to watch my soul
dance out to the shore
crashing lovingly against the rocks
eroding them, eroding them.

Ramblings in Trump Era America

"BRING BACK THE CONCENTRATION CAMPS!!!"

Screamed an irascible man on the streets of Boston. And yes, this is meant to Shock you for it shocked me…this is Trump era America we're living in… Hence I was inspired to pen the following:

A man's usefulness is contingent upon his ideals, in so far as he possibly can.

Am I just a memory of what a man used to be: strong, daring and courageous in the pursuit of his ideals? Or one who neglects his daring path, his contempt for inequality in a futile & clumsy Conciliatory NOT to be controversial and to make everyone happy?

Imminent sociopolitical divisiveness, hegemony and jingoism in America is NOT happenstance;

But why be afraid of my circumstance? My people have high pain tolerance…

In the drone of my dreams, Emily Bronte said to me: "No coward soul is [yours], no trembler in the world's storm troubled sphere, I see heavens glories shine and faith shines equal arming [you] from fear…with wide embracing love, thy spirit animates eternal years…"[1]

I am maddened by hints of deliberate and devoted affronts denigrations and disparagements of immigrants! Why not allow disharmony and deception to drown in the deep ocean sphere.

If you were only aware that anger is a snare, humanity would live in harmony.

Peace and love is the only SUPREMACY! Trump proclaims: "Make America Great Again!" But for whom? For Blacks? For Hispanics? For Asians? For Muslims? For the Jewish? For All immigrants? For the poor and disenfranchised? For whom?

America maybe GREAT for the bourgeoisie, the top one percent of society, but not necessarily so great for the rest of the country.

Perhaps we can "all" make America great by making our own unique voices heard by making moral and ethical contributions to one another; by aiding and not abetting the American cause, the American promise of life, liberty and the pursuit of happiness which belongs to all Americans.

Let's not forget that all of us, who are NOT indigenous American Indians, are descendants of immigrants. All of our ancestors came here from somewhere else, whether it was on the Mayflower or on Ellis Island in New York harbor overlooking the Statue of Liberty; we owe our lives here in America to the intrepid liberty seeking trajectory of the immigrants of this country!

Hence in the midst of all this, I retreat to holding onto a flower and the word Kumbaya, a transliteration for the prayerful plea to God: origination from Gullah CREOLE language tradition spoken by former SLAVES living on Sea Islands of South Carolina.

In America, atavistic slave labor generated a communal interdependence of nation-states misguided by self-serving notions resulting in fraudulent feudalism;

Creating the classist hierarchy of the nobility, the clergy and the peasantry.

Hence come by here and heal the supplications against injustice;

Come by and hear the delineations of prejudice;

Come by and hear the clamorous appeals for peace and justice;

Fortunately, I came from a business and property owning middle class family in Haiti;

Unfortunately, still I frown upon oppressive ideologies and business practices of the bourgeoisie.

The history of society is the history of RACISM;

The history of society is the history of CLASSISM;

Hence let's go back in time using history's retrograde memory before we make our way back to our present reality. Way back when, chiefly Africans worked 400 years around the clock building the American capitalist economy.

It is documented that slave labor made an 80% contribution to the building of the grand American wealth. And when Abraham Lincoln tried to remedy slavery with the onslaught of the Civil War and won, he was assassinated and the White Lives Matter More movement was born.

Never mind the fact that when America decided to free itself from the tight grip of British oppression, the first person who died for the American cause was a black Bostonian by the name of Crispus Attucks on March 5th, 1770.

Never mind that Black people have fought in every American war, even when they were told that their "inferior" genetics made them a liability and unfit to serve, hence they essentially had to fight to fight.

Never mind that after the American World War II triumph, when returning soldiers were handed hefty G.I Bills–which is designed to help service members, eligible veterans and their families cover the costs associated with getting an education or training–that allowed them to partake in the American dream that resulted in being able to buy houses in the suburbs with two car garages during the booming 1950s and subsequently the Black soldiers were denied their G.I. Bills and instead faced further indignities by having to endure separate but "equal" Jim Crow laws and a discriminatory practice that was generated by the civil war called The Black Code which meant that Blacks seeking jobs were to be turned away.

A practice similar to the "No Irish Need Apply" signs during the influx of Irish immigrants in the early 1820s. Which makes one wonder, how does a race that endured 400 years of slave labor, toiling seventeen hour days under the sun, while light skinned Blacks waited on Whites inside the plantation houses, and in the post slavery years were turned away when they sought legitimate employment be characterized & stereotyped as "lazy"? Besides, scientific evidence has traced the genesis of the human race and eventual diaspora all the way back to Africa 50,000 years ago. Hence this mere fact would argue that indirectly we are all connected. According to scientists, we are all 99.9 percent the same.

But in Trump America, "Brotherhood" is by another name…

Never mind that my Haitian ancestors fought in the American Revolution and were finally memorialized in Savannah, Georgia for their heroic service.

Never mind that the ruthless emperor Napoleon Bonaparte used the monetary funds he attained from the slave labor on the Island of Haiti to fortify the American cause against the British. Never mind that Haiti's victory over the French inspired American slave revolts in the form of Nat Turners rebellion and more successfully the Civil War; which resulted in the passing of the 13th, 14th, and 15th amendments meant to ensure Black equality in America.

Yet, here we are, in the 21st century, over 150 years post slavery, we are back in the streets fighting to matter. I once heard an unmasked white nationalist (as most of them are these days) asserting with a deceptively docile smile on his face, that he acknowledges the inherent worth and dignity of all people BUT… particularly people of European descent. Go figure.

If All Lives Matter, then why did America have to have slavery?

If All Lives Matter, then why did America have to have the civil rights movement?

If All Lives Matter, then why does America have to have the Black Lives Matter movement?

The history of America is the history of RACISM;

And it doesn't help that it was told by the victor who tells BIASED tales… Even Mark Twain agreed when he said:

"The very ink with which history is written is merely fluid prejudice."[2]

18th century philosopher Alexander Pope in Essay on Man Warns us to accept things as they are:

"All discord, harmony not understood;

All partial evil, universal good:

And, spite of pride in erring reason's spite,

One truth is clear, whatever is, is right."[3]

But is he really right? We can only hope that he had good foresight.

In Trump era North America, squawking black birds get SHUNNED OR SHOT!

Ignoring posts that dictate: NO HUNTING PERMITTED!

In Trump era North America, black birds besieged as foes,

American forests become a de facto hunting ground… Naturalists posit is this ideology or is this reality?

Capricious despotism has dawned a forest feast

In the urban jungles of the American North East!

Nevertheless, I must take responsibility for my own disposition since no one owes me tranquility; I must take issue with my own myopic course of self-destruction; patterns of deliberate insanity!

Permitting revolutionary ruminations to run amok in my mind like stone throwing anarchists!

I must FIGHT for the right of my community!

Who am I?

Raja Yoga Meditation teaches that I AM AN INFINITE LIGHT!

But are they right?

Jacques Fleury

Eckhart Tolle's epiphany preaches:

"The truth of who we are is not I am this or I am that but I am."[4] Is he right?

I say, "I am a human being. Human is what I do and the roles I play;

Being is who I am as the LIGHT of day and

When we pass away—to weave-in words from a Shakespeare play

Our ethereal souls will say,

"Put out the light then put out THE LIGHT!"

Our world denotes that a man with nothing is nothing;

Money creates his worth. However, Hermann Hesse said:

"The true profession of man is finding his way to himself."[5]

Please know, as far as things go, you are NOT what you do or don't do!

Despite what avaricious capitalists like Trump tells you!

Religion too, is a formidable catalyst for conflict from the on start.

Emily Bronte challenges belief systems when she said:

"Vain are the thousand creeds that move men's hearts... worthless as withered weeds to awaken doubt in one."[6] Religion bounds us in fear and fear signifies POWER!

Trump's religion of xenophobia is trumping on our power by binding us in FEAR!

On profession, Oscar Wilde made this assertion:

Do something "...practical and prosaic. It is better to

Have a permanent income than to be fascinating."[7] What's wrong with being FASCINATING?

Maybe I ought to venture into the woods, live on the land and write prose and poetry;

Would that make me both "practical" and "fascinating" in this society?

Even I must heed this warming, less my pure creative intentions become impure venal pursuits and why not throw in a nihilistic predilection for secular attention to boot...

I sense the stirrings of revolution in my veins...I see the dethroning of Kings and Queens...

I foresee a future for our friends and destruction for our foes; destruction that will

Spring forth the seeds of a new season, full of hope and full of reason;

Empty of Trump's propaganda and of derision;

Am I ideology? Am I EQUALITY? Am I liberty?

Or am I just FASCINATING?!

The thirst for liberation always supersedes oppression... Is there no God? No justice? No Peace?

We are told we are tolerated, we are told NOT to make waves,

Be conciliatory, surrender and placate the oppressor,

However, from revolutionary winds comes revolutionary waves...

Ebbing and eroding the gritty American shores full of

Folks fighting to stay afloat in tsunamis in Deep Ocean waves of injustice;

Proletariats unite! To form the working class, to organize a Utopia in which

All members are BROTHERS!

Black birds caged, their nests dismantled–try to outrun de facto hunting grounds;

Much like the young Hegelians in mid-19th century Germany,

Left wing extremists vie for a bourgeois reform in this our U.S. economy;

They amass like surrounding clouds of orbiting electrons electrifying

REVOLUTIONARY hearts and taking up justifiable space

Fighting corporate corruption and to eliminate the fallacious ideology of RACE!

Enlightenment philosophers like John Locke, Charles Montesquieu, and Jean-Jacques Rousseau Enacted theories of government in which ALL PEOPLE HAVE POWER!!!

The American political lexicon is forever indebted to 18th century French philosopher Montesquieu for his phraseology:

"Separation of Powers"[8]: the corner stone of the American constitutional paradigm Aimed at preventing overreaching corruption…share the power, share the wealth!

Montesquieu names two kinds of corruption:

One where the people do not observe the laws, the other when the laws corrupt the people.

That is where the grey area lies: determining when the individual or the law itself is unjust.

This philosophy of law and corruption is a Trump era America play on display… Elation requires dissention or happiness requires rebellion!

Is this script an act of rebellion or is it just FASCINATING?

Humanity's diaspora traced back to Africa,

So why not celebrate human UNITY right here in America! Humanity in AMERICA!

Let's live together as "one"[9] dictates the ideology of John Lennon.

"I saw an angel in the marble and carved until I set him free,"[10] said Michelangelo Set me free! I hail my own ideology, set me free!

From the frailties of impunity, liability and even alleged liberty!

Set me free from the inconsistencies of fraternity, the unpredictability of family, the low lands of life where bottom feeders dwell and all that encompasses heaven earth and sea; Set me free from all the debris superfluous to my tranquility!

And I will lay down in resolute surrender to befuddled woes here on earth and the hereafter… In Trump era America, I am no longer ideology.

In Trump era America, I am no longer reality.

In Trump era America, I MATTER and I am simply FREE!

#Living While Black

Man of color
Man of honor
Man of horror
Vying for valor

Bear witness to my marginal vision,
Something is vying for your attention.
Apparently some members of this *free-nation,* Thinks equality is *discrimi-nation.*

In this country,
If you're black,
SOMEONE will breathe down your back!
Such is the reality.

We are seeing in our nation, a rebirth of segregation,
Bear witness to the following demarcations,
See if you can see yourself in these situations…

In New York, a black teenage boy's backpack
Brushes against a white woman's back,
He wasn't fit for sight so they summoned the alt-right.
If you're black, **someone** will breathe down your back;
Take up your state Rep's time; make racial profiling a hate crime!

In California, an 8-year-old black girl sells water outside her home,
She wasn't fit for sight so they summoned the alt-right.
If you're black, **someone** will breathe down your back;
Take up your state Rep's time; make racial profiling a hate crime!

In Ohio, a 12-year-old boy mows the lawn,
He wasn't fit for sight so they summoned the alt-right.
If you're black, **someone** will breathe down your back;
Take up your state Rep's time; make racial profiling a hate crime!

In Oregon, a black lawmaker canvases in her district,
She wasn't fit for sight so they summoned the alt-right.
If you're black, **someone** will breathe down your back;
Take up your state Rep's time; make racial profiling a hate crime!

In Philadelphia, two black men wait for a colleague at a Starbucks,
They weren't fit for sight so they summoned the alt-right.
If you're black, **someone** will breathe down your back;
Take up your state Rep's time; make racial profiling a hate crime!

In Pennsylvania, a group of black sorority girls
Pick up trash on a highway; they weren't fit for sight,
So they summoned the alt-right.
If you're black, **someone** will breathe down your back;
Take up your state Rep's time; make racial profiling a hate crime!

In Missouri, a black man tries to enter his apartment,
He wasn't fit for sight so they summoned the alt-right.
If you're black, **someone** will breathe down your back;
Take up your state Rep's time; make racial profiling a hate crime!

Why must **you** be white?
Why must **I** be black?
Why can't
"We" just be
And have each other's back?!

In a town hall meeting titled **Living While Black**,
Former Obama white house staffer Darren Martin,
Whose neighbors were uncertain,
When he moved into his apartment in Manhattan,
Besieged the House and the Senate Judiciary Committee
Pleading for a hearing, boldly importuning,
To make a hate crime of racial profiling;
Apparently, his request is still pending…

On Writing Poetry in Trump Era America

I stumble words onto words trying to find my voice,
It suddenly occurs to me that language fluidity is a choice.
I retreat back into the oratory womb,
To find antediluvian words buried in its tomb.
I dust off the dusts by stomping on their bellies,
Pale greyish clouds rise amidst their melees.
I pick and choose my words carefully,
In order to compose a corpus like a visionary.
Words like *xenophobia*, *jingoism* and *hegemony*,
Aggregate to form my vocabulary.
Finally, I am armed and ready to write my poetry,
In this *their* supposed TRUMP COUNTRY,
Against *OUR* unfettered twenty-first century **DEMOCRACY**!

Identity Malady

Descending into a languid daze
Mesmerized by the sunny haze
I look around and in my daze
I find the world to be a maze.

Echos of propagation causing inflation
Mellow are those withholding their aggression
I take tepid steps around this notion
Only to find further degradation.

SUPREME Silhouettes decorate the flag
I can't seem to find my face in a SUPREME mag
My only hope for consolation
Is knowing I will find my way out of this desolation.

Man-made order of supremacy
Falsified notions of identity
And just when you thought you were happy
There comes the identity malady…

Random Political Musings

Trapped in the xenophobic world of political
Hegemony,
I abate the desire to be set free from its debris;
Simply for the sake of Conformity.
In a tumultuous jingoistic
"Democracy"!
I stand with the sun to see,
If "I", not "it", can finally set me Free!
From the imposed maladies of a crumbling Country!
I want I need I… I…don't know...
Anything anymore the more I grow.
In a society where most are in fear of living
Frightened!
Maybe this means I am finally
Enlightened…

Don't Hide in Front of Me

Don't hide in front of me,
I see *you* even if you don't see *me*;
Our ancestors have the same story,
They all came from another country,
To make gains on the terrains of opportunity;

Don't hide in front of me,
I love *you* even if you don't love *me*;
Our hearts are like magical incantations,
Wishing our rainbow-kingdom to action,
Against all forms of uniformed oppression;

Don't hide in front of me,
I don't hate *you* even if you hate *me*;
Our country is fraught with a malady,
Tainted by the stain of slavery,
That erected your capitalist economy;
If only you, if only me, better yet if only WE
Can come together
To make laudable the sound
Of mystical chatter,
Conjuring the clatter of laughter,
We would then be in recovery,
Deluding the fallacy of "The Enemy",
Ascertain an articulatory defense of a country,
Founded on the decree of colonial *fraternity*;

Don't hide in front of me,
I see *you* even if you **WON'T** see *me*,
Our hereafter hovers between sweet and bitter,
Less we make amends with each other,
Than we might roam the Elysian Fields together,
Be amongst the heroic and the virtuous forever...and ever!

The Seething Sage

This feeling just crawls into him: maladjustment, dis-ease;
A downward spiral of selfish self-deprecation and inattention to…
well E V E R Y T H I N G!
He sits under a willow tree to contemplate being
Buddha: master of thought and visceral wisdom and logic;
To know the feeling of inhaling serenity like a sage
And exhaling love like the song of a dove;
Eyes closed he imagines a world without
Conflict cunning constraints…
A world that doesn't sow the seeds of fear to reap the tree of hate.
Eyes closed he smiles to see the world unscathed by human pathology of
Greed envy jealousy…
A world where even in the jungles of Africa
The animals are diplomatic and benevolent;
So much so that humans gather to observe and
Emulate this miracle of manners.
A world with plenty so that no one ever feels empty of
Fraternity sobriety antiquity…
A disparate world without disparity.
And so he opens his eyes to face reality;
He rises from the tree and beat off the dirt from his sanctity,
Looks around in a circular motion and
Takes a step forward for humanity.

Hope Has A Place

Lacerate larceny defame defamatory
Instead of stooping all dreamy
Though much to be dreamt in dreams
When horses have wings
And man got swing
Who is to say anyway….?
All souls night all souls might
Scramble day and night
But what if they all just cowered in fright?

Wolves bask and howl under the moonlight
Calls of loons over the lake at night
But who is to say who will call back
When all is dark and no light in sight?
Dreary dreamer wonders into the forest
Flops under a tree rooted in unrest
White Anaconda slithers down and embrace his fate
Dreamer wakes up but much too late

Another dreamer dawns comes morning
Dreary eyed souls embrace his grace
Dare devil dogs' jaws drops a warning
The sun saunters out and takes its place.

Let Life In

"Life doesn't happen *to* you, life happens *for* you"
Says the butterfly to the flower.

A visceral light descends from nowhere land,
Like happenstance squatting on a cloud dance.

Let there be LIFE!

I am nothing if not the product of country and continuity.
Country lives within me I live within continuity.

What is life if not a series of continuous shenanigans from
Way back when, when life first began.
Be cautious but let them happen.
Hurt and hate,
Lust and love,
Money and Power,
Are portals to growth and understanding.

Don't waste time wishing for what isn't,
Bask in the glory of what is and
Let the moment delve into development.

Yank the shades,
Tout the horns,
Ring the bells...
Let life in, find meaning...
"Life doesn't happen *to* you, life happens *for* you!"

Nature

Your supple hands caress my cheeks
Like a loving mother
Your breath twirls across my eyes and
Slowly collapses like a graceful silhouette
As the dirge of song birds echoes in the darkness
echoes in the darkness echoes in the darkness
Then there came a cold chill as a wave of winter dust
descended deliberately from the mountains and
pierced right through me like a thousand needles
kissing me knocking me down so that my head
rested wantonly against your breast then I could
hear what I couldn't see the rustling of your leafy
fingers the rush of your wakeful breath over the
mountains
then there came the tree slayers I stood there
watching how their mockery and complacency cut
right through you like a giant persistent knife and
i watched you bleed
I watched you nurse your wounds
With a gentle elevated elegance
Then I watched you crumble
Only to see you rise again,
Just a little greener than before.

Chain Letter to America: The One Thing You Can Do To End Racism

Honoring Black history for all who have died fighting for equality

"The privileged majority thinks equality is discrimination."
-Anonymous White protester at Black Lives Matter rally

When you look at me, what do you see?
A black boy worthy of your pity? or
A Black Man replete with potential and possibilities?
I gather the former best suits your ideologies…
My usurped and chained African ancestors toiled this torrid place for four hundred years building
THE GREAT AMERICAN DEMOCRACY and CAPITALIST ECONOMY
on this great land of the "free" Chained by the chains of

Slavery,

Their darkest nights spent singing negro spirituals yearning for

Liberty;

Only Civil War could be expected
Between Northern ideals and Southern antiquity,
A respectable war for an unrespectable ideology.
Now hundreds of years later,
Descendants of Civil War soldiers
Are back in the streets fighting to matter; a disgraceful travesty
to the American promise of freedom and liberty! The United States
still "Divided" on racial unity. Some say: "Make America
great again!" When was America ever great?
Was it great during the displacement and slaughter of indigenous American Indians?
Was it great during the centuries of enslavement of African Americans?
Was it great during the terror, torture and murder of Black Americans at the hands of the
Ku Klux Klan?
Was it great during the Civil Rights Movement when Black protesters were horsed down,
beaten and
jailed
For having the audacity to fight for the American
promise of equality?
Is it great today when well fed past generational descendants of immigrants are denying under

fed present and future generations of immigrants the American Dream?
Denying them of economic opportunity?
Is it great today when Blacks are still
Fighting to matter?
Still fighting to "overcome" barriers of

White Power?!

Do me a favor…I don't need you to Validate
my human nature;
I don't need you to validate my existence;
I don't need you to validate my intelligence;
I don't need your intolerance; But I do need you.
I need you to continue marching right alongside oppressed peoples of all colors, men,
women and children.
I need you to stand by when White Lives Matter Neo-Nazis march into town with
signs screaming
"BLACK LIVES SPLATTER!"
I need you to stomp on ignorance;
I need you to stomp on prejudice;
I need you to stomp on hatred;
I need you to stomp on racism;
I need you to stomp on your fears of
Equality for all of humanity;
I need you to say TO ME publicly what you're saying ABOUT ME privately;
and then And ONLY then will we all be set FREE!
In the documentary "I Am Not Your Negro"
James Baldwin spoke of this American problem when he boldly stated:
"I am not a nigger! I am a man. If you NEED me to be a nigger than YOU have to find out
the reason why…and the future of America depends on THAT!"

Coming Home

Well, because a fall leaf fell before my feet today I see
In serendipity I yearn to live daily, Consider this my
soliloquy.
To awake to its bounty of unlawful acts of intrepid beauty
I yearn to taste the morning dew on my tongue at sunrise,
That is to feel again; to unfurl my wings like silver springs
And fly again; to sound out sounds yet to be heard;
Supposedly it's all been sounded,
Supposedly it's all been said,
But not by me so here I am, like a black-tailed deer prancing on wobbly legs,
Trying not to remember that I was once hunted so that I can
Imagine a world without hunters; but I do remember and that's how I got stronger.
I yearn to bay at the moon at night but not like a black wolf, But a white swan
flouncing on the foamy lake.
I want a world of butterflies and rainbows… Yes, I want to have my cliché and eat it too.
Poets! Allow me to harangue you:
Coveting prizes and publication can consume you!
Defy and denounce racism!
Confront and contain classism.
Confer and celebrate humanism.
Pursue the ultimate orgasm!
Happiness is accepting the life you see,
Be happy and enjoy your journey.
My heart has been doused in the dawn of new age reality:
Not unlike the reality TV that gave me a place to hide in uncertainty;
No one is talking.
Everyone is texting.
Social media: the new pathway to a social life. We are in a crisis of technological isolation!
So technically we are less and less connected
And more and more isolated.
Caught in the cross fires of neocolonial consumerism,
I want to live a life free of materialism, free of egoism;
I want to be like Buddha.
I want to meditate all day and sleep all night.
Keep your dreams alive!
I once publicly hid from love;
I yearn to love again like the moon tickling the midnight sea;
"You are a true Poet, don't EVER let them take that away from you."

They told me. Now here I am, battered and bruised, my silver wings have dulled
By the wear and tear of my new reality: not quite young, not quite old, not quite done;
Yet I've resolved to flail my silver wings again against the moon lit skies,
This time without worry,

And come home to my original love
Of prose and poetry.

Haiku: An Ode to the Ferguson Race Riots for the Unarmed Shooting of Michael Brown that Ignited the Black Lives Matter Movement

Wisteria gathers

Tinged boys die as mothers cry

Flower pickin' time…

House by the Lake

Incendiary tales
left at front steps
I open my door to sweep them out
Less I trip on them;
The wind howls and sweeps through
The cracks in my window
I let its whistling melody
Rock me to sleep deep;
The sun glares down at me
Daring me to open my gaze
And for an instance
I stare back in defiance
Less I go blind from non-compliance;
The moon emerges from a sleepy cloud
Highlighting a path for
dislocated crowds Less
they lose their way in
the winding grounds;
I beckon to butterflies
To amuse my visual fields
To nature's natural beauty I yield;
Only to come awake in a
house by the lake where
I will contemplate
Serenity For all who have been dislocated;
Serenity for all who have been aggravated;
Serenity for all wishing to be celebrated;
Serenity for all Humanity,
May you too dwell in a house by
the lake
Where you too may find shelter from
the hate…

Flight of the Broken

Under mists of the red, white and blue,
are jitters of jeering silhouettes;
looking like a reticent slew, in dread
of taking a stance; in evading their
circumstance.

In the distant dark there will
come a light that sparks a
bright red mark
against those who are refused flight;

the twilight is gloaming
morning is nearing the
sun is striving
to reach the dying;

Under the glare of white moon lit rays,
strolls in beaming sun shine days, out
of puffs of clouds in candor; to stand
mighty and proud in VALOR!

Cornucopia

I hear the sounds of heavy footsteps in my wake;
My ears jutted like jungle prey fearing their fate;
I start to toil in my sheets, anticipating the plight
of the meek.

I hear a knocking on my door,
I leap up bursting to implore;
and before I could ask what for
I was taken to the floor....

At first I resisted as much as anyone thirsty would;
But then was overpowered by a need for some hood;
And I could do nothing more than absorb a piercing
thrust; at which point I embraced the wayward musk.

After I felt down trodden,
I wiggled myself up from the milky satin;
At first I thought I was grumbling,
But then I realized I was really howling...

Shahk in the Dahk!

In liquid bliss it
Navigates in waves
You would never feel its whiskers
Because he never forgets to shave…
Comes twilight it
Twitches itching for a meal,
Careful when you're wading…
Cause you might just be served as veal!

Dawn in the Forest

The sun rises out of the belly of the earth
Like a giant orange over the mellow meadows
Birds singing their esoteric songs
Honeysuckles bask in the morning dew
A doe rustling to life after a long sleep
Caterwauling creatures echo over hillsides
Below the canopy are vanguards of activity
Supple blow of the wind weaving in and out of the trees
Conglomeration of broods chirping in their nests
Cryptic mating calls abound
The forest miniature wilds
From aphids to beetles slugs to toads
All on a brownish tarnished tray in disarray on the forest floor
Centipedes skulk through soil caterpillars chomp though leaves
Beetles pelt in their holes trailing and gathering in a
Resilient resolve to cling to life in spite of natural strife
In the deciduous forest that scraps its skin in the fall
Nature calms like a mother
Spring awakens
Chipmunks come out of burrows
Baby katydids and tent caterpillars hatch
Queen bumblebees collect nectar from wild flowers
Azure butterflies greet the dawn
Luna moth squirms and scratches within its cocoon
Green tiger beetles with large eyes jumping spiders with sharp eyes
Pounce on prey!
Between the ferns at your feet and the tree over your head
Is the leafy understory
It is the furrowed tree trunks weedy bushes brushing your shoulders
Old dead tree that lie on the floor expecting to be explored
Red spotted purple butterflies, ant lions and wood nymphs
Sunset descends as many animals become bed heads
Chipmunk heads to its burrow, cicadas stop singing
Birds fly to their resting place
Bush katydid shed its skin in nocturne
All insects molt so they can grow
Winter is here…
Woods are lovely dark and deep says Mr. Frost

And its inhabitants have NO promises to keep
Icicles sparkle on bare branches
Downy white snow manteau the ground
Mysterious eyes carved obsidian in the moonlit dusk
The geese robins and monarch butterflies fly south
While the animals that stay germinate winter skin to stay warm
The air is pure and clean like a mountain stream,
Now all bed heads head off to bed to sleep perchance to dream…

Walk for Haiti, Walk for Humanity!

Today, we celebrate the presence
And participation of the youth culture
The next generation for a brighter future
All joined together so that Haiti and optimally
Humanity can be better!
When I left Haiti I could not stop
From looking back in my rear view mirror
Leaving behind all the beauty and horror,
And I remember thinking to myself
There has to be more to life than constant strife!
So now I got poems burning on my breath
To cure misery and death like Partners in Health!
But I must emphasize,
Haiti for me was not all about death and debris!
It was also about beauty.
I remember staring in stupor
The dance of the Caribbean wind
Over the blue eyed sea a crystallized lagoon
Rising and falling with the grace of a ballerina,
The deep green elegance of palm trees,
Picnics by moonlight and sweet memories of mangoes,
The sounds of laughter resounding from the young
As they run about playing hide and seek,
A game adults knew very well in the face of
Domination and intimidation!
So now I got poems burning on my breath to
Cure misery and death like Partners in Health.
When I revisit these memories,
I can't decide whether I want to
Remember
Or whether I want to Forget.
I remember those who lived under
The roof of tragedy!
I often forget that I was lucky!
I lived a sheltered life since we
Were considered middle class.
Women had very few choices,
In Haiti, the heterosexist macho male culture

Does not make things sturdy for mothers
Defying gravity to rise above economic scarcity,
So they often turned to God for spiritual energy.
So now, I got poems burning on
My breath to cure misery and death
Like Partners in Health.
When I lived in Haiti,
Black outs were as constant as
The pain in the eyes of mothers
Watching their children starving.
Then the moon descended like a
Familiar friend to keep shadows in Misery's Company.
The children would all run around happy just to be.
Their carefree laughter inviting the winning shapes
Of eternity in their haunted voices. Then shadows
of the world would appear Attired in fear the
message was clear:
There must be something better than this!
So I like to remember the tropical sea
A blue hue at the end of Carfou on
Jean Claude Duvalier Avenue where we lived,
Coconut trees swaying with the wind to the
rhythm of beauty and brutality!
The sky separated in two: black and blue,
Under black skies, the moon hovered like
Halos over Haitian heads restless spirits
Searching through the night with darkness riding
Heavy on their backs
So they often sang their misery away
Their music bending the night to make
Room for a little light, I listened to
them sing their songs of hope and
inspiration:
"De Galilee, sa nap gade,
De Galilee, sa nap gade,
Jesus ki paret la, sa nap gade,
Lap retounin enko, sa nap gade"x2
I remember crying when I saw this sight.
I am sorry to have seen.
But glory has a history of curing misery!
And so I wait for Haitiâ€™s endless nights to turn
Into endless days,

And so I wait for Haitian children to shine like
The colors of May,
And so I wait for Haiti's hungry to be fed,
And so I wait for Haiti's sick to be cured,
And so I wait for Haiti's sun to shine like
The glossy innocence in the eyes of a child,
And so I wait.
With poems burning on my breath to cure misery
And death like Partners in Health. So today let's
all walk and sing until our voices ring ripples in
the Caribbean sea, so today let's all walk and
sing until Haiti is set free from torture! set free
from horror! set free from hunger!
A great man once said
"I fed the poor and the call me a saint
I ask why they are poor and they call me a communist,"
I say release all Haitian birds!!!
I've learned that some birds are not meant to be caged,
Their colors are just too bright!
The cross roads of time is on our side!
There will come a time when holy generosity will
fall from the sky,
there will come a time when the land of scarcity will
become the land of the plenty!
There will come a time when Haiti will reclaim it's
Original vision of bliss and beauty,
There will come a time when Haiti will be set free!
But for now, all I got is poems burning on my breath
To cure misery and death like Partners in Health.
Yet still I am compelled to listen to the sounds in the trees,
To the somber voices of our ancestors
Feeling compelled to say something to our generation
So pay attention!
Listen closely to the absent songs of democracy!
Go up to the hills of Haiti and there you will hear
Clearly hidden meanings humming in the wind,
So listen closely to the temptations of power,
So listen closely to the maltreatment of your brother,
So listen closely to the maltreatment of your sister.
No blood needs to be shed for Haiti to be fed!
On Haitian terrains we got mountains of pain
Dancing in the rain.

But one day, Haitian children will wake up to
Shiny silver mornings and hummingbirds singing
Promising a glossy wire string strong enough
To pull Haiti out of misery,
A glossy wire string strong enough to pull
Haiti back into its original grace and beauty.
Yet still I got poems burning on my breath
To cure misery and death like Partners in Health.
So thank you for walking, with each step
Haiti is brighter,
So thank you for walking, with each step Haiti
is stronger.
So thank you for walking to better the lives of the living!!!

Interiority

"He who looks outside dreams, he who looks inside, awakens." —*Carl Gustav Jung*

I wish this beginning would be the bulk of my story…
Landfills where fuchsia stars burst like
Beethoven's sonatas in the night,
Nesting birds basking in the moonlight,
Where the darkness and the light are both alike,
A marvelous silver against the dark horizon…
To know me look *not* through my eyes but where I gaze…
Disappearing in a cloud of mist alone and adrift in the big country;
Lulled by the sound of the sea;
The swish swash of life's longing to be;
Lying on my back on the soft summer sand;
I'd smile to the spurious dome above the land;
Grasping how glorious life is…
White waves crashing at my feet;
Seagulls squawking in retreat,
There, life would feel complete;
There I would write the following reprimand,
Not by intention but as if by happenstance…

Once brutalized you learn to run to what feels "safe";
You learn that to be happy is to create an enemy;
You learn that running from a challenge is safer than risking a change;
Feeling stuck in time you realize that
Sometimes you have to move to unstick;
You keep it moving like a boss
Knowing moving water gathers no moss;
You learn to take time to investigate your wounds…
Abrade the cut of the blade but don't be flabbergasted
If you feel bereft when your pain is vacated…
Because as human beings on earth,
We tend to cling to what feels safe.
Hence I decided to use my pen as a method of innovation,
As a form of meditative exploration of my internal tribulation…
In the immortal words of Frederick Douglas:
"If there is no struggle, there is no progress."
Cause don't you know?!

Life can be an array of endless tragedies
Obscured only by the occasional miracle;
But nothing comes without a warning;
Storms are often preceded by thunder and lightning…

And now…my story on interiority effective immediately…

Interiority implies self-acceptance;
Which is somewhere in the distance, contemplating misfeasance;
Hence in this instance I **must** take a stance against internal indifference.
I elaborate when I pontificate…
Interiority is: expressing inner strength through thoughts feelings and
Reactions…
To add context through humor and
Emotions…
So here I am,
Armored with prose and poetry in an attempt
To reveal my contempt for my affliction,
During this daring experiment to make sense of my situation.
Poetry: "Le mot juste" French for "the just word"
To speak of our inner world…

Before Socrates's killing
For his philosophical ruminations and extrapolations,
He professed that:
'The unexamined life is not worth living."
Sometimes it is necessary to venture and investigate
Your malleable human state,
Understand your triumphs and transgressions,
Deliberately descend into somewhere darker,
So you can eventually ascend to something better.

Self- examination can be connected to a delusion of reference,
That is if you think God is speaking to you through your television…
But like Socrates professed and his philosophy expressed,
It must begin with an admission of ignorance,
If we are to extrapolate meaning from our circumstance.
Whatever wisdom we possess
Comes from knowing that we know nothing,
It is from this point of knowing nothing,
That we can even begin to conceive of knowing *something*;

Life can be a whirl wind of WOW!
When you choose to live in the NOW!
Stop being a sycophant to that which stifles your advancement!

Prose and poetry speaks to the human condition;
An astute observer observes a sort of
Transactional quid pro quo this for that interaction;
Which then avails the opportunity for a transactional analysis;
A stimulant and respondent situation,
Mediating the roles we play…
Why leave it to the psychotherapists
To justify how and why we exist?
Our formalized schemas of action and *re*-action
From previous programming;
Interned by la di dah psycho-babble,
PSYCHO-dysphoria…PSYCHO-disturbia!
Just plain…**PSYCHO!!!**
You can clean up your own mess when you practice mindfulness.
I am conducting an action of self-renovation,
An exploratory mediation within my visceral nation;
Time is chasing me down, so it's time to stop clowning around…

Mindfulness means being able to bring open hearted awareness
To what you are doing *while* you are doing it,
Being able to tune into what is going on
In your mind, body and in the outer world moment by moment.
Haven't you heard?
It has become a massive metastatic movement…
So be mindful of your mortality and
Mind the moments of your humanity.

When you find yourself in an instance of cognitive dissonance,
Between your actual and ideal self that
Renders you irrational and dysfunctional,
Take a deep breath and clear your cranial activity,
Perhaps you'll find a remedial remedy
That is actually logical.

It's psychotic to sit here,
Lulled by water jutting from this American ground;
Trying to write the perfect poem;
That elusive beautiful beast…

It's all clear in my header,
But renders itself clumsy on paper.

Ugh! Numerous times I've considered abdication
Of this literary misrepresentation.
Why run when you can walk?
Why write when you can talk?
Perhaps my ego state wishes to celebrate its own fallacy.

"Don't break your neck trying to suck your own cock!"
I tell it in good deference. But in good ole ego
exaggeration, It takes it as an infraction.
"Tough!" I tell it.
"The best gift I can give you is THE TRUTH!"

Being an artist is becoming more and more tiresome…
But I must create!
Create my own fallacy!
Create my own cerebral society!
Less I become a menace TO society!
"I AM AN ARTIST DAMM IT!!!"

Artists: a bunch of brilliant psychotic eccentrics dying to get published
By even more psychotic publishers deciding
Who to exonerate and who to incarcerate.
"Oh yeah, sign me up!"

But here I am,
Regressing back to bygone years
In high school literary rebel circles,
Writing to matter, scowling on paper,
Mystifying narratives of pain and lack of power;
Feeling vilified like a stain,
Waiting to be cleansed by the rain;
Dwelling in the parched deserts of the dejected and deceived
By the touted and all too elusive American Dream;
The American constitutional promise of valor
And EMPOWERMENT for all people;
Not just those with idealized notions of melanin deficient skin color.
Admiring badass iconoclastic nonconformists like
Elton John and **Freddy Mercury**;
Hoping for an uprising from their divine divinity

Into an ARTSY statesman;
An emblem for the common man
With uncommon abilities;
Yearning to break the perpetual protocol of the
Oppressed and the *pathetic*;
Morphing into the *capable* and the *athletic*.
As if THAT will solve EVERYTHING!

Feeling like a distinction within the subculture of dysfunction;
I yearn to break from the acculturated self,
To embrace a deliberate self;
Or *programmed* self to *intervening adult self*;
Or **TO JUST GROW THE HELL UP!!!**

Feeling that labeled as anything "less than"
Is equivalent to putting out self-affronting pity signals
So you can feel sorry for me.

I am a literate loner dying…
To write the perfect poem;
That elusive beautiful beast…
Perpetually perpetrating a prima facie ruse,
Ineffable literary attempts,
Attempting to serve something subversive and
Simultaneously submerged in lofty liquidity,
But keep stumbling along the road of words…
I feel replete with incomplete;
Depleted of attention;
Surrendering my ascension;
Eschewing subconscious development,
In a desperate attempt at attaining PRAISE
From smug color-crazed capitalist narcissists!
Consumed by conspicuous consumption;
And in case you didn't already know,
In "*matters*" of anything racial…
We are all descendants of the
FIRST CIVILIZATION OF SUBSAHARAN AFRICANS
FIFTY THOUSAND YEARS AGO!
In case you didn't know…
WE ARE ALL 99.9 PERCENT THE SAME…
So STOP playing the race game!
Instead explore your *own* ideology of INTERIORITY…

THAT will be the only way to be set FREE!!!
And if "*why are you playing the race card*?" is your inquiry…
"Well that's the card you handed me!"
Because if we continue to do what we've always done,
We will continue to get what we've always gotten.
Remember, what you attack WILL fight back!
If race is a problem for you, don't attack it,
Face it, confess it, understand it,
That is the process to address this race mess…

Here are examples of blasé "conversations" between the races,
Manifesting what a person of color typically experiences…

Black man: "*We* experience racism every day…"
White man: "Well *I* grew up in a white, black and brown world
And *I* have black friends who take interest in
What *I* have to say…"
Black man: *We* experience racism every day…
White man: "Well *I* marched in the 60s during the civil rights
movement with Martin Luther King and *I* blended
with blacks who spoke in an educated way…"

Although white people are not the only people who
Perpetrate hateful stereotypes at the end of the day;
When it comes to sexuality…
Particularly in the black community;
If you're not a thug than you must be *gay*…
This is our human defray,
Our duality always keeps us in sway…
And just when you thought you were safe in your own home…
SUPREME POWERS tell you to go back to where you came from!!!
Forgetting that they too are descendants of people from another room…
"WE'RE GONNA TAKE OUR COUNTRY BACK!!!"
From whom exactly? Those who look like Barack?

In hatred's past and in its posterity;
Phony science of eugenics and polygenesis
Supporting white supremacy;
A justification for hatred and inequality;
Unequivocally proven to be a fallacy;
Yet in extant and in its posterity;
Have persisted in the twenty-first century…

Daguerreotypes of stereotypes put a dagger in all our hearts.
Despite our vehement use of force,
We all come from the same source,
In accordance with the laws of fate,
You become what you hate!
We are all part of the same "brotherhood"
So stop feeding on hatred like it was food!
Black and white, in spite of what you see on FOX,
Are just colors in a child's Crayola box…

Why do life fronting stoic heroics?
Why do life displaying plastic demotics?
Why do life dumpy and disconnected?
Why do life inert and disconcerted?
Why **NOT** live life *alert* and *elevated*?

Allow not the affliction of demagogue degradations;
Determine your right to sanctification and salvation;
Live life in light and in love, an atypical solution.
Be cognizant that HATE *incarcerates* LOVE **liberates**!
Change is *not* linear, it flows up and down like a stormy river…

The civil rights movement from the 20th century
Revitalized in the 21st century;
The oppressed and marginalized stand defiant in daring this country
To manifest its constitutional degree of EQUALITY!
Racism is at an accelerated rate of recidivism…
Which can only be chastened by acerbic activism
By malapert rogue poets and bohemian lots;
Whom does not disperse without a Parthian shot!

Script full of grit and pragmatic essence;
Poetry without patronizing pretense;
An artisan's temporary defense;
A benevolent remedy for malevolence,
While contemptuous consumerists
Construct coups for Cadillacs;
And congressional con men conduct convivial feasts
For fat materialistic maniacs…

It is said that Herman Melville insinuated at
The self-hatred instilled in all of us when he wrote **Moby Dick,**

Right or wrong, our projections of prejudice
Onto innocent persons proves that "**we are sick**!"

Good food good mood…
Nothing annihilates hunger more than food;
Nothing discombobulates evil more than good;
Find the good in your selfhood;
Understand before you can be understood…
Thinking good thoughts leads to
Doing good deeds for our brotherhood.
Our transient existence as Homo sapiens,
Which translate to "wise man"; which makes me wonder…
How "wise" are we to conceive that we are superior to one another?
What really "matters" is that our collective humanities
Are the only ties that bind;
Before you ponder your next attack just remember that
An eye for an eye leaves everybody blind!
"THEY" are you and *you* are "they"
STOP the blame game and find a better way!
Clear your name from this shame,
Understand that we are 99.9 percent the same…
So STOP playing the race game!

Your manifested American ideology of liberty
Will be indubitably contested by your hyperbolic hypocrisy!
Be a mouth piece for our democracy,
Designed to preserve our collective human dignity.
Stereotypes belong in a recording studio,
They ought not to be imposed on people…
The iconoclastic scientist Galileo Galilei
Hailed as the father of observational astronomy
He proved that the moon was
A place you could go and stand on…
Yet he was charged by the inquisition
When he challenged long held beliefs;
Much like modern day pioneers for racial equality
Who are stricken with grief when they are challenged
As they hail the clatter of
"**Black Lives Matter**!"
A retroactive attempt to reconcile slavery and stimulate conversation;
A counterproductive intent to dislocate confrontation…
I am a teller of truth while navigating this human journey,

A dictating dichotomy between
Metaphysical pursuits and *Existential reality.*
Or "Just doing the best I can" along life's lurid trajectory
While spewing pretentious perennial philosophy
Dedicated to the finite "truth" of our infinite diversity...
Hoping for a transcendent united epiphany of unity.
Let there be internal radiance in the face of external malfeasance
Transformative spirituality in the face of divisive oratory;
"Ils faut cultiver notre jardin"
French for "One must cultivate one's own garden",
Attend to your garden, be the change that you want to see,
Especially for the sake of the children...
Who will one day pluck a fruit from our implanted tree;
For "In sorrow thou shalt bring forth children":
Genesis verse sixteen chapter three.

Learn from the lessons of the past but let go of their context,
For they will only bring you distress;
Live in the moment let THAT be your truest test!
Remember as your fear of whatever decreases,
The higher in your power increases...
Forgive completely, live freely;
Contemplate unpopular concepts,
Please know fear is created when
You conspire to control so
You **MUST** aspire to "Let Go!"
Those you fear fears you,
Those who fears *you* fear themselves...
Build an entourage of courage,
Live your life like a sage.
In the dark and hallow hour,
Look to the tower of your higher power.
Remember to stay in the light,
Especially when you find yourself up all night.

Have you any notion of the bastion needed of a
Brain to go against the grain?
Enjoy the torment of being different!
And when you need to heal the pain... *S.T.O.P!*
Take three deep breaths,
Observe what is going on...
Proceed with awareness and compassion:

Deepak Chopra's prescription for perception,
Fuse it with your daily meditation.

Sit under a willow tree,
Perhaps in the lotus position,
Explore your identity,
See if you can find tranquility;
Mind your actions, take action but don't yield to *re-actions*;
Tension is a false notion of who you think you *should* be;
Relaxation is who you are truthfully.
Mindfully manage your freedom of choice,
Be the last person to evoke raising your voice.
When you interact with each other as
Sisters and brothers or as soeur et frère...
Remember to be mindful of exercising some savoir faire.
"Life is a whirlpool of WOW
But only when you own the NOW!"
Spend your time exploring who you are,
Before it's *your* time to say see you later or "A plus tard..."
Don't wait 'til you are in a procession on your way from hospice,
Remember no one ever said on their death bed
"I wish I had spent more time at the office..."
All work and no play...even God took a break on Sunday!

Stay focused and fight for your rights;
For in the poetic rhetoric of Robert Herrick:
"Go on fore right,
[But remember] it is the end that crowns you,
Not the fight."

I wish this ending was be the bulk of my story...
Landfills where fuchsia stars burst like
Beethoven's sonatas in the night,
Nesting birds basking in the moonlight,
Where the darkness and the light are both alike,
A marvelous silver against the dark horizon...
To know me look *not* through my eyes but where I gaze...
Disappearing in a cloud of mist alone and adrift in the big country;
Lulled by the sound of the sea;
The swish swash of life's longing to be;
Lying on my back on the soft summer sand;
I'd smile to the spurious dome above the land;

Grasping how glorious life is…
White waves crashing at my feet;
Seagulls squawking in retreat,
There, *I* would feel complete…

Notes

—Ramblings in Trump Era America

[1]   https://www.poetryfoundation.org/poems/43712/no-coward-soul-is-mine
[2]   https://www.brainyquote.com/quotes/mark_twain_105745
[3]   https://www.poetryfoundation.org/poems/44899/an-essay-on-man-epistle-i
[4]   https://www.amazon.com/New-Earth-Awakening-Purpose-Selection/dp/0452289963/ref=sr_1_1?ie=UTF8&qid=1532636248&sr=8-1&keywords=a+new+earth+by+eckhart+tolle&dpID=51dzTqj5fXL&preST=_SY344_B O1,204,203,200_QL70_&dpSrc=srch
[5]   https://boldomatic.com/p/Uf1yVA/the-true-profession-of-man-is-finding-his-way-tohimself-hermann-hesse
[6]   https://www.poetryfoundation.org/poems/43712/no-coward-soul-is-mine
[7]   https://www.goodreads.com/quotes/512994-unless-one-is-wealthy-there-is-no-use-inbeing
[8]   http://oll.libertyfund.org/pages/montesquieu-and-the-separation-of-powers
[9]   https://genius.com/John-lennon-imagine-lyrics
[10]   https://www.brainyquote.com/quotes/michelangelo_161309

Bibliography

Bartlett, Ray. Cape Cod: Martha's Vineyard & Nantucket. Third Edition. California: Avalon Travel, 2013.

Diangelo, Robin. White Fragility: Why it's So Hard for White People to Talk About Racism. Boston: Beacon Press, 2018.

George, Portia. Gifts of Our People: An Alphabet of African American History. Pennsylvania: Judson Press, 1995.

Stone, Gene. *The Trump Survival Guide*: Everything You Need to Know About Living Through What You Hoped Would Never Happen. New York: Dey Street Books, 2017.

Morrison, Toni. The Origin of Others. Massachusetts: Harvard University Press, 2017.

Jones, Van. Beyond the Messy Truth: How We Came Apart, How We Come Together. New York: Ballantine Books, 2017.

Woodard, Colin. American Character: A History of the Epic Struggle Between Individual Liberty and the Common Good. New York: Penguin Books, 2016.

Greene, Joshua. Moral Tribes: Emotion, Reason and the Gap Between Us and Them. New York: Penguin Books, 2013.

Elder, Delores- Rosalyn. Exploring the Legacy: People and Places of Significance. Second Edition. Massachusetts: African American Heritage, 2016.

Zinn, Howard. A People's History of the United States. New York: Harper Perennial Modern Classics, 2005.

Lobban-Fluehr, Carolyn. Race and Racism: An Introduction. Maryland: Alta Mira Press, 1776. p. 39.

The American Journal of Sociology. "Eugenics: Its Definition, Scope, and Aims". X (1): 82. Bib code: 1904.

*Eugenics is the science which deals with all influences that improve the inborn qualities of a race; also with those that develop them to the utmost advantage.

Popovic, Srdja et al. Nonviolent Struggle: 50 Critical Points. Belgrade: Canvas Edition of 500, 2007

Raphael, Ray. *Founding Myths: Stories That Hide Our Patriotic Past.* New York: The New Press; *Tenth Anniversary Edition,* 2014

Freire, Paulo, *Pedagogy of the Oppressed.* New York: Bloomsbury Academic; 4 edition, 2018.

Ford, Carin T. African-American Soldiers in the Civil War: Fighting for Freedom. Enslow Publishing Inc., 2004.

Glatthaar, Joseph T., Forged in Battle: The Civil War Alliance of Black Soldiers and White Officers. New York: LSU Press; Reprint Edition, 2000.

Davis, Kenneth C., *Don't Know Much About the Civil War: Everything You Need to Know About America's Greatest Conflict but Never Learned.* New York: Harper Collins, Perennial First Hardcover Edit edition, 2004.

Dubois, Laurent, Avengers of the New World: The Story of the Haitian Revolution. Massachusetts: The Belknap Press: First Harvard University Press, 2005.

Dubois, Laurent. Haiti: The Aftershock of History. New York: Picador; First edition, 2013.

Gilman, Charlotte Perkins. (1899) *"The Yellow Wallpaper"*, Digireads.com Publishing. 2017.

Wilkins, Mary E., *"The Revolt of Mother",* 1890.

Chopin, Kate. *"The Story of an Hour"*, 1894.

Cayton, Mary K., "Gender Roles and Relations", Encyclopedia of American Social History, 1998.

Rosenfield, Sarah. "Labeling Mental Illness: The Effects of Received Services and Perceived Stigma of Life Satisfaction", American Sociological Review, 62:600-72, 1997.

Link, B. G., Ph.D. et al. "Stigma as a Barrier to Recovery: The Consequences of Stigma for the Self-Esteem of People with Mental Illnesses", Psychiatric Services: 52, 1621-1626, 2001.

Media Sources (DVDs, Television, Websites etc...)

"Egalite (equality) For All: Toussaint Louverture and the Haitian Revolution", 2009 film

The Reiki Page, "What Is Reiki?":

http://reiki.7gen.com/index.html

The History of Haiti:

https://en.wikipedia.org/wiki/History_of_Haiti

Timothy Crumrin, "Women and the Law in Early Nineteenth Century Indiana" :

https://www.connerprairie.org/educate/indiana-history/women-and-the-law-in-early-19th-century/

Barbara Kantrowitz and Pat Wingert, "The Science of a Good Marriage" Newsweek:

https://www.questia.com/magazine/1G1-54488331/the-science-of-a-good-marriage

Trump: I am the least racist person anywhere in the world:

https://www.theguardian.com/us-news/video/2019/jul/30/trump-claims-least-racist-person-in-the-world

Elliot, Mary. "The 1619 Project" New York Times, 18 Aug. 2019, p. 4(L). SPJ.SP26:

https://link.gale.com/apps/doc/A596676232/SPJ.SPJ26?u=cam&sid=SPJ.SPJ26&sid=f7f2a3ab.

Watch: The Times Presents the #1619Project:

We're observing the 400th anniversary of American slavery. Watch a kickoff event with Nikole Hannah-Jones, Jamelle Bouie and more contributors:

https://www.nytimes.com/2019/08/13/magazine/1619-project-livestream.html

In 1864 "Le Figaro" published the tale "Le Joueur Généreux" ("The Generous Gambler") by Charles Baudelaire. The main character meets and converses with a manifestation of the Devil. Here is the link Scroll down pass the English translation to see the passage in French:

https://quoteinvestigator.com/2018/03/20/devil/

The History of Africa:

https://en.wikipedia.org/wiki/History_of_Africa#cite_note-http://newswatch.nationalgeographic.com/2013/10/31/getting-to-know-africa-50-facts/-2

Johann Blumenbach:

https://en.m.wikipedia.org/wiki/Johann_Friedrich_Blumenbach

Caucasus Mountains:

https://en.wikipedia.org/wiki/Caucasus

Catherine of Aragon:

https://en.wikipedia.org/wiki/Catherine_of_Aragon

Movie: I Am Not Your Negro, featuring James Baldwin:

https://en.wikipedia.org/wiki/I_Am_Not_Your_Negro

Jacques Stanley Fleury, is a Haitian-American Poet, Journalist, Theater Reviewer, Educator and Boston Globe featured author of three books available at The Harvard Book Store, The Boston Public Library & online. He holds an undergraduate degree in Liberal Arts and pursuing graduate studies in the literary arts at Harvard University online. His hitherto magnum opus **Chain Letter to America: The One Thing You Can Do to End Racism** is an omnium gatherum of essays, fiction and poetry espousing social justice and embracing multiracial-multicultural identities & their respective contributions to our society. He is published both locally and internationally in such eminent publications like the *Boston Globe, Poets Reading the News*, which was featured on National Public Radio (NPR) and published out of California and the *International Network of Street News Papers*, where his writings are reproduced and translated in over one-hundred and twenty counties within Asia, Africa, Europe, North and South America and the West Indies. He has made personal appearances at North Eastern & Harvard Universities among others. His CD *A Lighter Shade of Blue* as a lyricist in collaboration with folk group Sweet Wednesday is available on iTunes & Spotify to benefit Haiti charity St. Boniface. He is a Cantabrigian living in the great state of Massachusetts.

From the Introduction by the author

What this book is about is raising conscious awareness to our collective humanity and respective contributions to our country, with added focus on our multiculturalism and fundamentally our shared…constitutional ideology: **that we are all created equal…** In the midst of political and racial divisions in America, I heard a republican congressman speaking to the media, he said: "*With open eyes, open ears, open mind and you walk away with some understanding...*" while honoring our first amendment right to freedom of expression…through open minded and open hearted conversations… If you take one thing away from reading this book, I hope it's that our numerous races, ethnicities, beliefs and values manifested through comparative historical and contextual exploration can serve as a miscible advantage or a harmonious mixture when added together … a reconciliatory nod to our past and a meditative extrapolation, interjection and celebration of our …United States or '**US**'. Enjoy!"

Praise for Jacques Fleury's "Chain Letter to America…"

"A powerful strike on the doors of Justice. …" -Andre Emmanuel Bendavi ben-YEHU
—Poet, Translator

"Jacques Fleury's scholarship and writing ability are far above the average. Really worth paying attention to… Fleury really said a load in this broadly sweeping exposé of modern life awakening… Kudos!"

--Ronald W. Hull, Ed.D, Author *of Hanging by a Thread*

"Polarization and violence in our country make increasingly urgent a greater understanding of our history…So what lessons and what inspiration from our past can we draw upon to help us in our present circumstance?"

--Neil Calendar, Adjunct Professor of English

Printed in the United States
By Bookmasters